LONGSHOT

Brent,

Thank you for the path
you chose to take and
for always getting back
up when you got knocked
down.

Lance
Allred

LONGSHOT

The Adventures of a
Deaf Fundamentalist
Mormon Kid and
His Journey to the NBA

 L Squared

 **L Squared**

L Squared Productions 2017

Second Edition Print

The names and identifying characteristics of some of the people mentioned in this book have been changed to protect their privacy.

First Edition: HarperCollins 2009

Library of Congress Cataloging-in-Publication Data is available.

ISBN 978-1546317760

09 10 11 12 13   RRD(H)   10 9 8 7 6 5 4 3 2 1

Dedicated to my parents,
Vance and Tana Allred,
who took the Allred name
and made it their own.

It is not the critic who counts, not the man who points out how the strong man stumbles or where the doer of deeds could have done them better. The credit belongs to the man who is actually in the arena, whose face is marred by dust and sweat and blood, who strives valiantly, who errs and comes up short again and again. Because there is no effort without error and shortcomings, he who knows the great devotion, who spends himself in a worthy cause, who at the best knows in the end the high achievement of triumph and who at worst, if he fails while daring greatly, knows his place shall never be with those timid and cold souls who know neither victory nor defeat.

—Theodore Roosevelt

Contents

Foreword

The game that best illustrates my own basketball career occurred when I was nine years old. I would argue it's vaguely illustrative of some of what Lance Allred has fought through—and that's good because who wants to read about an episode from my third grade year when it's Lance Allred's book you have purchased?

Brian Foltz called the house and told me his team needed two players and two players right now. I ran as fast as I could to Jeff Whidden's place. We ran together up to Star Lake Elementary. We were ready to create, or shy of that, stay out of foul trouble. If this team was two players short, it certainly didn't need foul trouble. But right away we became a liability to this Boy's Club group of cagers. One or both of us had dragged in dog poop onto the gym floor. Some of it was left on the court just inside the foul line. The coach didn't want his stars blowing out a knee by slipping on some dog poop dragged in by one or both of these marginal free agents. We weren't even eligible. My parents never signed the permission slip. Neither of us was a member in good standing of Boy's Club. There was so much hypocrisy, we both should have just walked out and let that team forfeit. But we cared about the game too much to do that. We cared so much we helped the game tip off by running down the hallway and getting paper towels so we could clean up the dog poop near the foul line. I don't recall much about the action. It was a blur. Basketball moves so fast when you're in third grade and all the others except Jeff Whidden are in fourth grade. I do remember being very proud that I'd committed no fouls. I ran up and told the coach this after the game. And I'll never forget what he said: "If you didn't commit any fouls, you weren't trying hard enough." It hit hard. It must have because it's stayed with me for forty years. My coach, the guy I'd put myself on the line for, the guy who brought me into his program because I filled a special need (my existence helped withstand a forfeit) had shattered my fragile ego with eleven words. Thirteen words if you count the contractions. I was a scrub basketball player the rest of my existence in the game.

Lance Allred played at another level. And this is his story of making it to the highest level. Lance never dragged in dog poop, but he did get dragged through some bullshit. But he never gave up. Not on the game, not on himself, not on life. He's honest about it when the failings were his own but more often than not his life story is an inspiration for anyone who's ever wanted to succeed at anything that appeared out of reach. In reading his story, you'll find yourself rooting for him. You're rooting for him when he goes to the grocery store with his brother and father and, with dignity, they find a way to make five dollars worth of food last them a week. That lesson in economics would serve him well when the paymaster for some shady-sounding European teams did new math on Lance's income bracket. But he wasn't in it to get rich. He was on the journey and the journey had one destination: The NBA.

You'll find yourself rooting for Lance and his family when they make their break to a new life, when Lance gets his first kiss, when he embarks on a quest to find his identity through a game that brings him equal heartache and joy. Did I mention he doesn't hear well? Yeah, but his vision is precise. He has scanned through his entire life and found meaning in the smallest detail. When it comes to basketball, he'll tell you he operates best when there's structure. He wants everyone to know their role and fulfill it. It works that way sometimes when everyone is on a team and a man in sweats is blowing a whistle and actual plays are drawn up to be executed. But in life there's chaos and despair. There's disloyalty, jealousy, and hypocrisy to wade through. It's tough out there. There's the very real threat that you're going to walk directly into some dog poop. The trick is in being bold enough to jump over it. Or clever enough to step around it. But more than that, an exceptional few find a way to deal with it when it can't be avoided. They clean up the mess they might have caused, then they clean themselves up and face it again. Most importantly, they face themselves. If the journey is really going to turn out well, they face themselves and one day they like what they see.

The American sports fan has lost perspective on what it means to make it to the league. We've gotten so caught up in worshipping the stars as gods, we've forgotten the worst player on the roster is still a marvelous athlete. The worst player on the roster is a member of a tiny percentage of humans out of 300 million in this country, out of 6.5 billion on this earth. The worst player is himself uniquely gifted. LeBron James is rarer still. But we don't consider much the guys on the wrong side of that fine line that separates who gets in the league and who remains in anonymity. Lance Allred found a way to cross the line. But that's just basketball. You see, even if Lance won't admit it, even if he's going to tell you his unending passion was this game, this mere game, his success was not in the completion of a goal to play in the NBA. His success was in the completion of *himself*. Because if the only measurement of Lance Allred was whether his name would appear on the back of an NBA uniform, what would it say for his life had the need not been there? If that call had not come? For his sake I'm glad it did. But the journey was always going to be his story. The NBA finally needed him when he no longer needed it. I'm not certain he even knows this yet. But you will once you read on.

—Kenny Mayne

LONGSHOT

Prologue

Soap and blood. It mixes in an odd sort-of-way. It looks like tie-dye but then is magnified and stretched on the bubbles as you see your blood reflected back at you in prismatic schemes.

My life, my blood, wound down the shower toward the drain, sucking my dreams along with it. I let my tears vanish with the water needling my face from the showerhead, so no one could see me cry. I'm all alone in the locker room, a lowly Boys and Girls Club locker room in Boise, Idaho, on a late November night.

I turned in the shower, grimacing with each step as my tattered and flayed feet smarted from each new coating of soapy water. Each shot of pain was worse than the one before as more blood oozed onto the tile canvas of a sort of Van Gogh painting. I looked at my shoes in my locker, my shoes that had traveled with me to Europe and back. Those same shoes that I had been wearing for nearly a year, on which I had logged hundreds of miles on the basketball court. I loved those shoes, but that's not why I kept them and continued to practice in them: I just couldn't afford any new ones.

I asked them to do their best; I blessed them in the hope that they'd get me through this training camp here in Idaho—just a little bit further—before I got some free team shoes. They tried, but failed. They really did try. But they were so tired, those shoes, that well-aged calluses on my feet had torn without warning, without blistering, flaying my skin, tearing it fresh from my feet, like an Iroquois would've scalped a head.

This was in the first practice that morning, but I came back that evening for the second practice, daring fate to try me, as I laced those worn-out shoes one more time. I said a prayer before the second practice and teetered on the outside of my feet as I went back out on the floor, letting the blood and sweat crystallize in my socks.

It was all on the line—my life, my dreams. If this was my last run, it was going to be on my terms.

With the first day now over, nine more were left before the final cut. I was now alone, letting my tears flow as water pounded my back heavy with the weight of my dreams. Here I was, in Boise, trying to earn a $12,000 contract in the NBA Development League. $12,000. Was that my worth? This was the last run, the end of the line, and I knew it. A bloody bubble popped and gargled in the drain, gorging on my comeback dream, or had this been nothing more than a pipe dream all along?

Was there even a difference?

Part One

Utopian
Dream

Onceuponatime, in the heart of the Bitterroot Valley, there was a town.

On the surface it appeared to be like any other American town. When someone drove into Pinesdale, Montana, circa 1981, they would've noticed nothing out of the ordinary, the town's timber sign smiling at them and saying Welcome to Pinesdale in bold plastic lettering—save the first "i" and "e", which had been sourly painted on in a light tone of jade, discouraging any further juvenile shenanigans alluding to the male anatomy.

Dirt roads were lined with tin garbage barrels where the nice folk—those who were proper and sanitary—burned their trash on a nightly basis. Then you had those who simply let their garbage fill well past the brim, too lazy to light a match. And then you had the neighbors who didn't even have or use a bin, opting instead to simply hold trash bonfires on the dirt road in front of their homes from which they roasted s'mores and hot dogs.

This was Montana, where Ford trucks were what yellow taxis were to New York. You had the obligatory psychotic jackasses who liked to shoot dogs for sport, even before the neighbor's dog could cross into their yard—a preemptive kill they rationalized with a foreshadowing of Bushisms as they spat their tobacco and straightened their brass belt buckle. When there weren't enough dogs to shoot, they rounded up all the little kitties they could find and buried them in the ground, leaving their heads above the surface as game to run over with lawnmowers. NASCAR wasn't televised in this rural part of the country yet.

You had the folk who left skeleton frames of regurgitated capitalism of all shapes and sizes on their front lawns, with a pleasant collection of wood-carved bears to add a hint of serenity to an otherwise macabre setting. Garden gnomes were frowned upon in Montana, as this wasn't England. No time for tea.

You had the disheveled, dark-haired kids running wild without their pants who liked to break into your house and eat your cold cereal and play with your toys while you and the rest of the town were at church. Mom always said it was impolite to call them "gypsies."

We had a mercantile with a gas pump, run by the scary redheaded lady. We had community picnics and work projects to help those in need around the town. We had kids roaming the wilderness of thick pine trees between the houses, stalking prey in the ongoing pinecone war. We attended the town chapel every Sunday and sang Sunday school songs as we walked back through the woods to eat our large evening dinners at Grandmother's house.

Yes, this was just another American town. This was my hometown—Pinesdale, Montana. We were your quintessential 1980 rural American community, with one glaring exception: Pinesdale was a polygamist commune, a budding utopian society. It was a town full of fundamentalist Mormons who practiced the principle of plural marriage—reverently referred to simply as the Principle. It was a town that had been established in the 1960s by Rulon Allred, my grandfather, to escape persecution and oppression from government authorities, so that he and others could practice polygamy freely.

In 1977, Rulon was assassinated by the wife of a rival polygamist leader in his private medical practice in Murray, Utah. This happened four years before I was born. I never knew the man, but I was raised in his dream, his hope for a utopian society—Pinesdale. And in the 1980s his dream was alive and strong.

Outsiders called us Pineys.

We called outsiders Gentiles.

We called ourselves children of God, His chosen elite, whom He watched over personally. Only we could be saved, only we could reach the highest degree of glory in Heaven. Only we practiced God's true laws. Everyone else would answer to God when the Day of Judgment came. We were going to be rewarded for our diligence, behavior that was validated every day when we saw our neighbors practicing the same lifestyle, confirming our own beliefs and convictions. Our life was our religion, and our religion was our life.

My name is Lance Collin Allred. I was born in my grandmother's bedroom on February 2, 1981. The youngest of five children, I was, surprisingly, near death at birth due to an Rh incompatibility with my mother; none of my four older siblings had this issue. Noticing that I was yellow as flypaper, my parents took me to the hospital in nearby Hamilton, where I was kept in an incubator for two weeks and received several complete blood changes. We were incredibly fortunate in that very small town there was a young doctor, Dr. Stover, newly trained at Johns Hopkins, who knew how to exchange my contaminated blood for fresh, lifesaving blood. My titer count had been up to forty-five. There was no reason I was still alive; a baby is usually dead when the count reaches thirty-five. To this day, doctors scoff or give a skeptical look when my parents tell my story. Dr. Stover said he was hesitant to even publish the findings because no one would believe him. My oldest sister, Raphael, who is now a family doctor, has no scientific explanation for it, either.

When people ask me what is was like growing up in a polygamist community, I simply shrug and answer that it was a wonderful childhood and I wouldn't change those memories for anything. I loved everything about growing up in Pinesdale, except for maybe my Sunday school teacher, who thought it her duty to tell me that God had made me deaf as punishment for not being faithful in the preexistence. She believed I had sat on the sideline in the Great War between God and Satan. However, rather than sending me to earth as a black man, God had only made me deaf, and for that I should be grateful.

She was lovely.

I was a bastard of sorts, culturally speaking, as I knew my father, Vance Allred, to have only one wife, while those around me were from homes that had several wives and mothers. I never knew Colleen, my father's second wife, as she took her three children and left shortly after I was born, after investing eight years in a plural marriage with my parents. It's completely understandable to me now why a woman such as Colleen wouldn't wish to play second fiddle all her life.* But in my young eyes, it was acceptable for a person to live either a monogamous or a polygamous life.

If you sit in the kitchen of a polygamist home long enough, you'll see a whole soap opera unfold before your eyes. You'll witness sister-wives coming and going, banding together to force their shared husband and provider to grant a unanimous request. After promising to stick together and hold firm, one by one they will filter out, but not before speaking venomous words about the sister-wife who just left the room. It's amazing how many people assume others won't talk behind their back after they have finished doing the same. Once one sister-wife is alone with her husband, she will sell out all the other wives to get what she wants. Fascinating dynamics, and very entertaining to watch. You can't make this stuff up.

As an infant and toddler, I was larger than life—a ball of mass and inertia—and very photogenic. But, sadly, everyone feared me to be mentally challenged, as I was slow in developing my verbal skills and frequently screamed and hit others. I punctured my sister Raphael's cheek with my mother's stiletto heel. I hammered out my dad's car window at eighteen months. My mother needed all three of my sisters to pin me down to change my diapers. The family was coming to terms with the idea that I, their youngest son, as I grew older, would live a life relegated to simply tending the rabbits and living off the fat of the land.

In a last-ditch effort, my parents took me to a panel of specialists in Missoula. They poked and prodded and finally suggested that I be given a hearing test at St. Patrick's Hospital. It was there my parents discovered that their little hulk was severely hearing-impaired. To this day we don't know if the nerve damage within my ears was sustained because of the Rh incompatibility issue that I had with my mother before my birth, or whether it occurred when I came near death as a newborn.

As a toddler I inherited the crib my father built with his own hands, one that had served all four of my siblings well but met its demise with me. It made my life miserable, so I was determined to repay in kind. The night has always made me uncomfortable, even to this day, as I lose my sense of sight along with my hearing. I was always on high alert, waking at the slightest tremor, real or imagined. Insomnia is my companion.

While locked away in the crib, I slowly began wearing out the rail joints so that I could twist them back and forth, forcing pitched squeals. I actually became impressively skilled. I knew which knob to twist in what way to hit whichever note I desired. It must have been pretty annoying— inspiring as well—for my parents to be awakened in the middle of the night by their young child performing Beethoven's Ninth on his bed set.

As one lures a dog to its kennel with a treat, Mom did so to me with a bottle of milk. I needed my nourishment, and I loved my milk. I didn't simply suck my milk bottles; I ripped the tips off the nipples with my teeth and guzzled the savory refreshment. When a bottle was empty, I chucked it from my solitary confinement of a bed, hit the door, and yelled "Mo' miwk!" I was endearing.

My parents again sought professional help after being driven to a zombielike state of sleeplessness because I wouldn't stay in my bed. They were finally advised to put me back in bed no matter how many times I persisted. On the first night of confrontation I was put back in my bed and climbed back out on my own accord over fifty times. The next night I did so about half that amount. Then half of that on the third night. But, as the specialist predicted, I regrouped and launched a Tet offensive on the fourth night, breaking the fifty mark again.

But my parents never gave in and continued to put me back in bed, paying my behavior no heed, as if I wasn't distracting them in any way. After that fourth night, I never got out of the bed again. My parents were kind enough, however, to grant me the right of staying awake as long as I liked, as long as I didn't get out of bed. I happily concurred and sang myself to sleep each night, spooning my mangy, gutted bottle.

At eighteen months, I was fitted with two hearing aids that hooked over the tops of my ears. While we who suffer from hearing loss may not hear well, we can still feel pain in our ears. Aside from the torture of the plastic penetrating deep down my ear canal, the blast of sound that pounded into my eardrums and reverberated throughout my skull for the first time was enough to make a grown man cry. I wasn't even two, and yet I didn't cry: I simply took them out at every opportunity and hid them. I hated those HAs.

It got to the point where Mom would "release the hounds," dispatching the siblings to find my hearing aids, and then reward them with treats or even money. But I was not playing her game; they could have their quarters and cookies as long as I had my silence. I was able to enjoy the peace and quiet for several days at a time as my family searched for my HAs. Unfortunately, they always found them: in my mother's winter coat pocket in the middle of July; between the box springs and mattress of my parent's king-sized bed, as far in as my little arm could reach; in the tall grass beside the creek bank; even under the two-by-four framing in the sidewalk that Dad was going to fill with concrete the very next day. My sycophant siblings always foiled my schemes.

Only after I realized that I could better hear Alvin and the Chipmunks on Saturday morning with my hearing aids did I start wearing them voluntarily, only to "accidentally" lose them again once cartoons were over.

When I was three, I began speech therapy on a triweekly basis, and I would remain in speech therapy until I was fifteen. It was basically a friendly reminder that I was not normal.

I always knew I wasn't like my siblings. While they all talked really loud to me, it was when I encountered children outside of the home that

I really noticed my difference. Ours was a town where plural marriage was a way of life, and thus there were gobs of kids—hundreds of bastards scattered like little ants, rummaging through the forest, all running with their own cliques, like Smurfs. Some kids were very cruel, playing with my hearing aids and making fun of the way I talked. I always had to be on the lookout for a pinecone coming my way, on a path to embed itself in my head. The only thing that irritated me more than an unforeseen pinecone in my temple was people disrespecting Neil Diamond. This fact holds true to this day. I love Neil Diamond. I adore him and will fight to no end defending his honor. I'm being neither flippant nor facetious.

It's no surprise I became a very self-conscious, quiet, and introspective child. There was one place I loved to go to get away from it all, and that was down by the river, where I had not a care in the world. Mom and Dad took us down there on the weekends, where we played and watched the older kids jump from the bridge.

The Bitterroot River, which runs the spine of its namesake valley, is where my memories are. I spent many days lying on tubes, floating down the river with my father, letting my head tilt back and dip in the water, which had its own unique smell and taste; there's no other water quite like the Bitterroot. I loved to skip rocks across her wide channels, staring up into the Big Sky, and tell her that I'd never leave.

The Bitterroot River is my lifeline. It's where all my dreams and hopes are held most precious. It's where my heart will always be. It's where I will be when I die. And it's where my future children and loved ones will find me and talk to me whenever they need me. That's where I will be. I have already achieved immortality, for my memories are there in the water, in the bittersweet smell that emanates from the water and the banks of sage and rough sand. My memories are alive down there in the Bitterroot, and my memories are what make me.

2

The offbeat gait thundered down the hallway, reverberating throughout the house like a sledgehammer. Only my father could make that noise, and he made it only when he was unhappy, which was only when someone had distressed Mom. Due to earlier construction accidents, one of Dad's legs was shorter than the other, and this made his gait distinct. I knew he was coming for me. I sucked in a breath of defiant air. He pushed the door open, his beet-red face twitching in displeasure; his Tourette's was acting up again: his neck and eyebrows twitched spastically, inextricably linked like a marionette doll.

I did my best to stare back at him without fear, but the first thing I saw from the corner of my eye was the unmistakable yellow paddle: a foot-long, six-inch-wide, inch-thick paddle that my father had carved and my mother painted yellow, with bouncy lettering proclaiming Because We Love You. By this logic, I was a very loved child.

But I came to reason that my father's handy skills provided me with more comfort overall than the discomfort caused by one single yellow paddle. It was a luxury to have a father around who could fix any wire short, pipe leak, or wall crack, and, most important, it was a luxury to live in a home you could say your father built with his own two hands. I grew up in a Tudor-style home, one of many homes in the town my father built with his own hands, for free, for the good of the cause. This one he got to keep for himself. The house stood out like a beautiful woman in an all-boys school, among all the other trailers and half- finished houses that were to remain forever so because the patriarch had another home to build for another new wife and couldn't finish the job. After three good whacks—don't worry, New Age parents, I'm not scarred, and I will spank my kids, too—Dad sent me downstairs to apologize to Mother. I sauntered out, rubbing my numb butt, plotting and scheming how I was going to rid myself of that damn yellow paddle.

Once the punishment was over Dad told me I was going with him down to the local home-improvement store. I jumped into the gold Buick, the fourth installment in the endless line of beater A-bodies Dad bought and wore to their graves that for many years accommodated all seven of us Allreds at once. As we drove, the awkward tension of what had transpired an hour earlier—Dad cricketing my ass and all—was palpable, and not even the Fleetwood Mac *Rumors* album in the tape deck could break it. Deciding to be the man in the situation, all savvy and adult, I took control and asked, like any five-year-old kid, "Dad, why aren't the people in Russia free?"

We pulled up to Dunbar's. I loved that store. I loved the smell of fresh sawdust and Elmer's glue: it was euphoric, not to mention hallucinogenic. Dad made the usual rounds, collecting two-by-fours, caulk and glue, drywall, and other assorted items, while letting me play with his measuring tape, which rolled up in a heavy steel case bigger than my hand. That thing weighed at least three pounds. Dad got a lot of mileage out of it. It was the perfect babysitter.

After the bill was settled, Dad displayed his efficient packing skills, which I have yet to see matched. Somehow forgetting that his car wasn't a truck, Dad calculated its every crevice, positioning the newly bought plywood and two-by-fours just so, angling them in crisscrossed patterns, from one rolled-down window to another, and then drove home, entertaining me with stories of his childhood with his forty-three brothers and sisters, the parents of my four hundred–plus cousins.

I helped Dad carry in the wood and had grand visions of me swinging a hammer, all chiseled and buff, standing in sawdust and laughing at splinters that dared to hurt me. I was ready to be a man, to feel the sweet sting of sweat in my eyes. Sadly, none of my father's building and carpentry skills have passed on to his children. Hoping for a hammer, I walked up to Dad, who was working under the sink or twisting wire in a circuit, and asked, "Can I help, Dad?"

Never breaking away to make eye contact, Dad said with a grunt, "Not right now, but you can sit down there and watch." This was something every one of us kids was told. It was a rite of passage in the Allred home. Instead of giving me a hammer, Dad gave me a piece of sandpaper. I don't know why I ever let myself think it was going to be any different than the time before. Dad never let me handle his tools. Nope: sandpaper was all I got. By this time, at the ripe age of five, I had done enough sanding for my father to build a wooden battleship. Dad still won't give me a hammer to this day, just a smile and a piece of sandpaper.

It was after a second fall from a ladder, and a second break in his left leg, as he lay in a hospital bed crying, not knowing what to do, that my father decided to go back to college. He was poor, had eight children, and was going nowhere. My family isn't quite sure how they pulled it off financially, sending my father to college while building a new home. But they did. Three years later, my father graduated first in his class from the University of Montana, with a bachelor's degree in history and a teaching certification, and we had our own home.

My father's going to college was an outrage to the men on the Council. In the Allred Group, you didn't need education. All men in the Group held the priesthood—the power, given by God, to act in His name and with His authority. They held it in their hands when they gave blessing to others while being inspired by God. Those who were deemed God's most worthy followers were inducted into the authoritarian Council. The Council was also referred to by all members of the Group as the Priesthood with a capital *P*. All male members had the priesthood and could lead and guide their own families, but only the Council had the right to lead and counsel all Group members in all matters. That meant they could make decisions affecting everyone. As in "The Priesthood has decided that it is now permissible to marry first cousins." These Council members, some of whom did not even have a high school diploma, were very vocal about my dad's going back to school. His increased knowledge only added to his threat (and his being a son of the Prophet was threat enough). He was told that an education would destroy his faith. (At least they were right about *something*.)

But I looked up to and respected my dad. Dad always seemed to have an answer for whatever was bothering my young mind. I found him one day next to his most recent drywall project. "Dad, where did God come from? Who was his dad?"

"Well, son," Dad paused, staring at his aluminum palette heaped with joint compound that he held like Picasso, "that's a question every young boy and every forty-year-old man wants to know the answer to."

Dad taught me that we study history not for miscellaneous data, but to learn vicariously from other people's mistakes. Life is much easier if one is able to do that. But as Dad explained, many are unable to learn from others' mistakes, let alone their own, and often think they are the exception, allowing history to repeat itself. Through my father, I learned I was no better, nor of less worth, than the next person, and if subject A performs an action to ugly consequences and subject B earns a similar fate, I will probably experience the same.

Later that night, as everyone was filtering off to bed, which was when my mind came out to explore the world, I watched my father playing games of solitaire, reflecting in silence at the kitchen table as he shuffled the cards and then flipped them over to memorize them. He never maneuvered them; he just memorized them.

"Dad, isn't that cheating?"

"No. I'm just memorizing what is there so I can win."

My father had no qualms about rationalizing the fact that he was cheating at solitaire.

"Dad?"

"Yes, son?" he asked as he observed the one-eyed jack.

"Why was President Kennedy shot?"

The next morning my brother Court and I lounged in the kitchen with our Audrey Hepburn of a mother. "Boys, don't make noise just to make noise," Mom said, standing at the sink. I sighed, got up, and began to put away my pots and pans. They were my amazing musical instruments. I couldn't understand why Mom didn't appreciate them. But never one to be deprived of enjoyment, I quickly ran to my Tonka truck, which sat in the corner of the kitchen with long, worn treads in the linoleum where I had passed the truck hundreds of times before. "Lance, would you like to take this outside and put it in the garbage for me?" Mom asked.

"No." I was an honest child.

"Lance, I will try that again. Take this outside to the garbage, please."

Acting as though she were asking for my left eye, I got up and took the bag outside.

When I came back in, she handed me a plate of winter squash with brown sugar on it. "I have a treat for you!" she said enthusiastically. My mother: the queen of treats. There was no fridge, no cupboard too bare that my mother, the ever resourceful woman, couldn't scour to find a treat to make. I sat down and happily ate the squash; Court scowled at it, preferring something more junky—which would explain his bad teeth.

She came up to me and started lightly and repetitively smacking my head: "Oh, you're just so cute I want to beat you! Squeeze you until your head pops off!" A perturbed look covered her face, which conveyed the frustration she endured at not being able to properly express how much she loved us. These threats were known as "Allred terms of endearment." My mother, Tana Mosier Allred, was raised in the mainstream Church of Jesus Christ of Latter-Day Saints (LDS) in Salt Lake City before her parents went through a painful divorce. Following the split, which was due to my grandfather's infidelities, my grandmother was looking for something to hold on to, something to give meaning to her suffering, something greater than herself. She found Rulon C. Allred. She took her four daughters, my mother being the oldest at sixteen, and moved them up to Montana. She had an older son, twenty-one at the time and on an LDS mission in Japan, who would come home to no home at all. And she had an older daughter, long since married and on her own.

My father was twenty and my mother sixteen when their marriage was arranged by Rulon. My father was in love with someone else, a woman he met in college, a woman outside of his extreme faith. Though she was LDS, she was certainly not a fundamentalist. My father didn't wish to upset his father or family and went along with his father's wishes. After all, Rulon was a prophet of God.*

Mom gave birth to her first child ten months later, when she was seventeen. She quickly added another four, me being the final and most glorious project in her twenty-sixth year.

My four older siblings were Raphael, Vanessa, Tara, and Court. Court and I were the two boys, with three older, nagging sisters to delegate their chores to us and then turn right around and tattle on us at every opportunity.

Mom was kind enough to make me and Court some karate suits, which we donned whenever we watched *The Karate Kid* and then ran upstairs to imitate to the best of our ability the Daniel-san Crane stance.

---

*I do not believe that Rulon saw God, nor do I know that he believed that he saw God, but I know that many of his followers, members of the Allred Group, believed he did, and I know that he allowed them to believe that. I remember, as a little child in Sunday school, being taught that Owen, Rulon's brother and successor, spoke with God, and that Rulon did as well.

I do, however, have to give my grandfather credit for being a very charismatic man who had a dream, a vision of a perfect society, and gave his all in an effort to achieve that—all in the name of the Lord. It's amazing what the human mind can do when there's hope, when there's a dream—especially a dream greater than oneself.

Court and I would assume our meditation stances, each bowing to the other, and then I would often sucker-punch him in the gut, leaving him on the floor, gasping for breath in the fetal position, while I strutted out of the room, tightening my black belt.

When I was five, my parents took me to get my first dog, a Norwegian elkhound mix. I found the ball of fluff sleeping underneath the breeder's porch, hiding in the shade. We took him home and named him Szen, a minor mishap on my mother's part, who mistook it for "Sven" in a telephone conversation with a friend while they were talking about Norwegian names.

Although I won't always mention him throughout my story, let it be known that Szen was the perfect watchdog and my own personal protector, always by my side. He never slept on my bed but always beside it, within reach throughout the night. Even though a mix, he was a beautiful dog, smart as hell, and well mannered, thanks mostly to my mother's training. As a five-year-old I had kindergarten only in the afternoon, and Mom, Szen, and I passed the mornings away doing whatever we pleased until I left for school. He was my dear friend.

Notice that I spoke about the dog before I did my siblings. That was intentional.

Raphael, or "Ruffles," was the eldest and eight years my senior. We kept our distance, or more accurately, I kept my distance from her. She was a tomboy with attitude who rode horses and had a permanently braided ponytail. She had a fat black cat who was just an extension of her intolerant self.

Raphael showed no hint of emotion or love or anything of the kind toward me. She simply tolerated me. Every so often she would deign to speak to me, but usually in the form of a command. At the age of twelve, Raphael made the commitment to become a medical doctor and would lose herself, as well as her love of horses and Piers Anthony novels, in her studies because she was a dork. But she always found time, or made the time, to torment Vanessa, who in turn tormented Raphael by simply choosing to exist.

Vanessa, the second-oldest child, was my caretaker, my second mother. She loved for Mom to leave on errands so she could assume the protective role over me. She loved to show me off and take me places. At the school Halloween party, she took me by the hand and introduced me to everyone she knew. . . . Scratch that: just everyone.

If she could've taken me to school with her every day, she would've had me sit right at her feet and color while she learned algebra.

When I was old enough to enroll in the afternoon kindergarten program, I was able to take the bus home with all my siblings. The bus driver, George, was a scary man with a crow's nose and a perma-sunburned neck who yelled and barked orders from the front of the bus, eyeing us all from his rearview mirror. No one said a word on the bus, let alone moved or, heaven forbid, stood up. If there was a hint of movement in the mirror, George looked up to eye you and the hand that was scratching your nose. I'd freeze in terror, telling myself, "If I don't move, he can't see me."

If anyone acted up, George had no qualms about dropping them off and letting them walk the rest of the way home. I love Montana. George was Montanan to the core: he spent all day shoveling shit on his own yard; he had no time for anyone else's.

One day I climbed on the bus, melancholy from a long afternoon of stares and brutally honest questions from brutally honest five-year-olds who'd ask, "What are those things around your ears?" or comment, "You look funny" or "You talk weird." George said something to me that I didn't hear. He then barked, "What are you, deaf? I'm talking to you!"

Vanessa, right behind me, turned around with her fists on her hips and stared George down: "Yes, he is, as a matter of fact. Do you have a problem with that?" It was the only time I had ever seen a sheepish George. All the kids sat with their jaws dropped, amazed that my sister had stood up to George. Vanessa would've stood up to Satan himself to defend me.

Raphael and Vanessa were always regarded as "the girls" and allowed different privileges as the elder. Poor Tara, also a girl, was always regarded as one of the kids along with us boys. There was an incident where Tara called for my father while he was taking a shower and he kindly, unknowingly replied, "Yes, son?" Tara ran off screaming in trauma.

Tara was my enemy.

The poor middle child had some issues, mostly about wanting to be regarded as one of the girls and respected by her younger brothers. If I didn't listen to her or obey her every command, she'd hit me, as though *Days of Our Lives,* a massive hit in our estrogen-dominant, pant-wearing family, was a true rendition of life.

Mom and Dad bought Tara Care Bears to remind her to be nice to her younger brothers. They also got her a bunny—a live one. One Sunday morning, Mom thought it would be fun for Szen and the bunny to play and be friends while we left for church. We came back home a few hours later to find the animals still playing, albeit the bunny in a macabre state, being flung lifelessly up in the air by a very happy Szen-the-Dog. I don't think he meant to break the bunny's neck, but he did.

Tara ran into the house, screaming bloody murder at the top of her lungs, while the rest of the women stood in horror, covering their mouths, and I admired my dog's great prowess and killer instinct. But don't get me wrong: I was sad about the bunny.

Dad dug the rabbit a grave, and in the evening the family held a burial service that we all attended to pay our respects, except of course Tara, who had chosen to behave like a wife of Henry VIII. Her idea of mourning was screeching and spitting sobs of loss and sorrow from within her bedroom, leaving her window open so we could all hear her mournful wails. From time to time, just for good measure, she popped her head out of the window to make sure we all heard her refrain: "My rabbit's dead!"

To ease her sorrows, but mostly to get her to pipe down, Dad bought Tara a Cabbage Patch doll. Our lives of peace and tranquillity resumed.

Two days later Szen dug up the corpse and renewed his play.

My brother, Court, was a wonderful big brother to me. He was patient and accepting and always let me tag along with him and his friends. Court was the local tough kid. This was a truth undisputed by any of the kids in town our age, as Court had a Billy Ray Cyrus mullet going on that silenced any critics.

It's a wonder he put up with me and my pettiness for so long, as I was the type of younger brother that didn't want a toy until his older brother wanted it. There was a Christmas when Mom and Dad got Court a big fire truck, but he could never play with it because I'd always race to it if I saw him eyeing it. From then on, Mom and Dad bought duplicate toys for us every Christmas, and on Court's birthdays as well.

Court has always had a sense of right and wrong and what is fair and what isn't. He saw and still sees things only in black and white. There was a boy named Tyler Johnson who was the local bully. One day, Tyler stole Court's Big Wheel trike and threw it in the pine-needle-foliage bonfire.

Court came home in a fit of rage: "Mom, I hope Jesus comes and takes Tyler Johnson's body away." Jesus was omnipresent and broody, or at least our young minds believed him to be so. That Big Wheel tricycle meant a lot to us. We had long since worn out the treads on the plastic wheels that we peeled out on, and some parts of the wheels were so badly torn that a smooth ride was no longer an option, but still, we loved those wheels. Loved them enough to wish hellfire on someone else's soul.

3

There was a grumpy, redheaded lady who ran the local mercantile in Pinesdale. It was a thriving business, even though she made no profit off it, as it was the property of the utopian cause, belonging to the Council or, officially, the AUB (Apostolic United Brethren). The lady was big and strong, standing at six feet, with flaming auburn hair. The children of the town were terrified of her. Even I was terrified of her, and she was my maternal grandmother, Edith Mosier. We grandkids called her "Yaya."

She was stern, blunt, and a no-nonsense type of lady. Yaya was the incarnation of a Norman Rockwell painting. Whether it was her baking goodies, making chocolates and homemade turtles for her grandchildren, giving piano lessons, managing the town mercantile, or doing hard labor out in her garden in the rough Montana soil, every memory of her I have as a child could be frozen in a Norman Rockwell moment.

She frightened children. If a child came into the store not knowing exactly what they were looking for and instead moseyed about indecisively, Yaya would lean toward them over the glass cabinet that sheltered all of her candy, casting a shadow only Paul Bunyan could match: "I don't have all day."

She never seemed to get the fact that her standing there made the kids more nervous. "If you don't know what you want," she'd say, "then get out of the store and stop wasting my time. Come back when you know what you want." The customer always came first for Yaya.

She gargled hard liquor for cough syrup and was big on tough love. "Watch where you're going, ya' big dummy!" she would chide me, as I often tripped over things since my inner-ear imbalance lent me the gross motor skills of an alcoholic giraffe.

I was her youngest grandchild for six years. I had it made. She spoiled me rotten and loved me, but she showed it in an odd way: "What did I tell you? Go put it back in the kitchen. What are you, deaf?"

Yaya lived around the corner from us, but her place was even closer if we cut through the forest into her back lawn. If she wasn't home, she was at the store, a ten-minute walk.

I loved to go to the store and sniff around her office, which smelled of unfinished Butterfingers and pencil shavings. When no one was looking I'd lift Sour Patch Kids and Swedish fish, thinking I was being sneaky, stuffing as many as I could in my mouth and then a good sum in my pockets. Yaya always knew my game and placed pennies in the cash register later to make up for the losses. She also had a toy stand and from time to time would reward me with a fresh batch of ammo for my cap-gun revolver if I was a good boy and took a nap behind the iron bars of the post office, which was conjoined to the store, letting her get some work done.

It was a perfect life for a little boy.

I was and still am Yaya's favorite grandchild. While I mostly say this with an arrogant flair to get a rise out of my siblings and cousins, they have, one by one, collectively come to terms with this truth. Just as they now know that the snow falls in December, they know that Lance is Yaya's most cherished descendant.

In Pinesdale we had our own set of rules; we were above the laws of the secular world. We adhered to the laws of God, or at least the laws of those who were anointed to interpret the word of God for us. Those anointed men were our prophet and his Council. Most of those men were Allreds or Jessops.

In the Allred Group, the two main families were the Allreds and the Jessops. In Utah, the Allreds were unquestionably dominant. But in Montana, the Jessops reigned supreme. They outnumbered everyone else, not only in population, but in influence and privilege as well. Marvin and Morris were on the Council, and they, their six brothers, and numerous offspring granted themselves certain entitlements. Nothing was beyond their overreaching grasp: political or bureaucratic positions, church callings, or homes—vacant or not. Not even the Allreds in Salt Lake had that sort of clout.

I learned first-hand living in a socialist commune within a capitalistic country, why socialism does not work: different people have different senses of entitlement and work ethic. Someone like my father, who built four houses for the good of the cause without receiving a dime, feeling he could never give or do enough, would be exploited by those who felt they deserved more for less. Entitlement is a vicious disease. For all the masses of people who strive for a communal dream, it takes only one to destroy it with greed and entitlement, grasping for their piece of the pie, as the system will then collapse under its own weight.

In Pinesdale, my parents were protectors of the little people, those who didn't carry the last name of Allred or Jessop. People loved them because they treated everyone equally. They let each person know they were a child of God and were special in their own right. Morris and Marvin Jessop hated this.* After all, they had several wives and dozens of kids and were members of the Council, and though my father had none of those redeeming traits, everyone loved and listened to him.

Many expected, but never publicly acknowledged, my father to be the successor of the Allred Group. But he couldn't do so until he gained a second wife. My father was a scripture fiend who fanatically studied the Bible and the Book of Mormon and knew more about doctrine than the men on the Council. But alas, with only one wife, my father was ineligible to be on the Council. What was so remarkable about my father was that even though he could embarrass these "men of god" at any moment with scripture, he never did. He raised me to know that when we argue scripture, we lose its meaning and purpose and the spirit of Christ.

In my parent's world there was no hierarchy, no Allred or Jessop nobility. It was hard for me to reconcile the world inside my parent's home with that of the larger culture in which I was raised. Hypocrisies and inconsistencies occurred in our little utopian society, in that, although everyone was supposed to be equal, all of us children of God, we were, in fact, not treated equally at all.

Yaya's two youngest daughters, Sam and Audra, were a lively pair of girls. As they were teenagers in the 1980s, they wore curlers in their hair to bed, and kept beer in the fridge, not to drink but to add more life and shine to their hair. They had a collection of vinyl that any fan of the eighties would crave: Bryan Adams, U2, Jackson Browne, Heart, Air Supply, the *Top Gun* soundtrack, and the likes.

---

*Someday my father will finish telling his story and give you further insight into this way of life—how everything, work or play, was aimed to better our little utopian society and how by the age of twenty-five my father had built four houses and never made a dime on any of them, because it was all for the betterment of the dream. We were all preparing for the Second Coming of Christ—that much I knew.

In high school, Aunt Audra began dating Shawn Stoker. The Stokers were a rising, up-and-coming family in Pinesdale. One of the daughters of Marvin Jessop was married to Clyde Stoker, the patriarch of the family.

Life being what it is, Shawn and Audra replicated the Bruce Springsteen song "The River" almost to a T: they got pregnant. And back in 1986, in fundamentalist-Mormon Pinesdale: oh, the horror. It's not a far stretch to compare it to *The Scarlet Letter.* How people reacted, gossiped, hissed, and snarled. Clyde Stoker went into a rage, saying Audra had defiled and seduced his son and gotten him pregnant. He asked Marvin Jessop, his father-in-law, peer in age and superior in Priesthood authority, to step in and protect his family's honor. Marvin then told Shawn that he needed to take Audra off and marry her, to elope, for she was now his property as she had given herself to him.

My father came home late one night to see Yaya trying to pull Audra from a car while Shawn was trying to keep her in. My father got into the car with Shawn and Audra and drove away. He had Shawn drive to a quiet spot, stop the car, and calm down. Shawn admitted that he was following Marvin Jessop's instructions.

My father tried to explain that this wasn't the right way to handle the situation: the fact that a member of the Council said to do something didn't mean that it was right. Shawn respected my father, for although my father wasn't on the Council, he was the son of Rulon Allred. More important, Dad was an expert on the Mosier women and told Shawn that dragging Audra away in the middle of the night wasn't a good way to start a marriage.

Shawn answered, "But the Priesthood told me to come take Audra."

Dad replied, "Shawn, in five years the Priesthood isn't going to care whether or not you drag Audra away, and they won't accept any responsibility for the situation in which you'll find yourself. But Audra and all of our family will never forget, and you alone will pay the price. Is that how you want to start a marriage?"

Shawn went home alone that night instead of obeying Marvin Jessop.

When Marvin found out about Dad's intervention, there was hell to pay, for my father had undermined his authority. It got ugly. But where my father was concerned, it wasn't about egos and who was right and wrong: it was about Audra and doing what was best for her. For Marvin, it was the opposite: the charismatic son of Rulon Allred, whom everyone loved, had challenged his power. So Dad had to be taught a lesson, and Yaya needed to be punished.

My parents struggled to reconcile their understanding of what their religion was based on with this petty, arbitrary, and frightening position taken by these men who claimed to speak for God, these men into whose hands they had placed their lives. Morris Jessop adamantly told Mom, "If Vance ever wants the Priesthood to have any confidence in him, he simply needs to learn to do as he is told."

Suddenly, Mom and Dad felt as though their world was tilting drastically. Everything they owned was controlled by these men. More important, once it was clear that the Council had no confidence in Dad, Mom and Dad didn't feel that they could have confidence in the Council. If standing up for a young woman's right not to be dragged away from her mother was cause for Dad to be excluded from Heaven, something was surely not right in Pinesdale.

What had been a private family issue now became a public matter: Marvin had the power of the pulpit and used it to call my father down publicly, warning that no one—not even the son of a former prophet—could interfere with the power of the Council without incurring the displeasure of God. Dad was so troubled by the turn of events that he wrote an appeal to his uncle Owen, my grandfather's successor and the recognized prophet of the Group.

My parents drove to Salt Lake and presented their written appeal to Uncle Owen, who, rather than looking at the issues, also became angry with Dad for challenging the authority of the Council. Dad tried to explain to Owen that he no longer felt safe in Pinesdale: "If anyone has to be punished because Audra became pregnant, why is it Edith?"

"Because she's a woman," Owen said dryly.

When Dad tried to reason with Owen, it became very clear that Morris and Marvin had told a very convincing story, painting my dad as a meddlesome usurper. When Dad began quoting scripture and citing the teachings of Mormon prophets, Owen cut him off: "You're not in charge. The Council is."

My parents came home devastated, knowing that everything they had believed Pinesdale to be was now a sham. Rather than a safe haven for the people of God, it was a place where women were not safe in their homes. Rather than being ruled by the teachings of Jesus Christ, it was ruled by the whims and tempers of men. This was no utopian society, for those who wanted power had finally worked their way to the top. The dream was no more.

Dad became painfully aware that he had built our beautiful house on land he didn't own. When he heard the rumors that Morris wanted our house for one of his wives, Dad could see the writing on the wall. The many friends who had loved Mom and Dad began to separate themselves, fearing that the displeasure Morris and Marvin poured on Mom and Dad would spill over into their lives.

Marvin continued to battle my father from the pulpit in church and early-morning Priesthood meetings. He put forth some interesting ideas in his sermons, one being that through the plan of eternal salvation, God and Jesus could fail. Although God could fail, Satan would be redeemed and live with us in Heaven for fulfilling his role in the plan. We couldn't depend on Jesus, so we had to have faith in the Council and should never question its authority. Also, without much tact, Marvin spoke at the funeral of my uncle Louis, who had committed suicide. My father, who loved Louis, recalls that as the saddest day of his life. At Louis's funeral, Marvin said, "Because he was weak and took his own life, Louis will be in hell."

Through all of this and Marvin's other absurd preachings, my father never spoke up or interrupted Marvin, which made Marvin all the more hostile to him. Dad sat there in silence until the day came when he stood up in church, walked home, and told us, "We're moving to Utah."

Moving to Utah would mean more for my parents than just surrendering all of their utopian faith and dreams. It meant losing a beautiful house that was all paid for, one that Dad had built with his own hands and Mom had turned into a loving home. It meant that Mom, who had never worked, would have to become a working mom. It meant that our lives would change, for we would leave with nothing but memories of all that we had loved.

Some ask why we didn't leave the Group altogether at this point. And Dad, of course, looks back and thinks that if he could've just moved us to Missoula, where he used to teach school every day and had a good salary, my parents might not have had to endure the financial struggles that plagued them for the next twenty years. Why couldn't Dad have just said that he had had enough and thrown caution to the wind, hellfire and brimstone be damned?

He couldn't because he still believed that his father was a prophet. It was seven more years before my father came to terms with the fact that his father wasn't a prophet. He had to recognize that he himself wasn't a special descendant of a prophet, that he wasn't elite, and that he wasn't going to be exalted to the highest degree of glory in Heaven just because he lived Rulon Allred's way.

He will tell you that people want to feel special. They want to feel validated. They want to feel that their life is unique and that it counts for something. Being a part of the Allred Group—living in the idea, true or not, that you're God's chosen people, big fish in a small pond—is a scary thing to abandon when you realize that once you're in the larger world, you're just another person among many. Dad also had to tackle the fear of what would happen to you if you abandoned someone you believed was a prophet, and his teachings, when you were that prophet's son.

When I was six years old, my father wasn't quite ready for the great shift and simply moved us to Utah to reunite with his father's family and followers there, where Marvin Jessop would no longer have sway over his life. Marvin got Pinesdale all to himself, and his brother Morris got my father's Tudor home.

4

We moved to a house in Murray, Utah, a suburb of Salt Lake City, in the fall of 1987. It was a long eight-hour drive from Montana; it was light-years away from all that I knew. It was there, away from the security of Pinesdale, that I became aware of how truly different I was.

I attended the first and second grades at Grant Elementary. At the age of six, I was bigger than most of the kids in the school, and I had these large "things" sticking out of and over my ears, and I wasn't a regular Mormon—something they deduced, for I didn't attend church with any of the kids at school. Even though, technically, we were Mormon as we based our beliefs on Joseph Smith and the Book of Mormon, we were outcasts: any person caught in a polygamous marriage was immediately excommunicated from the LDS church. No one at Grant Elementary knew that I was of polygamist stock, as I never told, nor did I dare.

The kids liked to taunt me. There were these three kids, who were older than me, that liked to torment me, and take my hearing aids and throw them around and make me chase after them. One day they ganged up on me and trapped me in the bathroom, pinned me down, pulled off my pants, and ran out. Another boy walked in as they ran out with my pants and was kind enough to find a hall monitor. My pants were found and returned to me in my stall, where I quietly cried against the door.

I never pointed out my tormentors. I didn't want to be that kid. I wanted to fight my battles myself, or at least suffer the humiliation alone. I was more embarrassed than I was traumatized and didn't want my family to know that my pants had been taken from me. Court did his best to protect me. He was a wonderful brother, despite my pettiness towards him and my deliberate attempts to irritate him at times—things that younger siblings can't resist. I taunted Court as it was the only way I could feel tough, and Court was kind enough to let me.

With our new financials struggles, my mother had to take a job and could no longer be the stay-at-home mom I was accustomed to. She wasn't there when Court and I left for school in the morning, nor was she there when we got home in the afternoon. This life was so incredibly different from the cozy one that I had in Montana.

Whenever I had the nerve or gall to have myself a bad day and let it be known by being grumpy, or pouty, or maybe even shedding g a tiny, little tear my father would not only fail to validate that I might have reason to have a bad day, but would instead dismiss my problem with some bunkum and clichés about how I was the only one who could affect my attitude. Then one day after he was nearing the end of his repertoire of clichés, he finally figured how to deflect me and my moodiness with a catchy little question that stuck, followed, and haunted me for the remainder of my childhood. It ultimately became synonymous with me as a human being: "Lance, do you want to be the Big Lance or the Little Lance?"

My father read a story, in one of his "how to win friends and in-fluence people" genre books that were endlessly stacked in his library, about a man who motivated himself by asking, "Crusoe, are you the big or the little Crusoe? Little Crusoe, leave me!"

For reasons that are beyond me, my father never used this ploy with any of his other children. Nay, I'd be the lone subject of this hokey par-enting experiment. Whenever I was mad, *every time,* one of my parents would call, "Lance...?" with insinuating eyebrows, "Big Lance or Little Lance?" They asked this tedious question, feigning concern for my long-term development, when really it had just become for them a conditioned response, like a dog barking at a knocking door.

To their credit, it was a very effective conversation ender. Even if I had made the most staggering, incontrovertible point in an argument, it mat-tered little, for they'd always counter with "Big Lance or Little Lance?" Trying to get them to see my point was like trying to get a Baptist to read the Koran.

"But, Dad, we both know that Tara hit me and stuck her tongue out at me when Mom was disciplining me. You just saw it!"

"Lance..." My father would say indifferently as he clinked his sil-verware, as only my father can, against the bowl he held in his hand, scooping and chiseling for the last little speck of Grape-Nuts in his bowl. So focused was my father whenever he ate a bowl of cereal that he didn't care if he had to chip away and eat some of the glass bowl as long as he got that last little bit of Grape-Nuts. He then set the bowl down in the sink (no one fills up a kitchen sink faster than my old man) and pulled out his dental floss, proceeding to talk as he flossed his teeth, etiquette be damned. "Do you want..."—he pulled away the floss and then sucked from the floss some of the crumbs he managed to wrangle free from his gums—"... to be the Big Lance or the Little Lance?"

Or another scenario: "Mom, I don't want to go to speech therapy."
"Do you want to be the Big Lance or the Little Lance?"

Or another: "Dad, I think I'm bleeding internally."
"Big Lance or Little Lance?"

And: "Dad, there's a man in the back lawn giving me a creepy look while cupping his hands on the window."
"Son, do you want to be the Big Lance or the Little Lance?

Or: "Dad—"
"Big Lance or Little Lance?"

Or: "Dad! I just cured cancer!"
"Do you want to be the Big Lance or the Little Lance?"

This pep-talk technique that Mom and Dad used on me reached its zenith the day I learned my first bad word. It was a harmless word really. "Kids, come eat!" Mom yelled as we five hungry blonds poured down the stairs. The table was set, pleasantries were exchanged, a prayer was offered, and we each stated something positive about one of our siblings. The spaghetti was passed, with the sauce, hot in its pan, remaining in the center. Father sat at the helm with his helpmate across from him: "So, Raphael, how did your test go today?"
"Splendid, dear Father, I thank you."
"That's swell, Vanessa—"
"Pass the fucking bread, please."
One of my elder sisters had already started to pick up the bread when she stopped, having fully processed what I had just said. Gasps abounded, and a moment of incredulous shock crashed the tranquility of the dinner, as though we had all just witnessed a public hanging.
"Lance!"
"Lance!"
"Lance!" spewed from each open mouth circling the dining table, echoing off the walls in the sudden stillness.
"You cannot say that, not only at the dinner table, but anywhere."

I raised my hands to protest innocence: "But I said 'please.'"

"It does not matter," Mother reprimanded me. "Don't use that language in our home. Your friends may say that at school, but I don't want you to use that language ever."

The family stared disapprovingly at me, their black sheep of a child, the youngest of the batch, who was only trying to find a way to establish his own identity amid the dominant elder sisters who talked all night at the dinner table, never caring about anyone's accomplishments but their own, taking turns telling the parents about how awesome they were.

"OK," I sighed.

Silverware tinkled and clinked, chiseling through the icy tension of disappointment that hovered over the dinner table. Dad cleared his throat, his face still flushed from the previous moment's impudence. "So, Vanessa, did you answer that boy back yet, about prom?

"Well, not—"

"Pass me the fucking butter." If *"please"* didn't work, why use it? I reasoned.

"Lance! Big Lance? Or Little Lance?"

My father's mother, Myrtle, lived in Taylorsville, which was another suburb of Salt Lake, connected to Murray. We got to see her every Sunday when we attended Sunday school, which was held in the fourplex owned by the AUB.

Sunday school and church sessions were always fun in the Group. We used huge drinking glasses for the water that we anointed as a token of the blood of Christ, which we passed from person to person, letting each drink from the glass. There were a lot of old ladies at Sunday school, most of them widows of Rulon who wore really rich and thick makeup, including lipstick that spread like peanut butter. You waited for the glass to be passed around, up and down the rows, everyone putting their mouth on it, backwashing and leaving lipstick marks, and by the time you got it, you were rotating the cup to find a spot that wasn't marked with lipstick where you could safely place your lips. I always got to see Grammy at Sunday school, and she was one of the better widows, as her makeup wasn't too generous.

Grammy always said her favorite color was purple. I never believed her, because she was all green. Everything in her living space was green:

Green table, green carpet, green counter, green dishes, green wallpaper, green Tupperware holders that housed pumpkin cookies if it was the right day of the week. Green silverware handles, green sofa and love seat, and a green toilet to accompany the green soap on the green counter in the green bathroom.

When Grammy served food, she made sure you ate it all. She never let me remove myself from her kitchen table until I had finished my entire bowl of cornflakes. I'd oblige and drink my milk, but then she would grab me and say there was still more, pointing to the soggy, spongy, half-dried-up pieces of cereal that clung to the upper fringes of the bowl. After a weak protest, which was futile, I'd peel away the cornflakes like scabs, placing them one by one in my mouth, shuddering as each one leeched to the roof of my mouth.

With every meal she had home-baked wheat bread, cold butter, and homemade apricot jam. It's strange, but if I see any sort of liquid or gelatinous substance with chunks in it, like chunky jam or globby Cream of Wheat, I won't eat it. This, and my inability to eat meat from bones, are my two quirks when it comes to food. When I'm eating meat from bones and see ligaments and tendons rip from chicken legs, I recall all the sprained knees and ankles I have endured and lose my appetite.

Another issue with homemade jam is that jam jars are prime nesting grounds for fruit flies. And fruit flies are my biggest phobia. Dad always made himself a jam sandwich each morning before he left for work, but he *never* put the lid back on. After I woke up, I'd walk into the kitchen, hitting my head on an open cupboard door—which Dad never closed, either—only to discover that fruit flies had miraculously appeared out of nowhere. Seriously, where the hell do they come from? They mocked me as they congregated at the jam jar, circling about the open lid as though they were all having an intense philosophical debate, all the while enjoying a wonderful meal.

The focus of Grammy's living room was a shrine to Rulon and his many wives: a huge hand-carved oak board covered with a collage of pictures of the entire family. I often stared at it, examining all the black-and-white photos of my grandfather and his wives and children. I liked to play Where's Waldo? with photos of my father, looking for him in the sea of forty-four childish faces. However, Grammy, who was very savvy and saw into the future, knew this question of identity would become an issue, so she made all three of her sons of the proud Lloyd lineage

wear matching homemade striped button shirts in all their family photos. Consequently, my father, Vance Lloyd Allred, was pretty easy to
find, along with his older brothers, Saul Allred and Lloyd George Allred.
Grammy loved that Lloyd name.

Once you made an impression on Grammy, it stuck. For good or bad.
She had favorites. Some of her impressions made no sense, but not the
one she had of me. I was known as her "most polite grandchild." Neither the fact that this public coronation came when Grammy was well
lost in her senility, nor the fact that her anointing came at the tail end of
her most recent narration of her latest bowel struggle, made it any less
true. It was a title that was hard-won and maintained with integrity.

I was in the second grade when the tension between me and Tara reached
its apex. When Mom had to start working, Tara decided she was my sur-
rogate mother and began to boss me around all day. If I didn't comply,
she'd slap me. Being the little tattler she was, she loved to scamper off to
Mom at the slightest excuse. Mom would call me down and say, "Lance,
you can either apologize to Tara or have time-out."*

Without skipping a beat, I bluntly declared, "Time-out," and walked
to my stool in the corner of the kitchen to assume my post. I sat there in
silence, satisfied and content. Mom and the rest of the family went about
their business, while Tara, livid red, would stay, dedicating herself to the
task of standing watch over the timer to make sure I served my full punishment. But I was savvy enough to see I had won the battle. It was war,
and I was, and still am, a believer in self-sacrifice for the greater good,
for victory in the long run. No shame in moral victories.

One Christmas I came up with a scenario that I knew would blindside
Tara. Each Allred child received an Advent calendar with pieces of rich
milk chocolate behind twenty-four little doors. Each door was labeled
with a date counting down to Christmas. Being the calculating child that
I was, I snuck into Tara's room on the day we got our Advent calendars,
and found hers. I opened the last door—the twenty-fourth, the one with
the biggest piece of chocolate—ate my prize, and then sealed the door

*The physical spankings at the hand of the yellow paddle had become so frequent that my
parents, beginning to feel guilty, had instead embraced isolation and imprisonment as a sound
alternative.

shut. I waited with delicious anticipation for twenty-three days, my excitement rising each day, until the morning of Christmas Eve, when a shrill shrieking woke up the house: "Who ate my chocolate?!"

Although I couldn't hear exactly what was screamed, as I don't sleep with my hearing aids in, I knew it was Tara, and I just imagined her holding her empty calendar. I smiled, pleased that it had been as rewarding as I had hoped. I then yawned, leaned over and patted Szen, and went back to sleep. A few minutes later my room was bombarded by my mother—with Tara behind her, scowling, nostrils flaring.*

"Lance, did you eat Tara's chocolate?"

"Yes."

Mom had been expecting a denial. She raised her eyebrows, somehow still managing to be shocked after all my previous confessions about how much I loathed my sister. It was as though she could not believe I was admitting my guilt so freely, an obvious manifestation of how much I disliked my sister. I suspect that maybe Mom was even a little let down that I had not lied and made an incident out of it. I know Tara was, as it only made her more angry. She wanted me to lie so I'd be punished even more. "Well . . . ," Mom stalled, always managing to stay graceful, never stuttering, but thinking on the fly, " . . . then you'll have to give Tara your chocolate."

I played along, letting them think I was about to be taught a lesson. I rolled out of my warm bed on the chilly December morning and walked over to my Advent calendar atop my cluttered dresser arranged with various gum wrappers, paper clips, grimy pennies, G.I. Joes, and stone turtles. I retrieved the calendar and handed it to Tara. She had a malevolent look on her face that betrayed an eagerness for my last chocolate. I would've felt bad had I not hated her so much. Instead, I relished the disappointment that enveloped her face when she discovered that my last chocolate wasn't there. With foresight, I had eaten it the night before, expecting this moment to play out as it had.

Without having to be told, I walked downstairs to my time-out stool, my chin high and haughty, as though I was a martyr. It was one of my prouder moments.

---

*Although today Tara is a very pretty and charming woman and has grown into her nose, as a child her nose didn't fit her face. And her nostrils, if she wanted, could become as big as her eyes.

.   .   .

Twice weekly, my siblings lined the living-room window like codepen-
dent puppies, watching begrudgingly as Mom and Dad dragged me out
into the driveway and forced me into the car as I kicked, screamed, and
scratched like a cat avoiding bathwater. It was as though my siblings
believed that Mom and Dad were whisking me away to a wonderful
and delightful world of candy canes and gumdrops, dancing bears and
giggling midgets.

It was anything but. This is where I went every week.

Against my wishes I'm crammed into a dimly lit soundproof room,
forcefully seated, then wrapped with cords and cables and fitted with
tight headphones and plugs around my head that will fuse into my skin
after ten minutes. All the while some pleasant John Denver song
lingers in the background for good measure.

I look at all the pretty and enticing toys around me: the xylophones,
spongy puzzles, the thing made of little whirly slides and wires with
wooden shapes sliding around them. I never know what that's called.
What was that called? And of course, the obligatory stuffed monkey
with cymbals. I suspect a camera inside the monkey's head. Sometimes
I even expect the monkey to come alive.

Monkey aside, I'm tempted to play with the toys. But I don't, for I
know they're only a ploy to disarm and trick me into complacency.
I imagine someone's little Ricky or Timmy before me, picking up the
toys and dying in gruesome, unpleasant ways. Disturbing thoughts rattle
in my head until the guy that narrates those grisly and dark horror-
movie trailers comes onto the speaker: "Lance . . . can you hear me?
Nod if you do."

Sometimes it's a sultry female voice. But I know the game, and they
know I won't fall for the Eve tactic. If they're going to take me down,
I'm going to make it as unpleasant for them as possible. Scary-movie
voice fumbles with the microphone: "Lance, raise your hand when you
hear the tone. Can you hear that? Lance? The sooner you start cooperat-
ing, the sooner it will be done. Thank you. Good. . . ."

A few minutes of my feigned complacency pass.

"Wait! . . . Are you timing the sounds? Lance, you're not helping
us to help you if you're guessing at the tones. If you don't hear the
one, don't raise your hand. We cannot get a full assessment of your
hearing if you're going to cheat, and therefore your hearing aids won't

be as effective as you need them to be. Nod that you understand. Thank you."*

When phase one is over, a faceless tormentor returns to the booth, as I'm obstinate at his efforts to replace the current headphones with even tighter ones. I'm not going to make the bastard's job any easier. He mumbles something, but with my hearing aids out I cannot make out what it is that he says. I'm sure it's something less than polite.

Scary-movie voice (SMV) comes back on.

smv: "Lance. Can you hear me? Say 'Yes.'"

me: "Yes."

smv: "Good, now repeat after me. Doll."

me: "Doll."

smv: "Car."

me: "Caw."

smv: "Car."

me: "Cow?"

smv: "Jar."

me: "Jow . . . ? Oh, Jaw!"

The door opens once more and I'm lifted from the chair. After a stop at the Chinese water torture room, I'm led into another room, better lit than the sound booth, but still cold: two chairs, a steel table, and no windows, but another one-way mirror. Were they going to ask about the cinnamon bear I lifted from Dad's dresser? I didn't see the harm. Dad had an endless stash of them. Surely he wouldn't notice one missing, would he?

---

*It wouldn't be until I was sixteen—when I'd finally stop guessing at the hearing tests, trying to hide or mask my impairment—that I'd be fitted with a really solid pair of hearing aids. It was no one's fault by my own: in my pride and attempt at "normality," I thought it better to try to downplay my impairment and cheat on the tests rather than acknowledge it and be fitted with proper hearing aids. And my family had to suffer through my incessant whats and huhs and would always say, "Why don't your hearing aids work?" Or, "Lance, turn your hearing aids up"—even though they were already on full blast.

An attractive woman enters the room, wearing a two-piece business suit. She walks around the table and places files on the table with a landing that is soft, but accented enough to draw my attention: "Hi, Lance."

"Hi."

She pulls out the chair and leans over to scoot herself into the table, showing abundant cleavage while doing so, which is accentuated by the Catholic cross bouncing between her tracks of land—something that can only make a little boy wonder. It confuses me that a symbol of Christ, the Cross, triggers such improper thoughts.*

"My name is Christina," says the pretty woman, whom I now have a crush on. The crush does not last long.

"OK."

"Can you say, 'Hi, Christina'?"

I'm baffled at the narcissistic request until I realized there is an *r* in her name. "Yes, I can," I cleverly respond, making sure to use those three easy words that are free of that hateful letter *r.*

"Well, can you say it now, please?"

I feign confusion, and to avoid her request I calculatingly say, with slow precision to allow my mind to filter words with *r*'s, "I don't see why it would be useful now, since we have passed the 'hello' phase and it would just sound silly, don't you ag— . . . don't you see? We can't say 'hello' again when it has al— . . . just been said." I was good.

Christina raises her eyebrows, nodding. She knows what I'm doing, and I know I'm not fooling her. I know Christina has the 411 on me; it's evident from the many files on the table before me. I'm sure all my imperfections and sins are in those files: the time I lied to my mother when I told her I had brushed my teeth; the time I cheated at Stratego and looked at Court's pieces when he went to the bathroom; the time I mistakenly ate the ibuprofen tabs on the neighbor's kitchen counter, believing them to be M&M's.

"Very good, Lance." Christina says. "Please be sure to use my name the next time you see me, as it's polite to include someone's name when you greet them."

I'm aware of this social nuance, as Dad and Mom had just joined the Amway group, which is very into social edification. But even be-

---

*We Mormons do not embrace the cross as we believe it symbolizes Christ's death, when we rejoice in his living. So on the rare occasion when I would see a pair of breasts complimented with a cross, it was just that much more exotic.

fore that, my parents were very big into social appropriateness. I nod compliance.

"Thank you. Now, I'm going to give you a piece of paper." She pulls out a single page from the folder. "I want to you to read those words to me."

I look at the paper. Terror.

Car. Bar. Jar. Star. Dry. Cry. Try. Carry. Dairy. Marry. . . .

I'm aware I have trouble with r's, as has been made painfully clear to me by my classmates. What went wrong with my learning of the English language and alphabet was that I had to read lips to get the proper movement of the mouth in order to get the correct enunciation of each letter. I hear things differently, but I learned to read lips and to replicate with my mouth what I saw others doing with theirs. The letter r, however, is a tricky one. As I read people's lips, I cannot see their tongue curling in the back. When people use an r, their mouth will take the same shape as either a w or an o. Go look in the mirror and say red and then say wed. It isn't spot-on, but very similar. Then say run and one. The trick with the r is the tongue movement in the back of the mouth, a movement that one cannot see when reading lips. When I was developing my motor and verbal skills as a child, I didn't establish the curling movement in my r's. It's very difficult to retrain your tongue—much like asking an English speaker to roll their r's the way a Latino would.

I take Christina's paper and read: "Caw. Bow. Jao. Staow. Dwy. Cuay. Twy. . . ." Although this is how they sound to me when people speak, I'm experienced enough to know that this isn't correct. As if my humiliation isn't enough, Christina does the bitchy thing and repeats after me, with perfect diction, "Car. Bar. Jar. . . ."

In her eyes she thinks I'm just being lazy, like kids with a lisp,* and believes she can will me to get the true r sound in there, as if I had an on-and-off switch. I repeat each word again, and I really am trying to please her, until she says, "Watch my tongue. . . . Car."

"I'm watching. . . . Caw."

"No. Look at my tongue."

---

*I have a hard time with people who have a lisp. Two reasons: First, as I have to read lips and watch the mouth and tongue, when I see someone with a lisp let their tongue get trapped between their teeth, it all goes to hell, and I cannot decipher what they are saying to me, as the lisp will break the pattern and rhythm I have grown used to in interpreting the English language. Second, most people with a lisp can hear their difference. Whereas I, for example, couldn't hear the difference in the letter R but would often be treated as though I could.

"I can't see it behind your teeth; I don't know what it's doing." I did well on the fly to only have one *r* in that sentence.

"Watch," she says as she leans in, her nose nearly touching mine, "*Carrrrrrrr.*" It is so accentuated that it doesn't even sound like *car.* Instead, it sounds like she's gargling.

And so with that idea, I begin to gargle with my tongue, mustering a choked *r,* which is enough of a breakthrough for her that she feels as if she has just cured cancer. But soon that isn't enough for her. It isn't so much that she is displeased with the false *r,* but rather that I'm still unable to say her name as she wants it, as she is so in love with herself. She will be damned if I don't fully appreciate her beautiful name.

In no time at all, so overconfident in her ability as a speech therapist, Christina grows tired of my gargling sound, which I had only replicated from her and her dumb extended *Carrrrrrrr.* She then does the unthinkable: she literally grabs my cheeks and tries to steer my tongue. Absolutely humiliating. Here I am with this beautiful woman, and she's completely emasculating me—just the two of us, her perfectly manicured nails digging into my cheeks—as she exaggerates the *rrrrrrrrrrrrrr.*

I do it as well as I can, trying so hard to please her and to get her to stop holding my face: *Argggggggggggggg.* I'm literally choking on my tongue.

"Catch it, Lance. Catch the *r,*" Christina says, peering down my mouth and throat like a family pediatrician. Her hope of getting me to catch my *r* so easily was as much a lucid pipe dream as hoping to get me to be the catcher in the rye—or maybe even more of a stretch, along the lines of simply trying to have me catch the wind.

This went on and on. Every week we grew more frustrated until I finally taught myself to touch the bottom of my mouth with my tongue. I now curl my *r* 's down, tapping the tip of my tongue on that funny little ball that holds the middle tendon under your tongue. Instead of touching the tongue toward the roof like most people, I steer it down and tag that ball. It may not be proper, but it works, and Christina isn't a part of my life anymore.

And my siblings were envious of the times Mom and Dad whisked me away. . . .

5

In the fourth grade, upon my request, Mom and Dad let me return to Pinesdale to spend a year there.

It would be one of the most influential years of my life, transforming and drastically altering the way I saw myself, thanks to Aunt Sam and her young husband, Pax. Aunt Sam was, and still remains, a legend as a cradle robber, for she met her husband when he was fifteen and she was twenty-one. His name was "Pax" Virgil, Pax being a nickname for Edson, his cruel Christian name. Pax was my cousin on my father's side, being the son of my father's elder half-sister, and he married my Aunt Sam on my mother's side, so it's just one big web of relations. My siblings and I like to refer to him as "my cousin, Uncle Pax."

Pax was only twenty-one and Sam twenty-seven when I went to live with them. They were childless at that point, despite great efforts on their part to be otherwise. They saw having me live with them for the year as a great opportunity to hone some parenting skills. And boy, did I ever toe the line. I was their guinea pig. Nowadays I like to give Pax and Sam's daughter, Kjes, and her half-siblings grief for how easy they have it. Aunt Sam was very impatient with me. She never let me pout or whine, and if I did so, she only added more chores to my list. Sam was having none of my garbage.

Aunt Sam is sharp, fast, witty, and sarcastic, and man, could that woman make a Saturday chore list that put Luther's "95 Theses" to shame. I was the male version of Cinderalla.

- Clean the kitchen.
- Wash and put away dishes.
- Sweep and mop the floor.
- Vacuum room, hall, living room, and stairs.
- Clean bathroom, scrub counters.

- Clean up dog poop in backyard.
- Rake up pine needles on both front and back lawns.

The raking of the pine needles was the straw that broke my back. Unlike leaves, pine needles don't respond to rakes. I have raked up leaves and am well aware of how frustrating and tedious the chore can be. But raking pine needles is like trying to rake up leaves with a spade. They weave into the prongs and block the traction of the rake. Plus, they poke you. They just poke.

If I ever had qualms about my chore list, Sam was kind enough to explain the situation: "You're not going to pout and be a little baby. That may work with your mother, but not with me it won't. Each hour that goes by with all of these chores unfinished, another chore will be added. And believe me, I have lots of things I could have worked on right now."

All the while, Pax would sit in the front room, playing at reading a book, waiting for Sam's back to turn on him so he could drop his book a little, point at me, and laugh over the top.

Aunt Stace liked to starve me in an Oliver Twist sort of way. I was allowed only one bowl of cereal every morning and one Pop-Tart. "Two eggs!" she shrilled at me one afternoon upon finding that I was cooking two eggs for lunch. "One is plenty!" Thank goodness I didn't tell her those two eggs were actually my third and fourth of the afternoon.

Pax was just a twenty-one-year-old kid who woke up every morning at six and went off to work at his construction job building homes. He was healthy and lively, six-foot-four, strong as an ox, and enjoyed a good day's work, but he also wanted more. Though he struggled in school as a teenager, as he had a valid learning disability, you could always see intelligence behind his eyes, and a thirst for knowledge. He hated sitting in a classroom. I wouldn't say that he was agoraphobic, but he would go into mute mode when in large crowds. Understanding this trait, as I suffer from it myself, I can see why he was terrified or at least not interested in going to college and instead opted to build houses in the cold of morning; that's how much he dreaded school.

Every Monday at the Pinesdale gymnasium was basketball rec-league night. One January night Pax and I were walking to his game; it was winter, and there are few nicer things in life than walking in the dark of winter through the woods on a Montana night under the Sky. We always cut through the Medlars' back lawn, using the stepping-stones that had scraped many soft knees in our sporting endeavors. Pax and I were halfway across the lawn when Melinda Medlar, whom we affectionately called "Moolinda," opened the door to scream, "Get off our lawn!" No matter that the land was all part of a socialist, utopian community, all part of God's land.

Pax stopped, basketball in one hand, the other gesturing for peace, and called out, without skipping a beat, "Hey. Don't be rude and fat."

Dumbstruck, Melinda had no reply as she watched in silence, her frame outlined by the interior light of her back doorway, while we continued on our way.

Between Yaya's back lawn and the Medlars' was a twenty-foot-wide unclaimed strip of land that ran the length of our lawns. Both houses used this space for piling mowed grass and raked pine needles. It also contained a community clothesline. Yaya's yard was enclosed by a chain-link fence; Pax had put it up to keep his dogs in, lest one of his lovely neighbors shoot them.

During the spring of that year, Melinda and a couple of her siblings were playing in their backyard. Pax and I were sitting in our backyard, cooking on the grill, and Pax just had an urge, a longing. He went inside to his gun case and came back out with his pellet rifle, pumping it before he was even back out the door. He walked up to the fence, going to a prone position, well hidden from line of sight behind the drying laundry of the Medlars' clothesline.

Savoring the hunt, waiting at least twenty seconds, Pax finally fired his pellet gun. The first shot was absorbed by a damp towel on the clothesline. Showing his skill and conditioned patience, Pax calmly and quietly repumped his rifle while the unsuspecting Medlar children gaily continued on with their games, oblivious to the fact that there was a hunter, a predator, in their midst.

Not pumping to maximum power, Pax patiently waited for what seemed an eternity before finally pulling the trigger. Doing my best not to look suspicious or aware, I remained in my chair next to the grill. I noticed Chris Medlar stop midstride and reach for his back, but he couldn't touch that magic spot in the upper middle of his back that Pax had so skillfully aimed for.

Chris emitted a disturbing sound, a combination whimper, moan, and squeal that got lost in pain, and said to his half-siblings, who had not even noticed, "I think a bee just stung me!"

They all stopped what they were doing for about ten seconds, looking at each other as though they were expecting something to be done, feigning concern, waiting long enough in silence to validate his discomfort without seeming apathetic. They then shrugged and continued on with their play.

Pax waited for a moment, until I gave him the go-ahead with a nod indicating that the field was clear, and then got back into position. Again he took his time, and this time he hit one of the younger redheaded boys, Dustin, in the leg.

"Ow! Something stung *me, too!*"

Pax got off one more shot, and this time he hit Melinda. Where, I don't remember, but she was an easy target. Chris finally figured something was up, as I tried to sit too still. He walked over toward us and spotted Pax lying in cover behind the tree, gun in hand.

"He's shooting BBs at us!" Chris screamed as he ran back to their lawn. The children ran into the house—all but Melinda, who came running through the gulf between our lawns until she was halted by the chain-link fence. Like a vicious dog, she began screaming through the links, "You bastard! You could've shot my eye out! You're . . ."

Melinda continued to hurl obscenities and threats at Pax, who by this time had calmly stood up and emerged from behind the tree with a satisfied grin on his face, not even bothering to hide the gun or claim innocence. Instead, he just coolly walked up to the fence and met Melinda, his rifle resting on his shoulder: "Hey, hey. I was just having some fun with you guys."

Meanwhile, Fred Medlar came out of the house and walked toward Pax. I assumed my position by Pax, but not too close lest they all believe I had actually pulled the trigger as well.

"Pax," Fred called as he approached, "what is going on? What are you doing?" It wasn't aggressive or hostile, more along the lines of a professional questioning.

"Oh, Fred, I'm just having some fun with your kids." They exchanged some more words, but not before the mother hen, Debbie, emerged, yelling, "You asshole!" before she was even fully out of her door.

With his back to his wife, Fred sighed and went silent, rolling his eyes as Debbie approached the fence near a dead sprint, her red hair bouncing in time with her pear-shaped frame. She never even paused for breath, hurling obscenities at Pax, showing her great wind. If Moolinda was a lapdog, Debbie was a Rottweiler.

Letting the hollow threats bounce off him like Ping-Pong balls, Pax raised his hand in a token gesture of goodwill, asking for silence. Debbie granted him a brief moment as Pax calmly said, "Please be quiet. I'm talking to Fred."

It took a few seconds for Debbie to register what had just happened. Then she went apeshit. Fred held her off as she flung her fists toward Pax, who stood, unfazed, behind his fence. Fred urged her to go inside.

After a minute of pure pandemonium, Debbie finally headed back to her cave, baying at the injustice and humiliation she had just suffered, while Fred shamefacedly smiled down at his feet, trying his best to hide his amusement at Pax's defiance toward his overbearing wife. I could see that Fred was even a bit envious of Pax and admired him for the courage he had displayed in fending off Debbie.

While I have immeasurable love for my friends and family and my parents, I can say that there's no one I love more in this world that Pax Jessop, for the time he invested in me and the lessons he taught me. He taught me to embrace my hearing loss. He taught me that if I made fun of myself, no one could get the better of me for it.

The final month of school in Montana, Pax decided to take a second wife and got engaged to another woman, Sarah Stoker, the sister of Aunt Audra's husband, Shawn Stoker. Pax was more or less pressured by his father and uncles to pursue Sarah as a wife. It had become the elephant in the house: Sarah came over, and Sam knew things would be changing, that her husband would be marrying her friend.

I saw Aunt Sam silently crying in bed when Pax was gone on his honeymoon with Sarah. She was already alone and missing him. She was having to face the fact that she now shared her husband with another woman and would get to sleep with him only every other night from then on.

But it was the life we knew. And that was part of the deal. We lived the celestial law of plural marriage, and that was the price we—or rather the women—had to pay. They had to sacrifice. And Aunt Sam couldn't object or voice displeasure; she had to take it and accept it as part of life while living the higher law.

The year couldn't last forever, and the time flew by. I hugged Pax and Sam good-bye and went back to Utah with Dad when he came to pick me up at the end of the school year. I won't say that I returned from Montana as a shining beacon of manhood—I still had a lot of growing up to do—but I was better for the time I had spent with Pax and Stace.

6

While I was in Montana, Mom and Dad had declared bankruptcy and been forced to move in with Dad's brother Uncle Saul. We now lived on the secluded two-acre lot known as *the property,* which contained three homes: the fourplex that had been built by Rulon but now was owned and rented out by the AUB and was where we held Sunday school; the duplex my dad had built, which was shared by Uncle Saul and Aunt Susan with Uncle Mel, Aunt Laurie, and Aunt Margaret—and now us; and the duplex that Grammy shared with Uncle Saul and Aunt Ruthann. I personally was happy with the turn of events. At least now I was back in a safe little commune of people who believed the same things we did. I didn't have to constantly be trying to remember what I had to lie about and what I didn't.

Uncle Saul had been a wonderful older brother to my father when they were growing up in Salt Lake City, carrying my dad to his baseball games and practices on his bike, with my father sitting on the crossbar. The neighborhood kids thought they did this because Saul and Dad were poor, not because my father, who was a baseball prodigy, couldn't ride a bike.

When Saul left for Vietnam, there was no one there to encourage my father to pursue his dream of baseball. My grandmother told my father it was just a game and that he had more important things to attend to, like God's work and getting a real job where he could earn money and contribute to the family. He gave up baseball and dedicated his life to God's work, unable to resume baseball when Uncle Saul came back home from Vietnam.

Uncle Saul became very successful, owning a car dealership in the Salt Lake Valley during the 1980s. As a child, I thought it odd how Uncle Saul was smiled upon for having achieved his wealth while my father was told he needed to dedicate his life to furthering the work of the Lord.

Uncle Saul had two beautiful but very different wives. His first wife, Ruthann, gave him six kids. Uncle Saul adored her.

One of his sons, Steven, was a year older than Court. Steven could easily have been mistaken as the reincarnation of Ivan the Terrible, the brutal Russian czar of the 1500s who as a child liked to have his guards stand with their pikes upright beneath the ramparts so he could drop little puppies down and see them impaled. This isn't to say that Steven killed puppies. He did, however, have a macabre shrine of disfigured clay men. He created awesome men out of blocks of colored modeling clay, which he then tortured and mangled. Steven was the head honcho of the little clique of cousins our age on the property.

Aunt Susan was Uncle Rex's second wife. She was also very beautiful, but in a very calm, aristocratic kind of way, very sophisticated and properly mannered, as her mother was a first-generation German who immigrated to the United States. Danielle and Levi were Susan's only two children at the time. Danielle was a year older than me, and Levi was two years younger. Levi was a conundrum. He loved sports and could play any sport and was naturally good at them, yet for the life of him he couldn't put a spoonful of cereal into his mouth in the morning without leaving soggy frosted flakes on the chair and table where he ate. You always made sure to eat before Levi did, lest you lose your appetite.

Uncle Saul loved having people together and was thrilled when we moved in with them. He loved being the host and treating people, and he took us kids to Murray Park on Sunday afternoons in his most recent demo model. He always took us afterward to 7-Eleven and bought us Slurpees. I'd take my time with my Slurpee as we drove back home with the windows rolled down, Levi falling asleep on my shoulder, his Slurpee spilling all over him.

Court and I were young enough to simply enjoy the close proximity we had with our cousins. That summer was a fun one for us boys,* as we played football in the open lawn between the houses. And Szen loved all the open space he could patrol and lounge about on.

---

*Except for the day I accidentally boiled my turtle, Tory. I loved that turtle. I gave her a bath every day for two years. And one day, I mistakenly left a bit of the hot water running, because I couldn't hear the faint sound with my hearing aids, before I ran out to toss a ball around with Court, and when I came back she was dead, in scalding hot water. I was inconsolable for a week.

I'm sure by now many readers are wondering when I start talking basketball. Well, I wasn't much of an athlete in my budding years, to be honest. I was more of a Nintendo and Dungeons & Dragons type of kid. Sure, I'd play basketball with the guys, but I was terrible. I had no gross motor skills. I couldn't make a layup to save my life. I didn't know how to time a basic two-step stride to do a simple one-handed layup. But my fine motor skills were excellent!

We had fun playing on the huge lawn, with the horse pastures at our backs in the setting sun. Steven always manhandled us, as he was undergoing puberty at the age of thirteen and was just so much stronger. When we grew bored of Steven mauling us, we spent hours playing Nintendo together, which usually meant gathering around Steven while he played his single-player games.

It was nice to have a tight circle of cousins about me to protect me from bullying and ridicule at school. Allreds were healthy kids. You didn't mess with them as a group.

When I was in the fifth grade, Uncle Owen called upon Dad to become the teacher of the Priesthood meeting, which was held every other Wednesday evening. This was a huge responsibility and was Owen's way of anointing Dad his heir apparent as best he could. The Priesthood meeting was exclusively for men. Women were not allowed. Period. It was a very important meeting where the men gathered to hear the words and promptings of men on the Council.

Torn between his desires to get out of the financial bind he now found himself in and the burden of carrying on his father's legacy, Dad ultimately chose to commit to his new calling in the Group. He couldn't let his father's legacy go. He still believed that his father had been a prophet, and he still believed in the dream. He became Owen's right-hand man and confidant, much to the chagrin of the Council.

Dad spent that summer writing various sermons while crammed into a small laundry area in Aunt Laurie's unit, publishing theories and hypotheses and discussions regarding the "principle" and "true" interpretation of scripture. He became Owen's right-hand man, producing many volumes and manuscripts that he sold dirt-cheap as a part of his lectures and discussions at Priesthood meetings. My father now refers to those written documents as a pile of crap and cannot believe he actually wrote them. As an historian, he is embarrassed.

One day, my father came home with a concerned look on his face. "Owen came up to me," he told us, "and asked for my help. He took me over to his closet and showed me shoeboxes full of money. He told me he had over a million dollars there in his closet. He asked me to help him get rid of it and put it somewhere safe."

"What did you tell him?" My mom asked.

"That since I wasn't on the Council, I couldn't help him. That it was a matter for the Council."

One day that next spring, 1992, Dad came home with starry eyes. He gathered us all in his little bedroom in Aunt Susan's basement and told us, "Uncle Owen is going to let us move into the fourplex. And . . ." He paused, still unable to believe what had just happened. ". . . Owen is going to give us the deed to full ownership of the house."

"You mean let us live in it, right? Not own it really?" Mom asked, unsure of what she had just heard.

"Full ownership," Dad said.

The Allred Group owned hundreds of homes throughout the inter-mountain West under its official business title—the AUB—and they never let go of the deeds. They always held their believers hostage, so to speak, in that they held the rights to the land on which the believers lived. It was a subtle reminder that they could evict anyone from their home at a moment's notice. In a fit of peculiarity, Owen was ceding the land and house entirely to my father, removing the title and deed from the AUB and putting them into my father's name. No one could make sense of it, not even Owen when members of the Council berated him for his impulsive action.

It seemed that karma, God, or whatever had finally taken a turn and re-warded my father for all the homes he had built for the AUB over the years.

As a family, we could make sense of Owen's decision only by conclud-ing that God, in some way, led Owen to have a moment of uncharac-teristic good judgment. Why else would Owen give my father the house when everyone else, even members of the Council, lived on land owned by the AUB? It's the only thing that made sense. And we'd later see that God was drawing a path for us to leave the Group. Sounds superstitious, I know, but nothing else explains it.

We, as a family, moved into half of the fourplex. It was rundown and filthy, but it was ours. Dad got to work repairing and remodeling, com-bining two units into one, allowing each of us to have our own room and allowing Aunt Susan to have her house back to herself.

. . .

During my sixth-grade year, Aunt Ruthann kicked Uncle Saul out of the house. It was shattering to our little world, our paradigm, to see that our parents were fallible. The idea that Aunt Ruthann was leaving Uncle Rex brought about serious internal questions: If we're God's people, why would Aunt Ruthann leave? Will Aunt Ruthann not go to heaven? What will happen to the family in heaven? Is Aunt Ruthann going to hell?

Ruthann's son Steven was crushed. He moved out and into Ruthann's sister-wife Susan's basement. Steven was so angry that he wouldn't speak to his mother for years,. He wouldn't even talk about her. His mind was in torment. Even though I was only eleven, I could see that Steven was in pain.

Aunt Ruthann's departure was a foreshadowing of things to come. Our little heaven on the property was beginning to crumble. The shock of Aunt Ruthann's leaving was just a precursor to haunting truths and secrets that were about to be unveiled.

The summer after sixth grade, 1993, Mom and Dad ran Youth Conference for the Group, which was held for three days over the Fourth of July weekend. Hundreds of teenagers raised in the Group gathered together. It was a successful weekend, one that Dad would cap off with a slide show that ended with a giant picture of Jesus accompanied by Garth Brooks' song "The River." "Jesus loves each and everyone of you," Dad said.

Everyone in the audience was crying as they began to realize that love should be unconditional. "There isn't anything you could do that would make Jesus love you any more or less than He already does," Dad told them. This was a truth my mother helped my father realize over their years together, as my father had been raised on conditional love.

Many men in the AUB, especially those on the Council, didn't appreciate Dad telling their kids that they could have a relationship with Jesus when they themselves believed that their children needed to rely on and trust the men of the Council to get them to heaven. Jesus was just a side note. They didn't like Dad teaching their kids that they deserved to be happy and that they were loved no matter what, no matter their sins.

Three weeks later we all migrated up to Montana for Conference. Conference was an annual three-day event during which Uncle Owen and members of the Council would address the Group as a whole. It was basically an annual reunion for members of the Group.

Dad, Court, and I drove up through the night with Szen and with Court's new Dalmatian, Pongo. We found ourselves stopped at 4 a.m. at the top of Lost Trail Pass, over the Montana/Idaho border. Construction held up traffic, and I woke up at the crack of dawn in the high peaks of the Montana mountains. Once traffic cleared, we continued on, and just as the sun was rising Garth Brooks's song "The Dance" played on the radio. It was a powerful memory, and I remember how it seemed to be a warning. It was a foretelling of how life, as I knew it, was going to change forever the very next day.

I was twelve years old.

It was good to see everyone. Pax, Sam, and Sarah were doing well with their two babies, Kjes and Bud; Aunt Audra had recently given birth to her third child. Mom and the girls got there a bit later than we did, and there was tons of commotion while all the oohs and ahs were shared.

The next morning Dad called for a family meeting of Yaya's kids and grandkids. We all gathered in Aunt Sam's living room, some of us sitting on the floor as there wasn't enough furniture to accommodate all of us. A tearful Dad, who was in the know as Owen's confidant, came out and told us the names of men—men on the Council, men whom we believed to be men of God—whose daughters had just come out to say that their fathers had molested and raped them, repeatedly, for years.

Owen also told my father that there had been other claims by other daughters of the same men, but the Council had managed to keep those claims quiet. It completely shook my father's world, his paradigm. He had watched as the Group, after his father's death, became less about scripture and more about their own interpretation. He had seen power-hungry men gravitate to the Group, seeking weak people who would follow them, people who wanted to have someone to follow and hold their hands and guide them through life. He had seen many men abuse their power of authority to blackmail, to extort and intimidate so many. For a time Dad had been able to ignore the situation and tell himself it would get better, that good would prevail and the weeds would be rooted out.

My father had invested many years in the Group after his father's death, believing in his father's legacy, and believing that the sanctity of their cause would work itself out. But when he learned of the rapes and molestation, he could hold on no longer. He could no longer fight the tingling in his conscience that told him of the wrongs and the ills that had corrupted the Group. He could no longer ignore the elephant in the room that was hypocrisy and contradiction hiding behind piety. He could no longer disregard the spiritual torment and captivity in which the men on the Council kept their people, holding them hostage to the idea that they, and they alone, would determine if the people could get into Heaven.

Dad told us that he was no longer attending church and was leaving the Group, that we were all free to choose for ourselves, but as for him, he was done. He told Owen that he would give him one year to make significant changes, and that he would require signs of progress that showed the return of his father's family and his father's people to the correct and simple ways that Rulon had envisioned. He needed to see a return to the dream. If Owen didn't answer the ultimatum, Dad would move on. The changes, of course, never came.

Dad invested forty-three years of his life in his father's dream. He wasn't going to blindly give anymore. As Dad had only one wife, it was easy for him to make such a declaration.

But what about Pax and Sam? Were they supposed to say to Sarah, "See ya. Thanks for giving us Bud. You can either take him when you go or leave him with us, and you're on your own with the baby you're about to give birth to." It wasn't so simple. Not so black and white. Just like life in general.

Shawn and Audra were in the same boat, as two years earlier Shawn had taken a second wife, who had already given him a child. What were they to do? And what was Yaya to do? She was the one who had packed up her children and left Utah, bringing them to this polygamist culture, uprooting them from all they knew. Was she just to say good-bye to her daughters, whom she was responsible for bringing to the Group, and simply leave them behind?

The divide came, and the pain of separation was inevitable.

Over the years people have asked me if I witnessed any of the perversion. Luckily, I didn't, but I know of many who suffered. They then ask why it happens so often. Are all of the men sex fiends? No. Some men in plural marriages actually practice abstinence, having sex with their wives only for the purpose of reproduction, and thus get less action with seven wives than most average American men get with one.

When a man rapes a woman, it's for dominance. When an adult rapes a child, it's for dominance. Dominance is a natural tendency, an impulse that we have learned to curb through laws and the mores of our advancing societies. The reason child molestation seems to be so common in polygamist communes is that they're set in prime locations for molestation and incest—isolated areas with very little outside interference. Their own laws reign supreme.

In Pinesdale, and other communities like it, many men set their own laws, or claim to put God's laws above the laws of the land. Thus they no longer have to adhere to government expectations. Over time, without mainstream society's laws to restrain basic animal instincts, and without public schools to monitor children, molestation and incest creep in. Some might even wonder if people who have these tendencies seek out societies like Pinesdale, knowing they are flourishing grounds for molestation: parents can choose to keep their children at home and homeschool them because it's a common practice and no one will blink twice. A man with the power of the priesthood is trusted to run his own home in the manner he sees fit; no one will challenge him.

We packed up our car that day and drove home to Utah, no longer members of the Group, no longer disciples of Rulon Allred. The break from the Group was ugly. There were to be many angry and tearful arguments with our extended family. These arguments were mostly with my mother's side, as my father's side completely disowned us.

My parents felt like they were sinking in quicksand. They felt that their entire lives had been based on a lie. They had no firm foundation. What could they now have faith in? Could they trust their own instincts? How were they supposed to lead and direct their own children? Luckily, at this time, in Utah, they were befriended by several born-again Christians while trying to find some kind of anchor. As Mom began tearfully explaining to one of these new friends that their life was a lie and they had nothing to stand on, the friend said, "You stop right there. You have a remarkable marriage. You have five amazing children. That isn't a lie. That's where you start." Mom took one gasping breath, and her world was steady again. That was exactly where my parents started. With us five kids and each other.

Aunt Sam and I had only one clash. We argued for a good three hours in the car while we drove to Idaho one time, but it was just the two of us, and we were able to hash out our differences. I saw that she was trapped. Though she saw the fallacies and inconsistencies, what was she to do? Say good-bye to Pax? Or make Pax choose between her and Sarah? Between her and Sarah's children? She loved Pax too much to do that.

That day we both promised each other that no matter what, we were going to be spiritual, that we were not going to let the label of an organized religion determine whether we were God's people or good Christians or simply just good people. We were going to always remain Christians, first and foremost, and the rest was just details. God and Jesus could sort that out.

I feel that the greatest sin is simply being unkind. You can follow the letter of the law of the Gospels to a T and still be an asshole. Being unkind is the gateway to all the sins: murder, theft, lying, adultery, and so forth. There are people I know who are just wonderful and live a different lifestyle from mine, and I'd rather be in heaven with their pleasant company than with a broody, condescending, "perfect" individual who lived life by the book and felt himself superior for having done so.

Do you really believe God runs in cliques? If so, then you can have that God.

The God I know loves me and knows my strengths and weaknesses and knows my flaws and knows the hand I was dealt in life. I believe God judges us equally with regard to the hand that each of us was dealt and whether we each individually are doing the best we can. Someone is born with bipolar disorder, someone is born into a violent home, someone is born an orphan, and so forth. We don't all have the same start and finish lines. We all have our own crosses to bear, and God will know whether we did the best we could with the resources he gave us and whether we tried to help as many people as we could along the way. Were we good Christians? But more important, were we good people?

Religion divides us. Spirituality unites us.

7

"Don't go into the kitchen. Raphael is studying."

This was the theme in the Allred house my seventh-grade year. Why, as a college student, Raph had to always study in the most trafficked room in the house was beyond me. Well, no; quite frankly I do know: it was empowering for her, and she liked to hold us—especially me, a hungry thirteen-year-old boy—hostage in our own home. Raph never made it a secret—her disdain for me, her thinking I was a spoiled brat. And for some reason, she couldn't understand why a thirteen-year-old boy wasn't as mature and sophisticated as she had been at thirteen. She thought I was a little hellion because Mom and Dad would from time to time let me behave like a typical thirteen-year-old in our home, which was still my home.

When finals rolled around, we had to forgo the basic human ritual of dinner and were escorted into our rooms with Cream of Wheat by our parents, themselves wary of the monster they had created. I sat in my room, my growing body grumbling for some food, until finally, at 10 o'clock at night I'd had enough. With frail limbs that couldn't help but tremble with every step, I walked out into the kitchen, the rest of the house silent with trepidation, my trembling, shallow voice complementing my emaciated features, and said, "Please, dear sister, may I have a piece of bread?"

She looked up from her book, hissing at me, "Fine, but make it quick."

I walked into the kitchen, doing my best to make the least amount of noise possible, which consequently only magnified each sound I made. Every time I slowly closed a cupboard with a soft thud in the dead silence, it seemed that I was being more obnoxious than if I had slammed it shut. I noticed this truth at the very same time Raph did, at which point she looked up at me with a *Why do you choose to live?* look on her face: "You're more annoying when you do that. Just hurry up."

Even when Raph finally moved into an apartment, she still came home and studied in the kitchen during midterms and finals, hell-bent on making sure we couldn't have any fun with or without her, needing us all to acknowledge the sacrifices she was making in order to get into medical school. We should all have to suffer right along with her. If she wasn't having fun, she couldn't suffer it alone in her apartment; nay, she needed to come home and exert herself to make sure none of us could have fun, either.

One day, it all changed. Following her interview in pigtails, Raphael got a letter from the University of Utah telling her she had been accepted into the medical program. Suddenly, Raphael became a nice person. She had finally achieved her goal. After so many people had told her to stop wasting her time and everyone else's and start a family, she now could allow herself some kindness and credit. Now, looking back, realizing the pressure that she placed on herself to be successful when so many from the Group told her not to try, or belittled her, or judged her as being selfish, or simply laughed at her, I understand why she was quite removed from us. She wasn't at peace, as she wanted more; she didn't want a life of confines. Knowing she could do more, she wanted more.

In my seventh-grade year I didn't fit in anywhere and wasn't doing well in school. I was still not LDS, and I was no longer a "polyg" kid hanging out with my cousins, running in a clique. I had no friends other than Court. I still spent time with Levi, but the tension was there. Steven wasn't talking to anybody, such was his mental state following his mother's departure. My whole family just seemed to be coasting, waiting.

At this time Mom finally approached Dad as he was playing solitaire in the kitchen one spring afternoon and said, "I think we need to join the LDS church."

Dad replied, "I was just thinking the same thing."

Raphael came in a few minutes later: "I don't know about you guys, but I'm joining the LDS church. Anyone else who wants to join is welcome to come along."*

As a family we would soon begin taking missionary lessons at Grandma Ripplinger's house in Salt Lake. She was Yaya's stepmother, who raised

---

*The LDS church, it turned out, was embracing of Raphael's pursuit, letting her know that it was possible and more than acceptable for her to be a successful woman and still be a faithful servant of God.

Yaya and her four siblings after Yaya's mother, Tannie, passed away from cancer. Grandma Rip and the rest of Yaya's siblings were mainstream LDS. And though they vehemently disapproved of Yaya's decision to up and join the Allred Group, they still loved her and always welcomed her. It says a lot about them, especially when you consider that one of Yaya's younger brothers, Don Ripplinger, was a well-known figure in the LDS church as one of the Tabernacle Choir directors. They always let her come back and were never ashamed of her at family reunions. Uncle Don, whenever he was asked in church meetings if he knew or consorted with any who practiced plural marriage, would proudly answer without hesitation, "Yes. My sister is one. And I love her."

Yaya's grandfather John Baptiste Ripplinger was one of the first homesteaders in Driggs, Idaho, in the Teton Valley. There was a family cabin on the property that her father, John Henry, farmed during the summer and harvest seasons. It had been built in the 1940s, no more than fifty square feet in size, on the edge of the 160 acres he harvested. It had two tiny rooms that encircled a tiny kitchen. The place smelled of sticky flytraps mixed with mice droppings and old paint chips. But it smelled great in the mornings with fresh eggs and pancakes grilling on the wood-fire stove.

This place is a part of my heritage in a land I call "Wydaho," right on the Idaho/Wyoming border, on the western side of the Grand Tetons. The cabin was old-fashioned; its only plumbing was the outhouse, twenty yards from the cabin. It was fun to step from the cabin to see a full moon lighting the Tetons, and though it was always chilly, even on summer nights, you couldn't help but appreciate the beauty of the place—and then hold your breath as you went into the outhouse. I loved to look out over the valley, be it under a full moon or in the light of day, and notice how it looked like one of Grandma Rip's quilts, with patchworks of different material, grains and patterns making up the body of work.

The mice ran the place. That was the deal. They were fearless. They'd come out and stare at you while you tried to sleep or as you read a book. It was the living incarnation of Brian Jacques's Redwall book series.

When Pax and Sam were dating, he accompanied the family on a trip to the cabin. Yaya, being the classy, old-fashion gal that she was, made Pax sleep in the bed next to her and not with Sam. Pax, being the seventeen-year-old that he was, and restless to be with Sam, the warm and luscious twenty-two-year-old that he longed for in the room next door, couldn't sleep while Yaya read with the lamp on. He observed and stared down the mice that came and mocked him, daring him to do something. They literally came next to the bed and stood on their hind legs, sniffing and staring. Pax, being the chivalrous man that he is, felt his honor being mocked. He would state it so eloquently via e-mail:

As for the mice in the cabin incident, I shot several of those little buggers with my 22 cal. pistol from bed. In order to keep the bullets from ricocheting, I'd have to wait until they were between the door jamb and the north exterior wall so I was hitting wood floor instead of the concrete slab in the kitchen area. Good times. Talk to you later.

Pax

There they were: Yaya in her in curlers, reading a novel, and Pax in bed next to her, gun loaded and poised.

When you meet the children of John Henry, you have to admire and love their spunk and backbone. They each have an opinion about everything and love to share it. They love to sit around a table and argue and debate, but not rudely, just matter-of-factly, like civilized folk at a book-club meeting.

Yaya's sister, Aunt Jeanette, deserves her own paragraph. As a child, I saw Aunt Jeanette as a miserable, bossy miser. She told everyone what to do. But to her credit, she engaged in the labor as well. She wasn't a bureaucrat by any means. She has a love affair with England and has lived over there and frequently returns. She behaves like an English lady. She has picked up their mannerisms and terms of speech and expects everyone else to behave as such.

Aunt Jeanette has emerged as more than just another grandmother for us; she is my mother's mentor and guide, a financial contributor and investor in all of us kids, helping us in times of need. She has been, and I mean this with all of the love and respect I have for Yaya, a true mother to my mother.

Aunt Jeanette proved to be a fanatic for my basketball games. She became my number-one fan. She considers herself an investor in my future, and she truly is. She was always a fan of the game, but when I began playing in high school, she attended all the games she possibly could. Aside from my parents, who made the road trips in college, Aunt Jeanette has seen more of my basketball games than anyone else.

This lovely lady loves to horde things. There isn't anything she can't salvage. She is a squirrel among acorns who loves to shop at flea markets and secondhand stores. Aunt Jeanette will often appear at Mom and Dad's house to drop off a box of assorted books, board games, and other miscellaneous items—things that Mom doesn't have any room for. "I was at the store and saw these things, and I thought you and your kids might like them," she'll say.

Mom will breathe in through her teeth: "Um, maybe."

"OK," Aunt Jeanette will say. "You owe me ten dollars."

Grandma Rip did a wonderful job raising Tannie's kids and would give John Henry another four, one of them being Valeen. Valeen suffers from Down syndrome and is still alive and kicking at sixty-seven. She must be setting some kind of record. Valeen frightened me as a child, and to be honest, she still does to this very day. And I must tread carefully here on the topic of Valeen, for her siblings are very protective of her.

Valeen does not have teeth. And I need people to have teeth if I'm going to be able to read lips and to understand what they are saying to me. Plus, Valeen has a very high, croaky voice to accompany her lack of masticating utensils. This makes me nervous, because when I can't understand someone, I instinctively think it's because of my hearing loss and I grow paranoid and self-conscious.

Valeen is bossy as hell. She would tell the queen of England to pick up after her own damn self. Through the years, whether at the cabin, or when Valeen is visiting Yaya in Montana while I am, or when she is stopping by to say hi at Mom and Dad's house, tagging along with Aunt Jeanette, whose head is hidden behind yet another box of assorted abandonments, I quickly give my obligatory but affectionate hug and then run for the hills.

Many times Valeen would just come into my room, without knocking, to look around, raise her disapproving eyebrows at me, her chin flirting to touch her nose, as again she does not have teeth, and say, "Aafsdo uh aewliugfhafi." Or at least that's how I'd hear it.

I was usually so perplexed that I couldn't even muster a dumb "Huh?" and could only validate her verbal output with a petrified sideways stare that one might have upon waking from a terrible dream only to discover that there's a one-legged clown in the room.

She would then repeat herself, speaking a little slower: "Aosdfaakjfh akjha fskdkl jgha ilu." And I'd say, "Yes. OK."*

One time while I was relaxing in bed, Valeen gestured for me to do some physical act, and I just nodded, not knowing what she was getting at. Irritated, she came over, grabbed my arm, and physically tried to force me out of bed. And like a vegetable at an old people's home, I complied, my mouth stupidly hanging open. She then started cleaning up my room and expected me to labor with her.

There have been other times, while at the cabin, that Valeen poked her head in the room, busted me with my video games, as electronics are forbidden at the cabin, and turned me in. But nowadays, me being the delightful man that I have become, having won the affection and trust of the Ripplinger women, which I labored diligently for,† the ladies leave me to myself, much to Valeen's chagrin.

It's because of this proud lineage and heritage that descends from John Henry Ripplinger that we flock at least yearly to Driggs to pay homage to our roots. Court once remarked, "It doesn't matter where we have lived or what we have been going through. Driggs has been the one constant in our lives." It's where I intend to build my first home.

When Yaya's family heard that we as a family were taking missionary lessons, they were all very welcoming and eager to help.

---

*"Yes" or "OK" is my default answer upon failing to understand for a third time the statement or question placed before me, as I'm too self-conscious after that to once again ask someone to repeat themselves. Valeen, however, is an exception. She gets the VIP treatment and is immediately rewarded with a yes or an OK.

But, as I'm sure many of you are wondering, what happens if neither a yes nor an OK is the correct answer, and you find yourself blindly committing to something that you would in good conscience not want to be a part of. Well, I will usually find out what it is that's being asked or said to me after I give the default answer, because people will be so surprised that they will raise their voice and repeat it loudly with a "Yes, you'll . . . ?" preceding said question. And if in that moment I can recant my answer, if it's indeed a wrong one, by saying "Oh, I thought you said you *didn't* . . . ," no harm, no foul.

Whereas if it was just a statement and I say yes when there's no answer warranted, the recipient will usually give me a dumb "Huh?" and a moment of awkward silence will ensue.

†I have been quoted and scribed to have said, albeit affectionately, "Why do Ripplinger women insist on yakking my ear off, when I have only half an ear to begin with?" This statement entails not only the true Ripplinger daughters of John Henry, but their ensuing lineage as well. Yaya herself has a lineage of children and grandchildren, with a ratio of four to one in favor of women. I'm of the school of thought that believes that the male infants are buried upon birth to keep the female harpingly dominant in the Ripplinger clan.

We were still living with my dad's family on the property in Taylorsville, and the tension was growing palpable. Dad, having the right to do so, as he owned the home, canceled Sunday school, which was held in our basement. We didn't want people who harbored ill will toward us treading through our home. We heard that in Group meetings, lessons and sermons were being preached describing Dad as the great Judas, even an advocate of Lucifer. We were being condemned to hell by people we used to call family.

One night Uncle Saul sheepishly came knocking on our door and told Dad that Owen and the AUB wanted the house back and that they had granted him the house with the trust that he would never betray them. It was ridiculous, but then so were they, so you couldn't expect much.

Dad, not wanting to burn any bridges, said that he would happily let them have the house back for $60,000, far less than the market rate of $260,000 and a very reasonable price considering the renovations he had made over the last two years. Understandably, Dad couldn't just up and leave the house, as he had done so many times before for the AUB. He was getting older and couldn't just push the reset button all over again. He needed a down payment for a new home for us to live in. We kids were older and had needs that couldn't simply be brushed aside this time.

Saul took the offer back, and they refused.

We knew then that it was time to move. Tensions were just too great. We found a real-estate agent, who found a couple who would be willing to swap houses with us—the fourplex for a home in downtown Salt Lake. Dad still held on to the hope that Saul could get the Council to just buy the house back for $60,000 and we wouldn't have to swap houses. But the AUB wouldn't budge. It had nothing to do with the house. It was all about setting an example of Dad to his friends and family, drawing a line of loyalty. Word was coming that there was a lawsuit in the works.

It was May 1994. I was thirteen. It was a night where you could feel something was wrong. Everyone felt it. As verbal a family as we were, it was telling of the tension that was present that we didn't discuss what any of us felt. I myself had a feeling that someone was watching me through my window in the night, with hands cupped against the window, allowing their eyes to scope my room, smilingly mischievously at me.

The fact that I wasn't sleeping wasn't anything new, but had I gone from room to room that night, I would have discovered that no one else in the family was sleeping, either. But unlike all those other nights with imagined enemies and intruders, this time they were real. This night the enemies were all around us. They came from inside our house, from the old Sunday school room where the pictures of our prophets hung on the wood-paneled walls that led to the storage cellar; they surrounded the house, pounding on the roof to get in. Szen wouldn't settle. He kept pacing back and forth between my room, the front door, and my parent's room. He seemed to be making the rounds, making sure everyone was safe.

Szen and I finally fell asleep as dawn crept into the sky, but we were rudely awakened at 6 a.m. by my father, who hauled everyone out into the front room and sat us down. It would be the last time we sat in that beautiful room he had created. Dad told us how he and Mom had not slept that night, and how the girls had at first huddled in Raph's room but then migrated upstairs, consciously afraid of the closed door that led to the Sunday school room, and filtered into Mom and Dad's room.

Dad knew something bad was going to happen if we stayed any longer. We were leaving, and we had only the day to do it. He told us to pack up as much as we could, the bare essentials, and to leave everything else behind. He and Mom were going to go to work and tell their principals they had to leave for an indefinite amount of time.

Dad had been in touch with a local police detective, who spent much of his time in the field investigating polygamist sects and the violence and extortion that often follow. Detective Forbes was the man who had investigated Rulon's murder and had since been regarded as the man in charge when it came to polygamy and violence in Utah. He was the chief detective for the Salt Lake County Sheriff, and he had heard through his sources that Dad was a target or at least an object of malice. Dad and Vanessa had been working with Detective Forbes and others in the hope of possibly helping incest victims. Vanessa knew way more than she wanted to about the inner workings of some of the prominent families, and that was only increasing the Group's aversion to our family.

Dad was being described as the Son of Perdition—also known as the Antichrist—from the pulpit in the Group, and some of those sermons were suggesting that something be done. Having once lived in the Group and seen that lifestyle, and knowing that the leaders too often felt themselves to be above the laws of the land, we were very nervous. There's no limit to the violence that can erupt when people rely on someone whose interpretation of the Bible is based on a whim.

There's a whispered story in Pinesdale about a boy, Paul Garcia. Paul was a stepson of my father's brother Louis, the one who would later be made a member of the Council and ultimately commit suicide. Paul was a teenager when his father died, and much to his displeasure, Louis married his mother. One day, Louis wanted to give Paul a haircut. As Louis was cutting, Paul grabbed the scissors, stabbed Louis, and ran out the kitchen door. Louis was rushed to the hospital. He lost a kidney and was at death's door. That Sunday, Rulon gave a sermon proclaiming that a kid like Paul "deserved the law of Moses. For what he did, it would be merciful if his head were shaved and painted red." Though Rulon would say that he didn't outright order anyone to do anything, when you're a powerful and influential leader in an extremist religious society, anything you say becomes literal. A few nights later, as Paul was walking home in the dark, he was struck over the head, dragged into a nearby house that was under construction, and tied down.

As some of Paul's attackers hacked his hair off and covered his head with red paint, others tore his clothes away. After Paul was stripped, his genitals were mangled and painted red.

We knew people who believed in the biblical teaching of an eye for an eye—men who would have fulfilled a demand of blood for blood if the prophet had desired it. We knew enough to be fearful.

As soon as Dad told his principal at Alta High School that he was leaving for an indefinite amount of time, he called Detective Forbes. The very first words out of Detective Forbes's mouth stunned Dad.

"Vance, I'm so glad you called me back."

"I'm sorry? You called me? I was calling you!"

"Yes, I called [the school] and left a message for you—that for some reason, all night long last night, I couldn't sleep, as I had this growing sense of unease and felt that your family is in danger. You need to get out of there—today."

The fact that this man, who was doing his job and had seen this all before, would be alarmed enough to call us and tell us to leave, on the very same night we were feeling the same warning, isn't a coincidence.

Mom and Dad had to leave the youngest four kids at home while they cleared things at their jobs. They told us to not go anywhere alone and to always have a sibling accompany us. Raph drove to campus to collect her things. Vanessa, Tara, Court, and I stayed behind to quickly pack.

For reasons that I cannot remember, there was something we needed from the cellar, which could be accessed only from the Sunday school room. But no one wanted to go down there.

We went down together, for we were all aware of the aura seeping from behind the Sunday school room's door. The eyes of the prophets seemed to follow us as we walked across the room. The picture of Grandfather Rulon smiled down at me—and it wasn't comforting. Something was laughing at me, cackling menacingly, and although I heard it only in my head, it was real.

Now, no physical threat came to us that day. But, with everything that I know to be true, to exist, as sure as the sun rises in the east every day, I know that there was something there in that cellar. I know it and can feel it as I'm describing this memory and recalling the emotions and feelings that clawed from behind the cellar door. Something was there. And it wanted to hurt us.

Never—*never*—will I be more terrified than I was at that moment. Had a man with a hatchet walked in, it wouldn't have been more terrifying than the energy that lurked in the cellar. It was hate, rage, lust, malice, fury. It was darkness and evil. It was all of those things, combined with menace. It wanted to toy with us, then ravage and devour us.

We all held hands, opened the door, and turned on the light. The light came on and shadows formed, but the light was weak and could reach only so far. The darkness had life. Maybe it was my paranoia playing tricks on me, but I remember the darkness moving like smoke, thicker in some areas than others. I mouthed the words "In the name of the Only Begotten, depart." I had heard Aunt Susan once say that if there was an evil spirit, you could cast it out with those words.

Tara found what we were looking for, and we quickly ran out the door, slamming it behind us, not caring to turn the lowly cellar light off, leaving it to battle whatever form of darkness it was that hid in there. Whatever it was that stalked the cellar, it was real, and it wasn't happy we were leaving.

To this day, I'm uncomfortable in empty churches. I don't like being in an empty chapel, alone, by myself. Is it a subconscious reaction toward organized religion? Or is it a conditioned flight response from the Sunday school room and the cellar?

Detective Forbes soon showed up to stay with us at the house. He was schooled and experienced in polygamy and its corruption, had been around long enough to see its ugliness, and knew not to take this matter lightly. Extremists are extremists. Left-wing or right-wing, no difference; they're the same. They thrive in a warped paradigm and will do the unthinkable to protect it.

Mom and Dad finally came back home, Raph as well, and we all packed up and left before our cousins came home from school. We didn't say good-bye to anyone—not Aunt Susan, Uncle Saul, or Grammy. We just left.

8

When we fled from our home, our immediate possessions in tow, we drove to Grandma Rip's house. I couldn't tell you what frightened me more—going back to the Sunday school room, or the knowledge that I'd be living with Aunt Valeen. We arrived and started unpacking. It was the only time I ever saw my mom sobbing. Mom is a crier, but she never sobs and bawls. But this time she did. I saw it for only a moment before she closed the bathroom door behind her.

Word spread that we had fled, and Yaya called Mom, furious, telling her that she was being dramatic and irrational and that no one in the Group would hurt us. Sadly, as we saw with all of my father's family, and as we saw with Yaya that night on the phone, rather than siding with loved ones and family, they chose to keep their reality intact.

That night when we arrived, Court and I were sent to bed early, in the basement, sleeping on camping cots. Feeling the noises of footsteps above me as everyone crowded into Grandma Rip's kitchen kept me awake. I began crying, but silently. My cousins and best friends were gone. I no longer had a home. Where were we going? At least there were the seven of us: Mom, Dad and us five kids, indestructible.

Then Troy came downstairs. Troy was Grandma Rip's grandson from Uncle Leon, who lived on the other side of the fence from her. Every so often, someone does something that may seem so effortless that they don't know and will never know how profoundly they impact your life. Troy was one of those people, doing one of those incalculably valuable deeds. He pulled up a chair next to us in our cots and talked to us in the dark: "Hey guys. How's it going?"

Troy told us stories of pranks and incidents involving his days in high school and how the best joke to play on a girl is to sneak into the girl's slumber party and plant Jell-O in the toilet—but it has to be colorless—

and then stir it up and let it congeal. Later on, when the girls go to the bathroom, they will leave quite a mess. "Saran Wrap is outdated. People look for it now," he stated casually, like a stockbroker knowing yesterday's buy and sell. Troy stayed with us for a good hour, maybe two, helping to take our mind off things.

As the evening progressed, most of the family began migrating downstairs to see what all the fun was about, and it was there, in the dark, musty, pipe-filled room of Grandma's basement, that we found our refuge, with Troy Ripplinger telling grandiose stories of mischief. We were no longer Allreds; we were now Ripplingers.

Yaya's younger brother, Dan, a retired dentist who lived in Arizona, had a nice secluded cabin in central Utah, near Beaver, which he said we could use. After two days of hiding away in Grandma Rip's house, and to Valeen's relief, we packed up our things and headed down to Beaver.

When we arrived at Uncle Dan's cabin, we were in the wilderness. There was no electricity, as it was on national-forest land. There was plumbing, thank goodness, but all of our lighting, heating, and cooking was fueled by either kerosene or propane. Uncle Dan did have a generator in the basement for emergencies, which Court and I would exploit to the max to play our Super Nintendo. Mom allowed us to fire up the generator for a half hour every day, letting us play Mario Kart, but after that we had to find other ways to entertain ourselves.

We bonded as a family, being stuck in that three-bedroom cabin for a month. We also got on each other's nerves. Dad spent a lot of time going back and forth between Beaver and Salt Lake that month as he looked for an attorney. It was made well known that Uncle Owen and the AUB intended to sue us for the house, hoping to stall the sale of the fourplex. By June, Uncle Saul and the AUB had officially filed suit against us, placing a lien on the property and thus ushering in what was to be a three-year lawsuit.

But we all knew it wasn't about the house; it was about punishing us and, more important, about making us the "bad guys" in a lawsuit, thereby creating a gap between Dad and his family. To the AUB we were a cancerous region of free thought and questioning of authority. We were a threat, so they needed to punish us—as quickly, meanly, and loudly as possible.

In mid-June, not wanting to wear out our welcome, we left Uncle Dan's cabin and moved an hour south to the cabin belonging to Uncle

Dan's son, Gregg, and his wife, Diane, in Pine Valley, just outside of Saint George. We developed a strong rapport and kinship with Gregg and Diane's family, and although their kids were our second cousins, they moved into our lives as our "immediate-extended" family. They became our cousins.

It was a humbling summer for our family, as Cousin Gregg, Uncle Dan, and Uncle Don all invested heavily in us financially with absolutely no collateral. Over time Mom and Dad were able to pay them all back, but that was a huge act of charity and faith on their part. They really didn't even know us or know if we could be trusted.

Dad made several important contacts besides Detective Forbes—specifically, Jeffrey Swinton, a real-estate trial lawyer. We were thrilled when Jeff took our case, and humbled when Uncle Dan put up the retainer. Jeff, of course, originally thought the AUB would settle because they didn't have a case. We knew they wouldn't settle, because it wasn't about the house. It was about discrediting Dad, setting an example of their authority, and making us pay for leaving.

By August, the deal to swap our house for the one in downtown Salt Lake was coming to fruition. Coincidentally, or divinely, the house we were trading for in Salt Lake happened to be just around the corner from Jeff Swinton's home.

Jeff had spent many years involved with the Colorado City real-estate war, between Warren Jeffs, another Mormon fundamentalist polygamist leader, and other men he had banished from his cult. Not only was Jeff an expert in the law, but he was also well acquainted with the stubborn mind-set of fundamentalist leaders. Here is the best way I can sum up war with polygamist radicals: if they're drenched in water but manage in the end to get a cup of water on your face, they will cheer, "Ha! I won."

When we learned that the owners of the other house had accepted the house swap, we drove to downtown Salt Lake near the University of Utah, to see the outside of the house that we were told was to be our new home—and we fell in love with it. You could see that it had not had the attention it needed the last few years. It was plain, dull, rectangular, and run-down, and the bricks were scabbing paint, but you couldn't help but see that this house, built in 1902, was old and wise and, if treated kindly, would make you feel welcome.

In August of the summer of our exodus, all the women went out of town, leaving Dad, Court, and me to our own devices. Dad right away wanted to get started on the house by renovating the basement, which was listed as a third apartment but was currently vacant. The ceiling of the basement apartment was only about six-foot-five. The apartment was run-down and comprised two tiny rooms, including the bathroom, and a tight furnace room. It was dark, with rusty pipes and asbestos insulation, and my claustrophobia was on high alert. Dad was a visionary when it came to homes, and he told us we were going to dig out the stale dirt in the basement and build a nice little entertainment room. I couldn't see what Dad was envisioning, and I doubted him, thinking there was no way on earth he could make something out of this forsaken basement.

Dad put us to work in the basement. We each had our shovels, and we began digging and filling up old laundry-detergent buckets with dirt, carrying them outside, one by one. It was slow, tedious work. Even with our face masks, my nose was filled with dust and my snot was black. My hands were blistered, I was tired, and it was only the first day. We were going to sleep on sleeping bags on the ratty carpet and peeled linoleum flooring of the basement. But first we drove to Smith's, a local supermarket chain. Dad pulled out his wallet from the stretched back pocket of his dirty jeans.

He opened his wallet and pulled out five dollars. He looked at us meekly but determinedly: "Boys, this is all we have for two days." Having been on the run all summer, and having borrowed from many and not daring to ask for any more, Mom and Dad were stretched to the bone. I didn't realize how bad it was until then, as I looked at Dad's calloused and dirty hands, which always shook slightly from his Tourette's. Neither of us said anything, nor did we complain. Thankfully, the dogs were not with us that weekend, so we didn't have to worry about feeding them. With our five dollars we walked quietly through Smith's and bought cheap frozen concentrated orange juice, some Malt-O-Meal cold cereal, and milk. That was it. That was our empire.

For two hot August days we labored, tearing our hands in slow, stubborn progress as we chipped away at the dirt, which felt like cement, straining our limbs and backs with each trip out to the dumping pile, bumping our heads repeatedly on the pipes. But we didn't complain. While we sweated and sneezed, we passed the time laughing and singing through our masks, taking breaks to have small rations of cereal and orange juice, telling jokes and stories as we sat on our newly made pile of dirt out back, or listening to Dad's history lectures in the shade in the park across the street, our faces tanned with dust, silt, and sweat.

We were kings. We were building our new castle. And we did it all with only five dollars.

9

Jeff Swinton was the stake president of the new area we were moving into. A *stake,* in LDS terms, means a boundary of collective wards—churches or congregations—in a close geographical area. A ward is presided over by a bishop. There are usually at least three wards that form a stake, which is presided over by a stake president.*

Jeff guided us not only through the lawsuit, but also through our conversion into the LDS faith. He and his wife, Heidi, spent countless hours mentoring my parents, helping them rid themselves of the negative thought patterns and guilt they had developed while growing up and living in the Group.

With the new life I was finding for myself in Salt Lake, there was also another side of me emerging, one that I was scared of and that I tried my best to keep hidden from others. Before we left the Group, I had been given several lectures in Priesthood classes for twelve-year-olds about homosexuality and masturbation, and how masturbation was a sin and a gateway to homosexuality, which was the most abominable sin.

As I broach this topic, please know that today I have no issues with homosexuals. I know plenty, and one of my cousins, a wonderful person, is gay. But at the age of thirteen, while still trying to distinguish the old lectures I had received as a child in the Group from those I received in the LDS church, I wasn't so secure in my standing. My developing mind, which had endured a traumatic shift in religion and paradigms and a summer on the run, was beginning to have weird, conflicted thoughts. I now know it was the beginning of my obsessive-compulsive disorder (OCD). But at that age I had no idea what was going on. Throughout my life I had always tended to think and analyze things too deeply, but this was something altogether different.

*I won't bore you with any more details of the LDS hierarchy.

The first time I truly noticed it was one Saturday when Dad took Court and me to see Jim Carrey's *The Mask*. It was the first time I ever saw Cameron Diaz in a movie. She was gorgeous. Being thirteen and undergoing puberty, I was feeling some funny things. But that was normal, and I knew it. What happened later wasn't, though, when my mind engaged in this dialogue:

Cameron Diaz is so beautiful; I'd love to have her as a girlfriend. Women are so amazing, they're the most beautiful things God ever created, and I'm so glad I'm not gay. But . . .

And here is where it began:

But what if I'm gay? Lance, you know you're not gay. You're attracted to Cameron Diaz, and she is a woman. Yes, she is attractive, but what if I'm gay and I don't know it? Well, you don't have to be gay. Well, what if I have no choice, and I for some reason do something "gay"? Well, it won't be a problem, since you're not attracted to men. Yes, but what if I slip, and. . . . What if, what if, what if. . . .

I can what-if myself to death. What-if became my nemesis. What-if was and still is the hardest opponent I face. And here is the key to understanding those who suffer from OCD: we know that these stupid obsessive thoughts are irrational, but we cannot stop thinking them. Even though I knew that my thoughts about being gay were irrational, I couldn't stop worrying about it. I'd go through the whole dialogue every hour.

I tried talking to Dad about it, and he got confused. He, too, was in transition, as we were still emerging from the shackles of our extreme conservative mind-set. With a worried look on his face, his Tourette's causing a slight twitching, Dad asked, "Are you trying to say you're attracted to other little boys?"

This gross oversimplification of my question didn't help in the least. That my father would even raise that question made me feel like I was doing something wrong. I was convinced I was going to hell—I seriously was. And I went into the bathroom and prayed, tears running down my cheeks, pleading for my soul.

"Just stop thinking about it," Dad said, as though I could turn it on and off like a switch.

But I couldn't. I had to think about it. I needed to, or else— . . . I never knew that answer, but I needed to. If I didn't think about it, I might fall into complacency and suddenly become gay. I had to think about it. Telling me not to think about it was like asking an alcoholic to never have another drink. I just had to. If I didn't think about it, something bad would happen, but I never knew what. I knew only that something bad would happen, even though nothing ever did.

After the routine dialogue of what-if scenarios that I'd recite to calm my fears, I'd pray to God, this angry God, in fear of his hell: "*I'm sorry, I'm sorry. I don't want to be gay. Please don't be mad at me. I'm not gay, I like girls, please don't let me be gay. Please take these thoughts away.* "

The compulsive praying and internal dialogue helped at first, as they would calm my anxiety for a good few hours, but over time the soothing effect of the compulsion lessened, to the point where I was praying every fifteen minutes to my broody God. I didn't tell anyone, or dare to, after my little chitchat with Dad. I kept these thoughts and other obsessions to myself.

Had basketball not come into my life shortly after these thoughts began, I'd have deteriorated dramatically. But thanks to basketball, I was able to calm my obsessive thoughts and shameful fears, or at least channel them, on the court. I was able to attach a new identity to basketball, hiding my personal demons on the hardwood.

My obsessive thoughts didn't go away when I began playing basketball, but at least I could now dwell on things I could have some semblance of control over. I could now obsess about a bad play, bad pass, or bad call and would stay up late at night pondering and replaying, saying, "What if. . . ." I could obsess about basketball things and think about them without feeling guilty, as I got my mind off of "bad thoughts."

In a positive way, my obsession—my compulsion to play through scenarios of what I should've done on the court and what I'd do the next time—is part of what fueled me. My obsession demanded perfection, and it's what drove me and motivated me to keep working and working, to constantly make up for the mistakes I made on the court. I was my own worst critic and always will be. No matter what negative thing anyone says of me on the court, I have already have said something much meaner to myself.

I had always been worthless as an athlete. But that all began to change in my new setting, at Bryant Middle School. As I started eighth grade, I was five-foot-ten. I constantly got comments that I should start playing basketball—from kids at school and members of my new ward, and especially from the coach of the ward basketball team. I continued to grow. By December, I was six-three, and I was in a lot of physical pain, as my body was growing so fast.

They held tryouts for the Bryant basketball team, and I made it, but only because I was tall.

Let me be frank: I sucked. I couldn't dribble to save my life. I shot the ball before ever looking at the hoop. I couldn't time a layup. And if I did, I always jumped off my right foot to shoot with my right hand, which is just awkward. But every so often I pulled something out of my pocket and hit a miracle shot, then nonchalantly jogged back to the other end like I was a badass, knowing full well that the shot had been pure luck but managing to somehow convince others I had skill. Confidence is the name of the game.

Basketball didn't come naturally to me. The biggest challenge for me was simply being able to balance my overly large head on my rail-thin body. I was like Don Carlos de Austria, among the last of the Spanish Hapsburgs, who fell off a window ledge one night while trying to sneak out for some romping fun. His head was so large that it distorted his center of gravity, causing his fall. I could make it down to the other end of the floor, but that was about it. I was a clumsy giraffe.

I also suffered, and still suffer, from asthma, and it was never much fun to have my bronchial tubes constricting my airways, so I tended to stay away from sports. But an inhaler changed that, or at least made it easier. I always thought the other kids were having as hard a time breathing as I was, but then our longtime family doctor finally informed me that I was usually breathing for two, such was the pressure that I had to fight in my airways.

Not only was I now on the Bryant team, but I was also on a popular Junior Jazz rec-league team, named after our local professional team. I also played church ball, not only for the deacons' team, which was my age group, but also for the teachers' group, and then the priests'. I was on five teams. The Bryant team played Wednesday nights, and church ball was on Thursday, and then there was the Saturday rec team. Lots of games, but very little practice, so I really never got better. Strangely, I went from never having played organized sports to having them define my week.

I wasn't anything special, as was evidenced in a deacons'-team game. I got an offensive rebound and quickly put it back up, and missed it; and reached up and grabbed it again, and missed it again; and grabbed it again, and missed it again . . . eight times in a row. I was so much taller than all the other kids, who were just jumping beside me trying to out-reach me. I just stood there, nearly flatfooted, and played yo-yo with this ball that refused to go in. On the eighth try, when I missed it one more time, I gave up and yelled out in frustration, letting the ball bounce past me as the other team grabbed it and went the other way. I just stared at the rim that had defied me.

Although I sucked, I was on good teams, well-coached teams that won. Since we won, it was fun enough to keep me interested and not too frustrated with my uncoordinated body.

It soon became clear that I was up against more than my uncoordinated body. In my second official game we were battling a tough opponent in a nail-biter that was coming down to the last minute. We were tired and bloody, doing anything we could to pull out the victory.

An opponent was fouled. As he stepped up to the free-throw line, we raised our hands in the air, not waving or moving them. This was the rage back in the mid-nineties—to hold your arms up when you were the defensive team at the foul line, hoping that it might distract the shooter. It never did a lick of good, though. The only thing that's going to psyche out a foul shooter is himself.

The player shot it and missed. But the ref blew his whistle and gave him the ball back. He signaled that two shots remained instead of one, giving the kid a do-over. I didn't know enough about basketball and all its rules to understand what was going on. The kid shot his free throw again, but before the ball even hit the rim, the ref blew his whistle, pointed at me, and called a technical foul.

I raised my hands in confusion: *What did I do?* The ref was turned away from me, so I couldn't see what he was saying. A teammate came up to me and pulled me down, to speak into my ear: "Put your arms down."

"Oh." But it was too late, with the technical foul adding two more free throws on top of the original still left to be taken. The kid hit all four free throws to seal the victory. I felt terrible and walked out of the gym to find a safe corner to cry in. I had cost the team the game because I had not heard the warning.

Afterward, my father went up to the ref and said, "Excuse me, sir. What was the technical about?"

"That kid was ignoring me. I warned him, but he arrogantly kept doing what I asked him not to do, which was holding his hands up while the other team was shooting a free throw. All he had to do was put his hands down."

"I'm sorry, sir," my father said as he held out my large hearing aids in the palm of his hand. "That's my son, and he is deaf."

The haughty and stern visage of the official turned ashen: "Oh, shit."

That eighth-grade year, when we finally moved into the new house on 1300 East in downtown Salt Lake, we still had to honor the lease for the main-floor apartment, and so the seven of us lived in the upper apartment and the basement. Vanessa and I ended up sharing the living room—yes, the living room. We were cramped. Court had the dark and broody basement all to himself. I was too claustrophobic to want anything to do with it and its low ceilings.

When I graduated from Bryant, I had the choice of attending one of two high schools, East or West, since we lived in a neutral zone in the school district. Court attended East, which was much closer to us and had more middle-class kids like me, but for foolish reasons, I decided to attend West High.

I attended West only my freshman year. I broke my foot at the beginning of the basketball season and barely managed to play a few weeks at the end of the season. I was garbage. But I did make an important discovery during that year. During a game a kid tussled with me for a rebound and accidentally head-butted me in the ear. By this time, I no longer had the tubed hearing aids that wrapped around the earlobes and rested there; instead, I had smaller ones that, although they were still visible, had the mechanism itself fitted within the ear frame.

The force of the head butt shattered my hearing aid and cut up the inside of my ear canal. Several smaller fractured pieces were jiggling around in my ear. I had to go to the hospital, where they probed my ear with long, cold rods. Even though my ear canals are less sensitive than most people's, having become accustomed to having plastic or rubber shoved down them to a very uncomfortable depth just for the hearing aids themselves, it still hurts when people shove a rod down my ear. The only thing that would hurt worse than having a hearing aid explode in your ear, I imagine, would be having a contact lens shattered in your eye.

Since then, I have never played a game with my hearing aids in. Practice, yes; but in a game it's different. The surrounding sounds from the crowd and speakers during a game actually serve as an amplifier, pushing the immediate sounds toward my ear (for example, my teammates' or coaches' voices). When I wear my hearing aids during a game, the

sound is so loud that they actually shut down, overwhelmed by the mag-
nitude and the quantity of different sources of noise.

I don't like wearing hearing aids in practice, but I do, so I can hear
and communicate with my team. Aside from the fact that the echoes of
a gym mess with the microphone in your hearing aids, you also have the
issue of sweat damaging the machinery itself or frying the battery.

When you wear hearing aids while exercising, sweat will crawl into
your ear canal, tickling your ear as it winds its way against the plastic
tube of the hearing aid. You cannot simply reach up and scratch your
ear canal. Instead, you have to take out the hearing aid with your sweaty
hands and try to not mess up the battery with said sweaty hands, and
then scratch your ear and put the hearing aid back in.

When the sweat gets in behind your hearing aids, it tickles but also
creates a sort of pressure chamber, like when you're in a plane or under-
water, and you have to adjust your jaws to pop the pressure. This whole
process triggers your yawn reflexes and makes you want to yawn like
you'll never be able to yawn again. But I always try to refrain from doing
so as a coach may mistake me for being disinterested, take it personally,
and make the rest of practice miserable.

During my freshman year at West, the lawsuit with Uncle Saul and the
AUB came to a head, and it made it to court in the fall of 1996. It was
heartbreaking to see Uncle Saul and Grammy sitting on the other side
of the aisle from us. Several of Dad's brothers testified against Dad, telling stories and saying how much was owed to them, and how Dad had
cheated them out of money and never paid them back. Luckily, Dad
was a meticulous record keeper and kept track of all of his finances,
even through all the poverty. When we grabbed the photo albums as
we quickly packed up and fled that summer to Grandma Rip's, Dad
grabbed his records. In court, Jeff got up and showed the brothers who
testified against Dad the receipts of the claimed missing payments. Em-
barrassedly, one by one they blinked and said, "I must have forgotten."

Uncle Saul was the hardest. There he was, my uncle Saul, whom I
loved and adored, the one I had passed many Sundays with playing soft-
ball in the park. It was painful to see him up there, as Jeff then turned the
tables and produced files showing that Saul still owed my father a great
deal of money, not only for the home Dad had built and Saul currently
lived in, but for other services and appliances as well. A refrigerator had

become a sticky topic, as silly as that may seem. But when emotions are high and irrationality rules the day, silverware can seem paramount.

Jeff grilled Uncle Saul. Humiliated him. When he was done, and the brothers' attorney had begun to perspire from his continual refrain of "I object," the judge called for a recess. I had not been able to watch the rest of Uncle Saul's testimony. I began to sob so hard that I had to pull my shirt up to my mouth and bite it, hiding my head beneath the bench. Had it not been so traumatic, I might have enjoyed seeing Jeff grill Uncle Saul, making him the scapegoat, the one that all the AUB would blame when they lost the lawsuit—which they ultimately did.

But it was one of my most scarring memories. When the judge left for his chambers, Uncle Saul was escorted from the stand. He was shaking, barely able to walk. His face was red with anger and rage, and his eyes were dripping tears. "Liars! Your Dad is a liar! I did so much for all of you!" Uncle Saul screamed at us as the bailiff ushered him out.

We heard Uncle Saul sobbing in the bathroom down the hall: "I hate this! I didn't want to do this! Why! Why!" He had been a pawn. His sense of duty to the memory of his father had led him to destroy his relationship with us and his brother. He was angry. He was angry at the AUB, but he was more angry at Dad for not just being a "good boy" and complying—even though Saul, in his heart of hearts, knew the AUB was wrong.

After three weeks, the trial came to a close. Jeff had done a superb job. However, the judge threw in his bid for the presidency of Switzerland as he read out the verdict, which was completely neutral, saying the house was ours to sell and we were free to move on, thus effectively making the place on 1300 East our new home. But our countersuit to cover legal fees and expenses wasn't granted. Both sides lost. Uncle Saul and Dad lost the most.

Even Jeff Swinton lost, in that it was a long time before he made any money on our case. He had to borrow heavily to stay afloat himself through the whole trial. He truly invested in us, and he earned every penny he made on that case.

But the important thing was that we were free to move on. Once the AUB had achieved what they wanted, they left us alone. It was pretty much "out of sight, out of mind." We never showed our faces at Group events again. We simply began a new life.

Part Two

High School Hoops

10

I transferred to East High School, which Court attended. A week before school started, I arrived at 7 a.m. in the East High weight room. The basketball players were doing their squats and hang-cleans, lifts I had never seen before, and they were all in attendance together, laughing and mocking and taunting in good fun. I soon learned that Coach Kerry Rupp ran a tight, organized ship of dedication and attendance.

This was all new to me, as West High had nothing of the sort. There was no organized off-season team routine. During the summer you simply went home, enjoyed vacation, and then came back to school, and then you maybe played some pickup for preseason training. But at East there were weight sessions and skill development—things I desperately needed.

On that first day, after sheepishly lifting weights, I looked about at all the seniors and juniors who were united with purpose following their loss in the state-championship game the season before. The assistant coach, Coach Cowan, took me up to the gym to get a quick assessment of my skill level. It didn't take him long to realize that I sucked. He knew I wasn't ready to contribute to varsity.

I was handed to Coach Gardner, the sophomore basketball coach. Once the season started, I had to wake up at five every morning to go to sophomore practice, which started at five thirty. Never once did anyone in my family have to wake me; it was that important to me. I wanted to be good at something. I wanted to make my own mark in my family of high achievers. I slept with the clock radio on my pillow, turning up the volume to max, letting it erupt full blast when the alarm went off every morning at five. I made sure there was no chance I might not hear the alarm and sleep through practice.

My family took turns getting up when I was ready and driving me to the gym. They were all in line to help me chase my dream, which at that time was simply just to be a good basketball player, nothing more. In spite of what my parents always told me, I had no inkling that I could be good enough to be anything I wanted to be.

I went to those five-thirty practices, just like all of my other teammates, for the pure enjoyment of the game—all of us paying our dues just to wear a uniform, none of us knowing or dreaming we might someday be good enough to even play varsity.

Our coaches were often late for those practices, as we sat in the freezing hallway, wearing our winter coats over our practice uniforms, tying our shoes in silence, with the howling snow and wind tugging at the school doors. Coach Kernodle usually showed up first. He opened up the door to the gym with a grunt for a hello, his standard coffee and box of doughnuts in hand. Kernodle looked nothing like a coach. He was in his late forties, with an orange handlebar mustache and a beer belly that hung over his waist like a laundry bag of linen sheets.

While we performed his warm-up routine, running and sliding in the cold, dimly lit gym, half naked in our flimsy jerseys, our knees absorbing the cold shock that reverberated up our legs and into our spines from the frozen wooden floor beneath our feet, Coach Kernodle would be sitting over on the table letting his dangling feet singsong back and forth. His mouth full of powdered doughnuts and coffee, he would call out in a muffled voice, "Pick it up, ladies. . . ."

By the time we were done with Kernodle's obligatory warm-up drill, which he used to keep us occupied in the same way a bad parent uses a TV as a babysitter, Coach Gardner would arrive. Coach Gardner was a tank. Each of his arms was thicker than my chest, and I dare say each arm weighed more than my six-foot-eight, one-hundred-eighty-pound frame.

Coach Gardner's practices were fun, and he spent a lot of time with me those mornings, teaching me how to shoot hook shots and drop-step layups, as I had no sort of offensive post game whatsoever. He also taught me defensive principles in the post, which to my surprise and dislike consisted of more than just blocking shots. When I told Coach Gardner that I should not have to do any defensive sliding drills and would just block shots, he laughed, slapped me on the back, and said, "So much you still have to learn, big guy."

It was nice to be part of a team. In the fall before the season began, I had done well enough under Coach Gardner's tutelage, combined with the short amount of time I had with Coach Rupp, that I had actually turned into a somewhat decent basketball player, at least decent enough to be considered an offensive option in the playbook.

Halfway through the season, I was called up to join the junior varsity squad and practice with Coach Rupp. I still remained on the sophomore team and had to wake up and attend practice in the morning, and also had to attend practice after school, keeping me at East High from five in the morning until five in the afternoon. Two-a-days every day. Those were incredibly long days, and not surprisingly, my grades began to drop. You can imagine the displeasure that showed in my father's face when my report card came in the mail and showed a 2.7 GPA. I know that many parents would be elated to have their child bring home a 2.7, but in my family, we had high expectations, and all of my siblings before me had set a standard of academic excellence. Being the only child in the family to participate in official athletics past junior high, I was something of a new challenge for my parents.

It ended up being a good season, which gave me enough validation and sense of accomplishment to keep me going. The varsity team made it to the state-championship game for the second straight year that season and lost again. But Rupp lost a strong core of seniors, leaving many positions open on the team for next season. Coach Gardner called me to his room and told me I had a chance to start varsity next season, but that it was all up to me. I had to hold up my end; Rupp wasn't going to go out of his way to motivate me. When the spring came, I was going to be that guy who took advantage of an opportunity and who accepted full accountability for himself. I was baptized into the blue-collar world of Kerry Rupp.

When my time did come, the spring after sophomore season, I joined Rupp at six thirty every morning for skill-development sessions—a practice we continued faithfully for two years.

You either loved or hated Kerry Rupp. There was no in between. He was never insulting to parents, but he didn't fraternize with them. He was respectful, but he had been around long enough to see the ugliness of the sports world and all the greed, subterfuge, and backbiting that came with school sports and parental school boards. He was impressed by nothing but hard work and integrity.

"Everyone thinks their kid should be a star," Rupp told us on the first day of his summer basketball camp. "Make sure your parents, if they call, know that I will talk about anything except for what goes on the basketball court and playing time."

I grew to love the early-morning training sessions when it was just me and Coach Rupp with a ball in a cold gym, buzzing lights dimly illuminating the hardwood floor. Rupp met me at six thirty every morning before school. He had no reason to do it but that he loved the game and saw something in me.

When he gave the team days off, I'd still ask Coach Rupp if we could work out the next morning by ourselves. I knew it would be hard and painful, as he pushed me to the limit and many times past, to the point where I'd vomit right onto the hardwood. But I loved it. I loved the pain and discomfort. I loved the sense of accomplishment I felt once it was all over. I loved to sit by myself there in the bleachers of the empty gym and be lost in stalled thought, my mind and body too tired to think. It was my high. A natural high.

When fatigued, the body produces chemicals that send your brain and physiology into a different place. I love this natural high, when I'm too tired to think. I love sitting there, not having a worry in the world as I revel in the small victory and sense of accomplishment I have just achieved, even if it's only for fifteen minutes.

Those mornings were the purest form of basketball I ever knew. Just me, Rupp, and a ball. No money, no boosters, no politics. It was the pure love and innocence of the game, when it was still a game for me. We both worked and sweated, our shoes squeaking and echoing out the gym and down the empty hallways. I'd pay to have those moments again, those moments of hard work and sacrifice when I knew not what to expect as far as what my future held, with no sense of entitlement, no reward or motive in sight other than just the pure love of the game. I had no idea if I was ever going to be good enough to play college ball. We were challengers of the unknown.

I wasn't playing for the future on those mornings with Rupp; I was playing for the moment, for the present. I wanted to be good at something; I wanted to excel at something. Coach Rupp was right there with me, through thick and thin. Rupp knew I was going to play college ball, but he held only the possibility of it before me, like a carrot on a stick. He withheld any certainty he felt about my future—to keep me hungry, to never let me get complacent. But he would come to know me well enough to know that I'm my own harshest critic, my own harshest coach, and that he therefore had no reason to worry I'd become self-satisfied.

There were a few times in games that Rupp would get in my face and yell at me, but I never took it hard, and he never made it personal. "Look at me when I'm talking to you!" he once yelled at me on the bench in the middle of a game. A parent of a teammate leaned over to my parents, who were watching the interaction, and asked if they were OK with it. Mom and Dad simply nodded. They knew that Rupp had only the best intentions for me. They also knew that when I didn't want to listen to someone, I stubbornly looked away, my hearing loss helping me block out what they were saying. Rupp was smart enough to know that this was a coping mechanism of mine, and he would never let me use it with him.

A lot of parents had issues with Rupp, and I can understand why. He was very stern and ran a tight ship, with a college-style program at a high school level. Most teenagers just want to show up and play and have fun. With Rupp, it was more than just a glorified extracurricular activity. It was a commitment. How many kids want to wake up at 6 a.m. during the summer to go run sprints? Coach Rupp's tryouts were the entire off-season, not just the standard obligatory opening-week tryouts in November. His practices were intense and serious. We never goofed off.

For some kids this was too much, but for me, I loved it. I loved the sense of purpose and the camaraderie. I loved having partners in pursuit of a goal. I loved the feeling that I belonged to something, that we were a fraternity of men, all sacrificing time and fun, committing to each other, in pursuit of that goal.

Rupp and I didn't have many heart-to-hearts. Like me, Rupp wasn't very talkative or gregarious. "I'm paid to be your coach, not your friend," he'd say. "There are two thousand other kids in this school for that job." But we had a deep respect for each other.

Kerry Rupp was the greatest coach I ever had. The man knew me and taught me everything I know. Everything I learned under the great-minded Rick Majerus, who is a master of the game, I had already learned at least some facet of under Coach Rupp, who could've taught me even more had I been older and my mind able to comprehend. But most of the things that Rupp couldn't teach me were things I could learn only through experience.

Rupp never embarrassed you if you made a mistake—an unusual trait in a coach, as I would find out. If I made a mistake, he took me out or pulled me aside, and then simply asked, "Do you know what you did wrong?"

If the answer was yes, he would say, "OK, learn from it." If no, he would explain it. The only time Rupp would yell at me was when I wasn't playing the hardest I could. And with all the hours we spent alone, one-on-one, Rupp knew what my hardest was. Rupp demanded a lot of his players, but above all he simply demanded that you play hard. If you didn't, you would come out. He let you play through your mistakes—if they were honest mistakes, of course, mistakes of omission.

As long as I was playing hard, Rupp let me have a long leash, to learn from my experiences. I did well with that style of coaching. I'm so incredibly analytical and critical of myself to this very day. When you're worried about making a mistake, you'll make a mistake. Trust me, I know. Basketball is a game of flow, and if you're playing in fear, your body and mind cannot get into the rhythm.

Since our days at East, Coach Rupp has, like me, gone on his own journey and is well traveled. Like me, too, he has sacrificed dearly, with little reward other than his own personal sense of accomplishment. It's scary just how parallel our lives have been since those days of innocence at East High School. He taught me so much, and yet we both have had similar experiences of heartache and disappointment within our profession, though from different vantage points. But as Rupp taught me every morning to never give up, challenging me to chase down every missed shot and put it back in, we both, since then, have never given up.

In the capricious world of basketball, we challenged the unknown, but we did so with passion, and the journey has been the reward.

11

That day comes for all teenage boys—and yes, girls, too—when all they can think about is sex. And when they're sixteen, they get a sex-education class, where they can giggle and laugh at all the anatomical references and diagrams yet burn in their bosoms with desire and yearning for the pleasurable.

The time came when I was eligible for sex ed. I was given a disclaimer to take home to my parents and have them sign, saying they were aware and either encouraging or silently disapproving of my education in the science of procreation. I arrived in class and handed the disclaimer to my teacher. Those without disclaimers were excused: some piously held their noses high, clinging to their innocence and chastity, for which they believed God smiled on them; others wistfully looked back over their shoulders at what they could only imagine we were about to see, and what they wanted to see.

The lights dimmed. I'd no longer have to rely on the sketches my Dad had provided many years ago; they were surprisingly detailed, but still, they were sketches. The TV blared on. The film started. Ink blotches spotted the screen. A scratchy soundtrack crescendoed from the tatty speakers of the TV. The sound and musical quality of the track combined to create a score that you would only expect to hear as an accompaniment to a 1950s Cold-War propaganda 8 mm projector presentation.

The black screen then exploded to life, with a big white shining title: "The Miracle of Life."

I'm already disappointed. Disappointment soon turned to curious bewilderment.

What is all that hair? Wait. . . . Is that . . . is that a vagina? All that hair. It must be a monkey or an ape . . . nope, it's a woman. A woman with a very hairy vagina, so hairy that it looks like an Italian mobster's ass. Why doesn't she trim it? She knew she was . . . her vagina was . . .

going to be on camera, . . . didn't she? Wait, OK . . . this movie must have been made in the seventies.

Vaginas are ugly. Do they have teeth? Is it safe to . . . ? Wait, why is her vagina moving? Is that blood coming out of her vagina? Oh my gosh, it is! There's BLOOD COMING—. . .OK, there's now a big white something pushing open her vagina. Annnnnnnnd her vagina just ripped. More blood.

OK, I got it: the big white thing tearing up the vagina is a head.

Now, some might be surprised that I didn't receive any formal sex education until I was sixteen. But you should know that Utah County, aka Happy Valley, home of BYU, has one of the highest per capita teenage pregnancy rates in the country. But we ignore this. We don't talk about the bad things. We don't talk about the things that rattle our paradigm of bliss. Utah also is the top state in downloaded porn per capita in the country. Why is this? Because we don't teach, nor do some of us fully understand, nor are we properly taught, the consequences of sex. When something is taboo, teenagers, who will always rebel, will touch and flirt with it, in hopes of finding their identity.

Jared Sperry introduced me to porn. It was under his guidance that I witnessed my first taste of it on the Internet on his personal computer in his sequestered room, which he kept locked at all times. Our friend Greg Noble and I were sitting on Sperry's bed one day when he said, "You guys want to see something cool?" And before we could answer, an MPEG was flashing in front of us. When I registered what I was seeing, I crinkled my nose and flinched. Greg did the same, and we both turned away in disgust, holding our hands up to shield our face. Had we been warned beforehand, we might have been able to enjoy it, but as it was, it wasn't enticing.

Sperry loved to play pranks on us: sending in a subscription for Greg to Playboy and having it delivered to his house, where his mother would receive it on a day that should have been just another quiet weekday; having Astroglide sent to the neighboring Maxwell house; or logging on to a gay porn site at my parents' house and then purposely leaving it on-screen for my father to come home and see and grow even more concerned about "little boys in the shower." Can you imagine the awkward moment of shame and the words that cannot quite roll off the tip of your tongue as you try to explain to your father that it wasn't you who logged on to a gay porn site, but rather a friend of yours who did it as a prank—especially when it's the oldest excuse in the book to point your finger at your absent friend in order to avoid being reprimanded?

In our senior year, Greg and I were in a computer-science class where we had to make up our own Web pages for our finals. Greg did his on aviation, and I did mine on basketball. Sperry was a brilliant computer-science nerd who knew tons more than I will ever know about computers and said he would help us. The night before the project was due, Jared and I reviewed the page and what I wanted on it, and the three required links to related Web pages, which on my page were ncaa.com, espn.com, and nba.com. When we finished up, Greg showed up to work on his project, and I left them to their own devices, my project complete.

The next morning in class, I logged on to my Web page via the Internet and did one last look-over to make sure everything was in order before presenting it on the overhead projector. All the links were working, the sounds and graphics were up and running, the comment board was functioning—all was great, until I clicked on nba.com.

The screen slowly began to fade as a Flash player was activated. While the screen was black, a looped high-frequency audio clip squealed out, "Lance Allred! Lance Allred! Lance Allred! Lance Allred!" My peers looked up from their monitors as I fumbled for the speakers, but not in time to cover the screen, which flicked on to show a skeezy-looking man with a black handlebar mustache, in ass-less chaps, gazing over his shoulder with a come-hither look. He had the studded leather necklace and the Nazi biker cap, a leather vest, and a perfectly waxed rear end that fit snuggly in the holes on the chaps. Sperry had created a gay porn site, recording his own voice saying my name and then tuning it to a high frequency to make it sound like a little boy's, which was creepy enough to deprive anyone of sleep for a good forty-eight hours.

The site was on a timer that caused it to gradually fade in to full sight over the course of a good ten seconds before you could even close it. All I could do after I finally managed to turn off the volume was flick off the monitor. The teacher popped up: "What was that?"

Frantic, I removed my arms from around the computer, looking down to make sure the screen was blank before finally letting go. I downplayed: "Just some silly e-mail my friend sent me."

Greg was leaning over in his seat, facing away from me, hugging himself as he laughed hard and quietly. He had been in on the prank. When I had left Sperry's the night before, he and Sperry had conspired against me, to humiliate me. Fortunately, I had done my routine maintenance check beforehand. If I had not done so, and all had gone according to Greg and Jared's plan, my name would've shrieked through the classroom as a Chester-child-molester in ass-less chaps appeared on the classroom wall looking lustfully at all the innocent boys. Those ten seconds would've seemed interminable, with utter chaos and madness ensuing.

Before I could voice my displeasure, I was called to give my presentation.

"Ah," my teacher, Mr. Stoker, said as my Web site came into view, the montage of various University of Utah basketball players appearing before the class. "Here is a theme that's dear to his heart."

I spoke nonchalantly, doing my best to downplay my shock and even more so my fear that the link would be found and I'd be labeled a porn addict, sent to the office, and confronted awkwardly by my father yet again about my phantom homosexuality. "Yeah, as you can see," I explained, "I have my basketball icons here and a comment and suggestion board up and running and various links and info about all the players and statistics for the University of Utah." I continued on, saying nothing important as I clicked on various parts of the page, including ncaa.com and espn.com but purposely skipping the treacherous nba.com. The teacher bought my performance, making no further comment as he nodded at my page.

"Well done, Lance."

"Thank you."

Greg raised his hand.

"Yes, Greg?" Mr. Stoker asked.

"Yeah, what's on nba.com?"

High school is a difficult time even when you're not (a) hearing impaired and (b) a freakish giant. I was trying to make a name for myself and establish a firm standing at my new school. One night after a football game, I found myself walking home with Jeff Adams, one of my teammates. Jeff had dated a girl named Jamie Stephensen throughout junior high, but they had broken up freshman year, and Jeff wanted her back.

As Jeff and I were walking, he told me he had overheard during that night's game that Jamie and two other friends were sleeping over at her house, babysitting her younger brothers for her parents. It was then that I was introduced to the term *stealthing.*

Stealthing: the act of moving in a group of two or more people (never just one, as this is part of the definition of *stalking*) in reconnaissance around a fixed parameter, which encases a group of the opposite sex (never just one, as this is also part of the definition of *stalking*) to gain knowledge of the general consensus or feelings of the targeted party in regard to various topics such as boys, school, teachers, rivals for affection, and so forth.

I had never spoken to Jamie before and didn't think she even knew my name, but I knew who she was. More than wanting the potential of socializing with members of the opposite sex, I welcomed the opportunity to fraternize with Jeff. And so I tagged along. We made it to Jamie's house, where most of the lights were off. Since Jeff knew Jamie very well, I assumed we were going to knock on the door. But he had other plans. Jeff wanted the truth, and in his search for it, nearly in a crawl, he found his way up the driveway and stopped around a lit basement window. He leaned his head next to the glass.

"I can hear them talking, but I can't make out what they're saying," Jeff said, rubbing his knuckles in frustration. The suffering was too much, and he was aching to know if Jamie still thought of him, because he did of her.

I then had an epiphany and saw a golden opportunity to present my worth. I pulled out my hearing aid, leaving it on, and handed to Jeff: "Here, try this out. It should help you hear a little better."

I don't remember what he heard, but as sophomore year ended, Jeff and Jamie got back together.

The summer after sophomore year, while most of my teammates were on vacation, I met Coach Rupp every morning at seven thirty in the weight room and the gym. Later in June, Coach Rupp took me with him to the Rick Majerus Big Man–Guard Camp. It was the first time I ever saw Coach Majerus, the University of Utah's head basketball coach at the time. Most people, upon first seeing him, notice how fat he is. But that wasn't what I saw. I noticed how, when he first entered the gym, it went silent and he went to work right away, before he even stepped on the hardwood—barking orders, directing traffic, having us sit around the perimeter as he conducted drills for his players. He ran it like a perfectly well oiled machine. I love organization.

After witnessing the attention he commanded and the knowledge he possessed, I knew that I wanted to play for him. Big Man Camp was intense. It was a forty-eight-hour camp, and you slept only twelve of those hours. Hundreds of big men, many bigger and some exponentially better than me, were there going through the drills, demonstrating their skill.

There were a few really good players there, men who are well-known NBA stars today, and I saw how much they respected Majerus.

I knew that if I was ever welcomed into the graces of Majerus, I'd be in good company. Throughout the camp, Majerus showed us a wide variety of big-man skills that he had his players demonstrate. His team was coming off a run to the Elite Eight, and his star player, Keith Van Horn, had been the second pick in the NBA draft that week, behind Tim Duncan.

I saw how brutal Majerus was with his players in such a public setting, but in a sick and sadistic way I wanted to fill that role someday. Because I knew that if Majerus was riding you, in your face, demanding constantly from you, then you knew he cared about you and that he felt you could be a good player. If he didn't have high hopes for you and felt you had limited potential, he would let you do your job without much conflict. But he demanded perfection from those he thought had talent.

We'd sit for long minutes in a defensive stance, basically a squat position, while Majerus told us to hold it as he walked around, his belly peeking out from under his shirt and slouching over his cotton waist shorts. He sometimes stopped to climb up onto the shoulders of a kid who wasn't low enough, to emphasize his point. His language was shocking, as he used the word *fuck* in those two days more than I had heard it in my entire life up to that point.*

When the summer was over and school began, I saw Coach Gardner in the hall, and he came up to me. "Is it true?" he asked.

"What?"

"That you had one of the best off-seasons in the history of the coaching staff?"

I could only smile. Rupp had complimented me from time to time but had never hinted at anything like that to me. Rupp had a habit of doing this—constantly challenging me, keeping that carrot on the stick, pushing and pushing me to go just a little bit more and then a little bit more after that, but never using negativity as motivation.

---

*I'm not offended by the "F" word; I simply find it mundane and boring. I have heard it used in every grammatical way possible—as a noun, verb, adjective, adverb, pronoun, preposition, and much, much more. It's too easy, too convenient a word. If "Fuck" is the most clever thing you can say, you really should pick up a dictionary.

12

When the junior season began, I was in high spirits. I had invested a long summer with Coach Rupp and was feeling good about my individual game and confident that I'd be able to contribute. After a solid fall work-out regime with the team, training camp came in November, and to my frustration I saw that I wasn't picking up the offensive plays as quickly as the others, who had been in varsity practices the year before.

Noah Eyre was my age but had played on the JV squad the year before. He was much better than me. Plus he was also the most popular guy in school: tall, dark, and handsome. By the time the first game came, Noah was starting at center and I was getting only a few minutes in a game. I started to feel depressed. *There's no "I" in team.* I know the saying as well as anyone. My depression, though, wasn't that I felt I should've been a star, but that I was looking back and asking, "What is all this for? What was all that hard work for?" It felt like I was in exactly the same place I'd have been in had I given only half the effort. Was Noah simply more talented? More experienced? Maybe both. But the root of my insecurity was that I had invested so much time the previous summer that I was now that much more emotionally involved. I saw myself only in one light, and that was as a basketball player. I felt that it was my only redeeming trait. I was so invested and eager to do well that I became crippled with apprehension, afraid to make a mistake. I was thinking too much.

Noah had a completely different personality than me. He was well rounded as a person: he had so many other things going on in his life, and he still worked hard in basketball. He was always able to put things in perspective, so that while he did care if we won or lost, he also knew that if we, and he, lost, there was still life after the game, and friends and family awaiting him.

I held everything on the line, feeling that my future hinged on every game. With that kind of pressure on myself, whenever I entered the game for Coach Rupp, I was paralyzed with nerves. You can't play basketball when you're afraid to make a mistake. Basketball is a game of constant mistakes, and while your coach may not forgive you for mistakes, you have to at least be able to forgive yourself and move on to the next play. Otherwise, you'll fail.

More than faith from your coach, you need faith in yourself to be a basketball player. If you can honestly answer that you did more good things than bad things in the game, you have won. I used to overlook all the good things I did and just dwell on all the bad things, replaying them in my head after every game. I wouldn't sleep after games, emotionally flagellating myself with what-ifs. What if I had just been one more step back while blocking out my man? The ball wouldn't have bounced over my head, and. . . .

But all you need is one good game, one good shot, and then you're rolling. My opportunity came a few months into the season when Noah was injured, against region-leading Olympus High School. I came out of nowhere and scored eleven points in the fourth quarter. Yeah, I know— whoop-de-do, eleven points! But when your head is in the tank, any-thing, anything at all, will usually do to help turn your self-perception around. Quicker than the blink of an eye, I was running the offense smoothly, my confidence was up, and I was playing slowly and under control. I was finally able to apply all of the skills I had invested in de-veloping with Coach Rupp during the summer.

Eventually, Coach Rupp began to start me alongside Noah and I be-came the low-post option that Coach Rupp had planned for me to be. And in spite of the team's rough start to the season, with a six-eleven record, we were finally able to climb back into the playoff picture.

Unfortunately, I pulled my hip flexor two days before we were set to play top-seeded Provo High, and I couldn't play in the first round of the playoffs. Even though I had wanted to play and tried to warm up, I couldn't get the hip loose, and the pain was too great. I hated myself when I had to tell Coach Rupp before the game that I couldn't go on.

I went and cried in the bathroom. I had bled, sweated, and sacrificed with my teammates all season long. We were committed to each other, and I had to abandon them as they went off to battle. We lost that game by ten points.

When the game was over, some of us went to a local burger joint. We all sat there in Hires, not realizing that it would be the last time we'd all be together as a team. I have enough of those moments since then—when a team is disbanding for good—to know them when they come, and I make sure I take in the moment.

Basketball bonds people, and ten years may pass before I run into a teammate, but I can still walk up to them and give them a hug. And while we may sometimes lack things to talk about except for the standard updates, there still is with us that bond that no one else knows, that only we share.

I joined high school choir only because everyone else was doing it. Sure, I love music; I love the notes and the harmony. I can hear those note shifts, albeit not like most people do, as my off-key singing will attest. But I hear the change in notes just as I hear the change in vowels when people are speaking. Still, this wasn't why I joined choir.

Anybody who was anybody—the cool kids, my friends, the pretty girls, jocks, even regular kids—everyone was doing it. It was a chapel of tolerance, bringing people from all walks of life together, according to height. No matter what clique you ran with in the halls, at lunch, after school, it made no difference, as nature and genetics assigned you your new friends, who were very similar in height to you. Luckily I had Greg on my left. Greg Noble is to this day my dearest friend.

The mirror faced the choir bleachers. It put a spell on you, and you couldn't help but look. It was a safe place that invited us to divulge our thoughts, secrets, and egos, and it would never betray us. Choir was really just a showcase of vanity, as we would all be lost in the gamut of mirrors in front of us, tilting our heads slightly from side to side to better appreciate our features. It gave immediate validation, as we could compare ourselves to someone else and have the instant gratification of realizing, *You know what? I'm comparing my features and looks to Ben Johnson, and I really am much, much better looking than he is. What do all the girls see in him? He is small, doesn't play football or basketball, but soccer. Soccer! Oh well, I'm gorgeous! Not as gorgeous as Noah, though.*

When you weren't immersed in your own visage and facial structure, you could also pass the time playing eye tag with a cute someone, staring at their reflection in the mirror and then quickly looking away. It was very convenient for puppy-love purposes. Even if you were busted for checking out a girl, you couldn't be held accountable, as the mirror was a safe buffer zone and couldn't be used against you. Was some girl really going to say, *I totally busted him looking at me through the mirror in choir today!* The mirror was a deflector—not only in light, but in accountability as well.

Mrs. Applegate, the choir teacher, was scary and mean, very intolerant and impatient. She often stopped to call someone out. One time it was Greg as he was tiredly nodding off. Mrs. Applegate stopped class, not saying anything, but simply staring at him, while poor narcoleptic Greg had no idea the music had even stopped. Ten seconds passed while two hundred of his peers all looked in the mirror to see what the sudden silence was about. All eyes on him, I finally nudged him awake.

"Huh?" Greg said sleepily, wanting to know why I had ruined his nap time.

I motioned with my head toward Mrs. Applegate, who was staring at Greg with a look a stepmother would give a redheaded stepchild. "Care to join us today, Greg?" Mrs. Applegate asked, giving us a we're-not-amused look while marking the roll-call sheet, letting us both know we had been "unsatisfactory" for the day.

"Ya, sorry," Greg said politely. But it didn't matter, because Greg never made a sound when he sang. He was in the choir only because he didn't know how to draw. Greg was truly the only person who didn't take advantage of the mirror. He didn't care about girls. Whenever Greg caught me looking at myself in the mirror, he would turn and look directly at me to let me know I was incorrigible, rolling his eyes in the tired, annoyed way that only Greg Noble can.

While Greg just lip-synched, I was the maestro of the bel canto, wowing the world with my off-pitch vibrato, a sound that only a deaf person can make. I sounded like what you would expect a deaf person to sound like. With growing frustration, and to no avail, Mrs. Applegate scanned us with her calculating eyes to see who owned that beautiful voice that she heard but that eluded her every day—the sweet, painful, melancholy voice that, if harnessed correctly, could bring the world together. I never let her know it was me. When she looked at me, thinking she had finally found who had this majestic voice we're speaking of, I went mute, mouthing the words. But when she turned away again, I resumed my singing, which carried so much emotion, it created waterfalls on the other side of the world.

I was afraid of the spotlight. I just wanted to sing with my friends, and to myself, alone in the shower. I was afraid of success. I didn't want my peers to envy me for the power and beauty that nature had bestowed upon the sounds my vocal cords produced, as I was already blessed with size and a fine, classical facial-bone structure.

When it came time for auditions for small groups—barbershop and madrigals—I opted not to try out. Even though Mrs. Applegate asked me to, I humbly declined, as I didn't want any extra school activities to conflict with my commitment to basketball.

I'm sure many of you, mostly my female readers, are wondering when the female protagonist will come in. Well, the reason you haven't seen one is that I was terrified of girls. I wasn't like, "Girls are gross!" No, I was a big fan of the ladies and had several crushes on them throughout my childhood. But I was so self-conscious of my hearing. I struggled, and still do, to hear high-pitched sounds even with my HAs in. I communicated much more easily with my father than I did with my mother mostly for this reason. Girls' voices are just higher-pitched than boys'. If I tried to talk to girls, I'd often mishear something, and, thinking I had heard a question or comment correctly, I'd respond with something totally random and make a complete fool of myself.

Back in high school, when I overanalyzed everything and was so self-critical, I took everything personally. I made it all about me—not in a selfish way, but in an "I have to be the one to fix things" kind of way. If something wasn't working, it was always my fault. If a girl wasn't talking to me, it was my fault because I wasn't saying the right thing. If a girl was going to like me, it would be because I had won her affection. If a relationship was going to fail, it was always going to be because of me or something I said or did. It was all my fault and responsibility.

I was a wreck, a big ball of analysis, and I'm glad, for the sake of all girls, that none of them dated me in high school—not from a danger standpoint, but from an emotionally draining standpoint. I was too intense.

Midway through my senior year, I discovered that I was missing some science credits to meet the University of Utah admission criteria. Wanting to get the most out of my education, I enrolled in the freshman-level physics class. In lieu of papers, I made two epic movies for the class. They really were amazing. Let's just say my movies involved me, Greg, and Jared, in the canyons near Park City, in the snow, with guns and dry-ice bombs and a clown mask.

When I enrolled in the class, I discovered to my relief that there was another senior in there with me. We even sat at the same table. Her name was Sharlie Ingles. She was very beautiful and tall and had the classical long neck that, if focused on directly, looked kind of odd but, in the context of the whole, was perfect. Sharlie was one of the student-body officers and editor of the school newspaper and yearbook. However, she wasn't peppy and annoying. She was very mature and had her priorities straight, and though she was acquainted with the wild girls, she herself was never into drinking, but neither was she into the whole beautiful-people, backbiting scene. Sharlie just kind of fit in wherever she wanted.

Little by little, Sharlie and I came to know each other in physics class. We'd playact as junior high kids, passing notes back and forth, which actually began to turn into flirting. I could tell that Sharlie was coming to like me, and I liked her, too. But I was so awkward. I had no idea what I was supposed to do.

I was so passive and hopeless that Sharlie was forced to make the first move and asked me to the prom, which was girl's choice. My friends were excited for me, but I was nervous. I was also in the middle of a basketball season that wasn't going according to plan.

It came time for me to answer Sharlie about the prom. One of my friends came up to me on my eighteenth birthday, the very same day I was playing my old school and rival, West High, and said, "Dude, Sharlie wants to kiss you for your birthday."

This was also the very same day I was arrested for truancy. Yes, I was arrested.

Greg's mom wanted to cook me a birthday breakfast, and so three cars full of my posse all packed up to drive to Greg's house. Greg and I were riding in a jeep belonging to Preston Hayes. Our jeep was the last car in the caravan to leave the school parking lot. Incidentally, it was also the only car that had an expired license plate.

Right as we pulled out of the parking lot, a truancy cop pulled us over—having grounds to do so thanks to the expired license plates. We tried explaining that it was my birthday and that we were en route to a birthday breakfast at a friend's house. He was having none of it as he called it in, while behind him a score of the usual troublemaker kids made their way to the 7-Eleven across the street.* While the truancy officer was telling us that he was going to take us downtown, I, as politely as I could, pointed to the kids at the 7-Eleven and told him he might have better luck with them.

Preston, Greg, and I sat in the juvie hall for two hours while this peon of a truancy cop, who wore a leather jacket, tight jeans that were stretched from the wallet he kept in his back pocket, and black Velcro sneakers, interrogated us. Each of us was taken aside to be grilled individually by the booking officer, who was too old to have a real job at the police department. He warned us of the slippery slope we were traveling, of how truancy led to drug use, which led to killing hookers, which led to a life behind bars and lots of child-support payments. When he was done, we were escorted back to our arresting officer.

When we sat down with our Tom Cruise–wannabe officer, the dialogue went something like this:

truancy officer: Why were you skipping school?

me: It's my birthday.

truancy: Sure. Now if it was your birthday, where were you headed?

me: To my friend's house, as his mom was cooking me a birthday breakfast.

truancy: Mmm-hmm, sure. Did you clear it with your parents or do you have an excusal note?

me: No, I have a 3.8 GPA. My parents both are schoolteachers and trust that I will take care of my schoolwork, and they don't care if I skip school as long as my grades don't fall.

truancy: I see. So you have no excusal note?

me: No. You can call my mother at work, and she'll tell you that I have her permission, and you can let me go.

truancy: Well, she needs to be down here herself, or another adult whom we can release you to. In the meantime I need some info. Address?

*You know the kind, the ones that wear Oakland Raiders jackets and spit every third step.

me: 32 South 1300 East.

truancy: Date of birth?

me: [Incredulous silence]

truancy: Date of birth, please.

me: Again, that would be today . . .

truancy: Mmm-hmm, sure.

Preston Hayes's father finally came and we were released into his custody, as my mother had given him permission over the phone. When we left the building, Preston's dad said only one thing: "Sorry, guys. This is my fault. I should've had the license plates renewed." Much ado about nothing.

When we landed back at school just at the end of lunch break, one of the assistant principals met us at the door. He was much smaller than the rest of us, and was putting on a big show about how we took our education for granted and how just because I was a basketball player, I was no more special than anyone else and I wasn't above school rules. He was going to make an example out of us. When he finally got me alone, he looked at me with a proud smile on his face: "By law, you're now ineligible for tonight's game."

He led Greg and me to the principal's outer office, where I sat and fretted, worrying about what Coach Rupp was going to say and how I was letting my teammates down. I was near tears—on my eighteenth birthday.

It didn't last long, as Principal Kay Peterson, whose children had been taught by my father at Alta High School, saw me out of the corner of his eye. "Lance! Get in here," he said. "I haven't measured you in a while!" It was a tradition that whenever Peterson caught me in the hall or near his office, he dragged me into his office, stood me up in his chair, and measured me with a yardstick, then marked my height with pen on his wall.

I complied, and Greg, being Greg, was along for the ride and quietly stuck by my side. The assistant principal followed us into Peterson's office, worried he was about to lose the fish on his line. He began grumbling his head off that I needed to be held to the same standards as the rest of the student body. He was fruitlessly yakking away until Principal Peterson looked at him and then down at me from atop his chair: "Why were you skipping school, Lance?"

"It's my birthday, and Greg's mom was going to cook me a breakfast."

"Really? Happy birthday."

"Thank you, Mr. Peterson," I said as he palmed the top of my head, penning the wall.

"Well," Principal Peterson said, stepping down and taking the form from the assistant's hands, "I think we can worry about this another time. Maybe some lunch duty? How does that sound?"

"I can do that." My eyes twinkled with joy. "So, I can play?"

"Sure, just because it's your birthday," Peterson winked at me. "But on the condition that you get a double-double tonight, you understand?"

"Yes, sir."

"All right, get out of here and go to class."

I nearly skipped out of the office. Greg, who may as well have been wallpaper, scooted out behind me, hoping not to draw attention to himself. I don't think Peterson ever noticed that Greg had been in the room. The assistant principle could still have gone after Greg, but where would the fun have been in that when you nearly took down the basketball star?

I went and played that night and had a great game. It was all swell, except for the part where one of the kids from West High School, while guarding me, blatantly punched me in the testicles, which my father happened to catch on tape. There was no reason for him to punch me, except that the West High players hated me, for I had betrayed them and transferred to East. I didn't even exchange words with the kid. There was no dialogue at all. (There rarely is dialogue with me, as I'm deaf.) There wasn't a thing to warrant his random ball punch. I keeled over in pain but was able to make it down to the other end of the floor, where I was subbed out of the game. Coach Rupp came over to me as I lay curled in the fetal position behind the bench. "What is wrong?" he asked.

"He punched me in the balls!"

Dad by this time had come down, his face red with rage, holding out the tape to Coach Rupp and Principal Peterson. I was taken to the locker room, where I vomited. It really was a hard hit. I can't tell you how bad it hurt, as it was spot-on. His knuckles got both of my guys. The officials reviewed the film during halftime, and the kid was ejected.

After the game, all of my friends showed up at Mom and Dad's house. I walked in and they all gave me a hug, and then my friend Jon, in front of everyone, said, "Sharlie wants to kiss you. Let's go!"

"Um . . . ," I said, hesitantly.

"Go!" Mom said as she tried to shove me out the door.

"Well, I can't just show up and act all cool, like she has to kiss me!" I was panicking. Put me on a basketball court in front of hundreds and I was fine, but put me in a room alone with a girl and I was a wreck.

"You have to answer her for the prom, right?" Jon asked. Greg and Jared, along with my friends Max and Jake, were standing behind him, smiling and nodding.

Do it, Greg mouthed.

"Ya!" Mom said.

Jon was savvy. He came up with the idea of writing the word *yes* on a one-inch piece of paper and then laminating it. Then, just before I saw Sharlie, I'd put it on my tongue. I'd let her see that my prom answer was on my tongue, and then she'd have to kiss me to get the answer.

Everyone clapped with excitement as I shook my head in disapproval. Dad was giggling to himself as he quietly read in his library, sipping his Pero—the fake coffee beloved of Mormons. "That'll be fun!" Mom commented. How embarrassing is it that my parents were involved with my first kiss?

We all loaded up Max's Club Wagon as Mom and Dad waved good-bye from the front door. As we were driving over to Sharlie's, I tried talking myself out of it. Max was egging me on, saying he wouldn't turn the car around, nor was he going to leave Sharlie's house until I kissed her. I was terrified, shaking.

"Dude, Sharlie is so hot, I totally would," Jared piped from the back of the wagon.

"Totally what?" Greg asked.

"Totally do more than kiss her," Jared declared as though he knew the ladies, when in fact none of us in the car had ever kissed a girl and I was about to be the first. I was going to be the first guy, of everyone in the van, of all of my dear friends, who would lose his virgin lips, a fact that both thrilled and scared me.

We pulled up to Sharlie's house. I cowered as I leaned my head against the window and stared at the house: "I can't do it. I'm not going in."

"Dude. You're such a [female genital]," Jake taunted. "Get your ass out there and do it. I will drag you out there myself if I have to. She is hot. That's a woman in there waiting for you, and you need to take advantage of this as everyone else in this van would if they had the chance. It's your duty as a man!"

I turned around in my seat: "Would you guys do it?"

"Yes," they all said, in flat unison.

"I'd throw her," Greg said in a matter-of-fact tone.

I stalled some more while all my friends called me various terms for the female reproductive system. Jon finally took the initiative and jumped out of the car. "Where are you going?" I yelled.

He didn't answer but went straight up and knocked on Sharlie's door. She answered. I could see her talking to Jon and then looking out to the van as he pointed at it. She laughed and then went in and got her sweatshirt. When she came out, she was wearing her snow boots. We were past the point of no return.

"Do it!" Jared yelled.

"I'd throw her," Greg whispered again, mostly to himself as he wistfully looked out the opposite window in deep introspection. He was tired. He had had a long day with me, what with our arrest and all.

I took out the laminated *yes* and put it on my tongue as I got out of the van. I walked up to Sharlie and Jon.

"Hey," she said, smiling brightly. She really was cute.

"Hey, I got something for you," I said. I looked at Jon, who was standing only two feet away from us. I looked at Jon some more, waiting for him to get the cue that he could leave. But he just kept staring back and forth between Sharlie and me, wide-eyed with excitement.

"Jon?" I said finally.

"Yeah?"

"Can you give us some room?"

"Oh, yeah. Sorry." He took a step back.

I saw no point in delaying the awkward moment and just stuck out my tongue. Sharlie cocked her head back with a *huh?* look. She then looked closer and saw the *yes* on my tongue and laughed. She reached up and grabbed my head, pulled me down in front of all of my friends, whose faces were longingly pressed against the windows, and opened her mouth as she took my tongue between her teeth, bit, and sucked off the *yes*.

We could've gone longer, but hey, I was new at this. It was weird, yet fun at the same time. But I mostly didn't want to continue, with Jon standing right there in front of us. She took out the *yes* from her mouth, smiled, and said, "Happy birthday."

"Thanks."

"And thanks," she said as she pointed at the wet *yes*.

"No problem." We awkwardly stepped back from each other, said our good nights, and went to our respective doors. I climbed back into the safety of the passenger seat, while all my friends chided me.

"Weak."

"Lame."

"So lame."

Jake leaned forward: "Dude, get back out there. You can do so much better than that!"

"I know!" I said, not needing any encouragement as I quickly opened the door and ran across the snow and up to Sharlie's door. I banged on it. She opened it, and before she could even say anything, I took her head, pulled her to me, and kissed her like a beautiful girl ought to be kissed, with my friends hooting and howling from the Club Wagon, which was rocking emphatically. We kissed for a good ten seconds. I pulled away. "I knew I could do better," I said.

I walked away like a man.

By the time the dance came, I was painfully sick with mono and pneumonia. Sharlie's dad rented us a plane for that night, which was totally awesome. However, while we were in the air somewhere over Park City, looking at all the pretty lights and with the fog spreading through the canyons like a spider's web, I threw up in the plane—all over my suit and Sharlie's nice dress. Good times indeed.

13

Midway through my junior year, Coach Rupp called me into his office in the middle of the school day and sat me down by his desk.

"I'm hesitant to give this to you, as I don't want you to stop working: I want you to stay hungry."

He pulled a letter out of his desk and handed it to me. It had my name on it, and on the return address stamp was an Aggie, the mascot of Utah State University. "If you want to play Division 1 basketball, Lance, you're going to have to defend, and that means more than just blocking shots. You can play at Utah State, and you can play well, but it's up to you."

I walked out of the office, stunned. I was ecstatic, but also disbelieving. While every basketball player wants to play in college and then professionally, and while I had thought about it, I had always assumed it was nothing more than a pipe dream. I was just focused on being a decent high school player. I couldn't believe I had my first recruitment letter from a Division 1 college.

When the season was over, Noah Eyre was recruited to be on the FranklinCovey AAU basketball team. The Amateur Athletic Union, or AAU, is designed to promote and develop amateur athletes. Their off-season tournaments are made up of teams who have sponsors that are usually unrelated to, but supportive of, sports. The FranklinCovey AAU team is a perfect example. A group of Mormon businessmen developed the FranklinCovey business firm, which likes to sponsor Mormon high school basketball players from around the country.

Noah had to back out of the first spring tournament because of family obligations, but he was kind enough to tell the FranklinCovey coach, Coach Wardenburg, that I would be available to fill in for him. With a few days' notice, I committed to flying out to Los Angeles. It would be only my second time in an airplane and my first road trip away from home or family.

The first game in California, I was starstruck, seeing college coaches in the stands whom I had been watching for years on TV. Of course I was nervous as it was my first game in front of college scouts, and I totally sucked. After the game was over, I apologized to Coach Wardenburg and said I'd do better next game.

"Oh, Lance," he said, "the point of these things is to get better over time. By the end of the summer you'll be playing more confidently. Just give yourself time."

Time wasn't needed, as the very next game I exploded. I think I might have scored thirty points, but I cannot recall accurately. When Coach Wardenburg subbed me out at the end of the game, he just gave me a scoff: "I had no idea. Noah told me you were good, but not this good."

"I told you I'd play better the next game," I said assuredly, proud that I had honored my word.

He smiled and patted my shoulder: "Don't do anything stupid, and don't talk to anyone, as the recruiters are going to be hard on your tail now."

When I arrived home from the trip, Dad came up to me and said, "Well, I just got a call from Coach Wardenburg, as he has been receiving calls about you." Dad then pulled out some sheets of paper fresh from the computer printer. The text was from the West Coast Hoops forum of Scout.com, a recruiting/scouting service that traveled to all the AAU tournaments. "And the best player I had never heard of before this weekend was Lance Allred," I read.

I felt I had played well, but not that well. I was young and impressionable and felt minuscule compared with all the high-leaping, long-armed athletes that were there on the court with me that weekend. I had not even considered that I might be a recruiting prospect, thinking I was just a stand-in for Noah.

The mail began to come, and soon I was hoarding letters from universities all around the country, universities that I had never imagined would know my name. However, the letter that I most wanted, the one from the University of Utah, never came. BYU, with its inside position and boosters in the FranklinCovey enterprise, recruited me the hardest. I really liked BYU's Coach Cleveland, but I had no desire to attend the institution itself.*

---

*But, Lance, you're a Mormon, you should want to attend BYU. First, if God had wanted me to go to BYU he would have named me Allblue, not Allred. Second, I'm a big fan of the con- cept of free agency, a concept publicly embraced in the LDS church. Free agency states that we

That spring the U of U made it to the NCAA national championship game, defeating Arizona and North Carolina along the way before they fell to Kentucky. The Hunstman Center, where the U of U Utes played, was only four blocks away from Mom and Dad's house. I had one of the top ten programs in the entire country right in my backyard.

Yet why wasn't I getting a letter from the Utah basketball offices, which were only four blocks away, instead of from North Carolina and Wake Forest, both three thousand miles away?

Junior year ended, and I continued to play in tournaments with the FranklinCovey team. When June came, I attended the Rick Majerus Big Man–Guard Camp again. Majerus didn't show up until the final day. He called me out and pulled me over to talk to him: "Lance, I love the fact that you're trying to go for the dunk. I want aggressive big men, but I also want skilled big men, so take these drills to work on, and improve the other things in your post game." I simply nodded my head, amazed that he even knew my name. I was speechless. I felt I was standing before genius. I knew he was regarded as one of the best "X and O" men any-where. He could make those Xs and Os come alive like a general before a map on the eve of battle. He knew the tendencies of every player and had them foiled after watching only one game tape of their team. His whiteboards where lined like hieroglyphics with plays, using Xs for de-fensive men and Os for offensive, creating a story, a game plan.

When camp was over, Dad came down to the court from where he'd been watching from up high with all the other parents who had come in to watch and pick up their kids. He gave me a hug. "You can't take him home with you yet," Coach Rupp said.

Dad smiled and nodded, and I looked at Coach Rupp, who knew some-thing was afoot and wasn't telling me. Just then, Majerus came out of his locker room and pointed to Coach Rupp: "Kerry, come on inside."

Coach Rupp began to head to the locker room. Then he stopped, looked back at me, and gestured for me to follow. Like a puppy, I did.

---

all have the right to choose between right and wrong and that's how we learn from our mistakes and develop character and accountability. It's strange how free agency and accountability are a big part of the Mormon doctrine, but at BYU they step in and manage every aspect of your daily life—your dietary habits (no caffeine or any other addictive chemicals), your clothing (no shorts above the kneecap), your freedom of speech (no swearing), and your personal grooming (no facial hair). I found it too ironic as a teen, having escaped a polygamist cult, to jump back into another environment where religion was around you 24/7. I don't drink and party, but I like having the option of doing so.

The room was empty. Coach Majerus was sitting down and motioned for us to follow suit. He shook my hand and in vintage Rick Majerus style got right to the point: "There's a scholarship for you here if you want it."

The University of Utah wanted me.

My mouth went dry, and it felt like there was cotton in my throat. All I could do was nod to show that I understood.

"I saw you on film when I was recruiting another kid you were playing against. I saw you dive into the stands to save a loose ball. I called up Kerry that night and told him that you had a scholarship."

That game had been five months ago, and Coach Rupp had known that a scholarship was awaiting me at the University of Utah but had not told me.

"We want you here, Lance," Majerus continued. "You're my type of player, and I already know that you're ahead of the game, as you have been coached by Kerry Rupp, the best coach in high school, and you'll be ready to step in and play. And I know I could've done a better job recruiting you, with all the fuss flying around that we don't really care about you—but we do. I honored Kerry's request that we wait before letting it be known to you that we wanted to give you a scholarship here."

Rupp drove me home. I was doing my best to remain calm, trying to not show too much emotion. I asked, "Coach, how long have you known?"

He tried not to smile when he said, "I had a scholarship for you in February."

We pulled up to the house, where Dad was watering the lawn. He smiled at me as I got out and ran up to Szen and scratched his head, burying my face in his neck, my heart full of excitement and joy that I had achieved a goal that I had committed to when many, even myself, doubted I could reach it.

"He has something to tell you," Coach Rupp said to my father as he backed out of the driveway.

"What is it?" Dad asked excitedly.

"Come on upstairs. I need to have Mom with us before I tell you." Szen and I ran into the house and upstairs into the kitchen. I saw Mom and began to cry. I hugged her and just sobbed.

Mom had not seen that they were tears of happiness and accomplishment, and feared they were tears of sorrow. "What is it?" she asked, concerned.

I took a step back and a long breath and wiped my eyes: "Majerus offered me a scholarship!" Mom squealed, clapped her hands, and began to cry, and Dad gave me a big hug. Szen could see how happy I was, and he just wagged his tail and stood right beside us, twisting and turning, showing more energy in his old age than he had in a long time.

"We were wondering when they were finally going to let you know," Mom said.

I stopped and took a step back: "You knew?"

Mom smiled a little sheepishly, and Dad just stared at me proudly: "Coach Rupp told us a few months back that you had the scholarship, but he asked us not to tell you. He wanted us to know, just to make sure you didn't give up."

In late July, having endured a long summer of the recruiting process, traveling, and workouts, I hesitantly asked Coach Rupp, "Would it be OK if I took a weeklong vacation to go back up to Montana?"

"Please, go! Get the hell out of here. I was about to tell you that you needed to take a break. You haven't had one in over a year."

It was as close to a vacation as you could call it, before the recruiters tracked me down at Yaya's house and her phone began to ring early in the morning with college coaches. When I came home, my room was piled with letters, and though in my heart I wanted to go to Utah, I also felt it would be foolish to limit my options to only one avenue and not give any others consideration, especially when Stanford came into the picture. I mean, come on: Stanford. I was planning on majoring in history in college, and anybody who knows anything about history knows that the Stanford history department isn't to be ignored.

I was planning on making my recruiting visits in the fall. I had it narrowed down to Utah, Stanford, Kansas, Purdue, and BYU. Until I got a phone call from Coach Rupp.

"Lance, there's another big guy who wants to commit to Utah. Coach really likes him, but he likes you more. He will give you twenty-four hours to make a decision."

I had wanted to keep my options open until I was fully confident that I was making the right decision. But in my heart of hearts I wanted to play at Utah, and so I had to make the move and commit, lest my spot no longer be available. Majerus had to look out for himself and his program. Could he pass up another big guy he liked who wanted to play for him just to wait in uncertainty for me? No.

The next day, I walked with my dad and Coach Rupp into Coach Majerus's office. "So," Majerus began, "obviously you know the situation. I like this big that wants to commit, but I like you more and I want you.* I'm choosing you over him. I think you can have a great career here, and you get to stay home and have your family to support you. I'm saying this on the fact that Coach Rupp told me you're ready to commit."

"Yes, Coach. I want to play for you and the University of Utah."

"Coach, if I may," my father interjected. "We're entrusting our son to you, in confidence that you'll help him become the best basketball player, student, and person he can be. We're not only committing to the University of Utah, we're committing to you."

Coach Majerus nodded his head: "And I can promise you that I will do my best to help Lance achieve those things. First and foremost, I will make sure your son gets an education here at this institution, as it's one of the best public schools in the West."

We talked a while more, and then I finally asked what had been on my mind for a long time: "Coach, what are the chances of Coach Rupp coming up here with me?" I choked up as I asked. I was excited to play for Majerus, but I was also scared at the thought that my time with Rupp was limited. Though we still had another year together, the idea that our deadline was nearing was haunting. This commitment to Majerus seemed only to solidify the fact that I couldn't have Rupp in my corner forever.

Coach Majerus answered, "Kerry is the best there is at his level, and he deserves to be successful. When his time comes, it will come. It may not be with me, but it will come."

Coach Rupp looked at me: "Don't worry about me, Lance, this is your time. Today is about you and what you have earned."

I wanted to say so much. This day was as much his as it was mine, and I'd be nothing without him. Not only is basketball about talent and skill; it's also, and mostly, about timing. Are you in the right place at the right time, and do you have the right coach for you? I had that time— the perfect synch with Coach Rupp. I'm a basketball player, nothing more. I'm not a baller, nor am I a track star. I'm only a basketball player who needs a system around him to survive. I'm only as successful as my

*In the basketball world, a *big* is a center or possibly a power forward.

coach. He truly made me into the player I was and influenced who I am today. My scholarship to Utah, as far as I was concerned, was just as much his as it was mine.

A week later, my senior year began.

Life was changing at a rapid pace: college was in sight, I was growing up, and Szen was growing old and tired. A boy's childhood is measured in dog years as well.

The day came when Dad told me the vet would be coming in a few days to put Szen to sleep. Dad knew it was time. Szen was now thirteen, his sight was going rapidly, and his hips were not functioning anymore. He could barely endure a walk around the block. Szen had stopped coming up the steps to sleep in my room, as it was too hard for him to make the climb.

I had been ignoring these changes in Szen. The winter before, Szen had wanted to stay outside for a while, and I had impatiently grabbed him by the collar and forced him inside. Szen hated the new house in Salt Lake; he hated being inside all day. He wanted to be back on open land, where he could stay outside all day and not be chained up or forced inside. Mom told me that I needed to be gentle with him now, as he was getting old and it was hard for him to move. It hurt that she had needed to tell me that, as I had always been my best with Szen, and this time I had gotten impatient with him. I guess I was just unable to accept the fact that my Szen was getting old. I didn't want to accept that I was no longer a kid, that my childhood was ending. Szen marked my childhood. I gauged it by him.

When the day came, I skipped the last two periods of school and came home and took Szen and Pongo across the street to the park. I lay with Szen in the grass for two hours, lazily petting his beautiful coat for the last time. He was too tired to sniff around like he used to and—alpha dog that he was—mark his territory. He was happy just to lie with me.

He was my best friend. He was my buddy. It hurt so much to see him going from my life. He understood that we were saying good-bye as he pushed at my face with his paw. He saw that I was already mourning him.

Mom and Dad came home and joined us in the park. Mom brought over pot roast and let Szen and Pongo jump around for it. The vet, who had been kind enough to agree to come to our house, finally pulled up. Szen was such a smart dog. He knew his time had come. He knew we were saying good-bye. His wise, kind eyes stared at me with fear but also resolve as he bade me farewell. If he could have had his way, he would have stayed with me forever. And I felt the same. And then, just as an eye blinks, my friend was gone.

The vet left in silence, allowing me time with my dog. Dad got up and let me have a few moments with him as well. And I just cried.

I immediately regretted what I had done, wishing I could have my dog back, that I could have let him live and die naturally. But really I knew that would've been selfish, as his quality of life had diminished so terribly those last few months.

After about fifteen minutes, Dad told me it was time to go, patting me on the shoulder. We carried Szen to the grave we had dug for him in the back. We placed Szen, wrapped in his blanket, in his resting place. Dad gave me the shovel and let me cover Szen with the first layer of dirt. He then took back the shovel, hugged me, and just let me cry. I never cried harder in my life. It was my first taste of death.

As he left, Szen taught me one more lesson about life. And it was his greatest lesson: always leave things on good terms; always treat your loved ones as though this day will be the last. I was angry at myself for the times throughout Szen's life, especially those last years, when I could've been nicer or more patient with him. As I became a teenager and started playing basketball, Szen had become less of a priority—not consciously by any means; it was just that life was changing for me.

I can recall just a few memories of life before I had my dog. Szen was in nearly all my memories, and now I was having to face the fact that he would no longer be in my life and I'd be making new memories without him.

It was that moment of good-bye, that memory of good-bye, that haunts me. The pain of knowing that change was coming. Yet Szen understood and was gracious.

Saying good-bye to Szen was the most painful experience I ever had. The fact that I ended my dog's life, and that he loved me and trusted me, is something that haunts me to this day. He was more than my dog. He had been more than my friend: he had been my protector. The mean dogs, the late-night indistinguishable sounds that he growled away, my depressions and feelings of isolation as a child—Szen had protected me from all of them.

. . .

When our senior season started and opening week came for practice, I pulled my hip flexor again. It was the very same injury that had finished my junior season prematurely, and it was now coming back to delay my senior year. It had remained dormant the entire off-season throughout the camps and recruiting tournaments, where I must have logged in well over a thousand miles running.

The preseason rankings had come, and we were ranked number two behind the defending champs, Provo. I was eager to get out there and confirm the expectations that were placed on our team.

After missing two weeks of practice and the first couple of games, I finally was able to come back. The team had split their first two games without me, and when I came back . . . we lost three straight. Sure, I scored thirty points apiece in two of those three games, and that was nice, and cute for the papers, but we were still losing.

As a senior and co-captain of that team, I took full responsibility for our losses.

When we kept losing, rumors and biting comments began to crop up that I didn't care about the team and was happy just to get my stats, that I was already up at Utah emotionally. It hurt. I didn't go out and party, and I wasn't dating girls. No, I went home every night and I watched film.

They were counting on me, and sadly, I wasn't able to deliver.

I grew so stressed and anxious that I stopped sleeping again. And I got sick. By the end of the senior season, I had contracted pneumonia, mononucleosis, and strep throat all at the same time. I was dog sick. And yet I still played. I didn't play well, only adding to the criticism and disappointment, but I did play.

I could've sat out and thought, "I'm going to protect my stats" or "I'm going to show that the team cannot win without me." But I wasn't spiteful. I honored my commitment to my team, and I played. One night, after we lost to Highland, I passed out in the hallway on the way to the locker room. I was taken to the hospital by ambulance. I was so tired, so exhausted. Flashlights were buzzing around me as my eyes, which I couldn't hold straight, were opened and evaluated. I couldn't focus and was very dizzy. I stayed in the ER for a few hours, where they gave me a few IVs to counteract the severe dehydration I'd experienced.

We made the playoffs that year, but we lost in the first round and exited with a whimper. I sobbed in that locker room, realizing that my time with Coach Rupp was over. Our paths were separating, at least for now.

In a sad way, I was actually relieved when the season was over, as I now could finally sleep. I'd no longer stay up late blaming myself. I had become so reclusive, lost in critical thought, that many, including my teammates, thought I was being snooty, aloof, and condescending. I didn't talk to my teammates because I had become completely engulfed in the guilt that I wasn't able to help bring us to victory; they, on the other hand, took my silence to mean that I thought they were not worth my time.

When it was all over and I was getting some rest, Coach Rupp called me in to visit with him. He told me with concern that I had not been voted MVP by my teammates and that Noah had. It crushed me. While Coach Rupp would award me at the end of the year with the Hunsaker Award for most outstanding player, and I'd be named the Utah Gatorade Player of the Year as well, I felt that my teammates, whom I had fought for, through pain and fatigue, didn't appreciate what I had at least tried to do for them. Maybe Noah did deserve it more than I did. He was lighthearted and had such a good perspective on things outside of basketball, which I didn't, that he was able to be a positive outlet for many of the younger guys. Noah came to me and told me he felt bad that I didn't get it, which is exactly why he was the one they voted for. He was like that. He really was an incredible person.

I didn't care about the trophy in a physical sense. What hurt was the disregard or even spite that some of my teammates had for me, blaming me for the disappointing season. But no one blamed me more than myself for the senior year that had turned into a train wreck. There wasn't a thing my teammates could say about me, to my face or behind my back, that I had not already tossed my way internally.

To this day, I look back on my senior year with regret, feeling that I could've done better. I wanted to do better, and there are many things I know now that I could've done to really change things around. But because of those disappointments I've learned how to deal with such adversity. I only wish I could've gotten Coach Rupp his state championship trophy.

Part Three

Sound and Fury

My time at the University of Utah was one of the most profound seasons of my life and played a large role in shaping who I am today. As I talk of, and as you come to know, Coach Majerus, I will discuss his strengths and his flaws. Coach Rick Majerus is the most complex figure I have ever encountered. He is a conundrum. He was brilliant and eccentric, yet cold and aloof. He was charitable and caring, yet brutal and hurtful. He was charismatic and endearing, yet terrifying and intimidating. Simply put, he was two people. Almost borderline schizophrenic really, if you saw how he changed, from the way he was at, say, a fun low-key dinner gathering, once he stepped onto a basketball court or behind closed doors. The man could humiliate you to the point of tears in practice and then be stuffing your face with food two hours later, patting you on the back. He could turn a switch in his head that allowed him to compartmentalize things, even his own actions, store them away for another time, and enjoy a present moment with no concern. While his love was conditional—as Majerus had a high rotation rate of players leaving his program, with an average of only one out of every three players from a freshman class graduating as a senior in his program—Majerus did love to dote on the players that were in his good graces at the time.

I mean this when I say it: Majerus loved his players. Did he have favorites? Yes. Was I one of them? Yes, *for a time.* He loved his players, and he loved to develop them, but he was also abusive to them, verbally and emotionally. And when you admired someone like him as much as I did, wanting to do anything to please him, yearning to receive even just a little praise, he had that much more control over you, and his criticisms were that much more crushing to your emotional state. I idolized the man. He was my God—not in the sense that I worshipped him, but he was my first thought and my last thought every day for three years. I wanted so badly to please him. And he broke my heart. But part of that blame lies with me, as I never should have let him have that much control over my life.

It was a custom in the LDS religion that, at the age of eighteen, a young man began to prepare to serve his two-year mission, dedicated to the converting of souls looking for answers in this world in regard to spirituality and life after death. I was not excited about going on a mission, but I felt that I had to. Having battled many demons inside my head while escaping the Allred Group and no longer letting dogmatic religion be a guiding factor or source of guilt in my life, I found the idea of going on an LDS mission, with religion ruling my every thought, day and night, 24/7, not an appealing one. But I played along for a while, convincing myself that I would eventually be excited to go. I even told Coach Majerus that I would be going on a mission.

As my senior year came to a close, Majerus called me up to a meeting with his entire coaching staff. "Lance," he announced, "as I respect you going on a mission, I have laid out a plan for you. I have Chris Burgess from Duke who wants to transfer here, and the only scholarship that I can give him is yours. And since you're planning on leaving on your mission, and rather than using your freshman year this upcoming season, then losing the practice as you leave for two years, I have decided that it would be better for all parties involved if you took a 'gray shirt' year, meaning you'll forfeit your scholarship and go to school part-time for the fall semester, paying your own way, and then you'll leave on your mission in the winter, when you turn nineteen. And that way, Chris gets a scholarship and can come play here and have a good experience. And then I get four straight years with you, without any interruption once you come back."

While I knew this was a reasonable compromise, I really wanted to play for the U. It was my dream, and now I was being told I wouldn't play basketball again for three seasons. That's a long time. Basketball is all about timing and momentum.

That summer, I had very little motivation to do anything. What was the point in my spending the summer at the university weight room knowing that all the work I put in to get stronger and in good condition would be in vain, as I was leaving for a mission that coming winter? I became depressed and lazy. I attended weight-training sessions half the time I was expected to be there, and when I was there I put in half effort.

Mom and Dad never placed expectations on me, nor did they ever really talk to me about serving a mission. The expectations were from myself and the society I lived in. Having served on the seminary council my senior year at East, I was just that much more visible; and having been asked to be in such a visible position in the church, I felt it was my duty to continue to set a good example for my peers.

I was enrolled in fall classes part-time, as per NCAA rules. According to the rules, because I had signed a letter of intent the year before and then chosen not to accept the immediate scholarship for the year signed in intent, I couldn't just walk on and practice with the team, nor could I attend school full-time (twelve hours or more a semester). I also had to pay my own way.

The first day of school, Coach Majerus called for a team meeting. We were all seated in the film room, and I showed up just in time. I immediately felt out of place. I was just that freshman kid who didn't have a scholarship and thus wasn't really on the team. I took a seat in the back. Coach Majerus came in and shook all of our hands. When he got to me, he said, "You need to get your ass in the weight room."

Majerus walked up to the front and then began to address us, telling us about his expectations, then asking who had had a good summer, and then who had had a bad one. When it came to the bad one, he began with me, understandably. After he chastised me, going on to say he had given me a scholarship only because I was a hard worker with not a lot of real talent, he asked what good I was to him if I wasn't even willing to use what he considered my only redeemable attribute. I knew that what he was saying was true.

Then he asked me a direct question that wasn't rhetorical. The following ten seconds would in essence capture the problem with the next three years and why I failed at the University of Utah: "Lance, do you not feel that you have not been given the same opportunity as everyone else here to be successful in the weight room? Has Coach Kenn [the weight-training coach] not given you a fair chance?"

I sat there. For ten seconds I sat there replaying the question in my head, Do I not feel that I have not been given the same . . . ? There I was, sitting in silence, thinking, OK, this is a double negative, so I cancel out the two "not"s and ask the question "Do I feel that I have been given the same chance ..?" But does Coach know that? Is he expecting a "no"? But I have been given the same chance. Should I just not say either "yes" or "no" and just say, "I have been given the same chance"?

I sat there for ten seconds in frozen terror, analyzing a pithy question, a question that foreshadowed my experience at Utah. I failed at Utah because I thought and analyzed too much. Basketball is a thinking man's game, but it is also not. When you think as much as I did, it becomes crippling. And when you admired a man like Coach Majerus as much as I did, wanting to please him and be in his good graces, you would be even more self-conscious and worried about making a mistake.

Coach Majerus barked, "Lance, I'm talking to you. Don't sit back there and pretend that you cannot hear me!"

I heard him all right, but Majerus assumed that I was playing the deaf card, trying to sneak by a confrontation by pretending not to hear, which is something I have *never* done. I made a commitment to myself when I was a kid: if I wanted to be successful and normal and functioning in the real world, I could never fall back on my disability to bail myself out. I tried to clarify to Coach: "No, I can—"

"Speak up!"

I raised my voice. "I heard you, Coach."

"Then why didn't you answer me?"

Was I to be honest and say, Coach, I was analyzing the double negatives in your question and determining whether or not...? How was I supposed to explain that, when I was already red with embarrassment?

"Yes or no, Lance!" Coach barked.

"No!" I blurted out.

"No?!" Coach exclaimed. It was obviously the wrong answer. "You don't think that all the coaches here have not been at your disposal?"

There was the double negative again. "No," I said.

Coach was getting mad and impatient now. "No?!"

"I have been getting all the same treatment, Coach," I clarified.

"Then why did you say no?"

Was I supposed to delve into the analysis of the negatives in his question? All I could say was, "I was just wanting to be sure that I answered your question right, Coach."

"What is there to question, Lance? It's a simple question: yes or no?"

And it was there, on that spot, that I learned how to answer Coach's double-negative questions, which were standard and frequent: by saying yes and then repeating the question. "Yes, I have been given the same opportunity as everyone else."

"Good."

For the rest of my three years at Utah, Majerus would never let that incident die. He often recalled what I'm sure he thought of as the time Lance pretended like he couldn't hear me. Majerus had a memory comparable to mine, but we obviously remembered the incident differently. No one could beat a dead horse like Coach Majerus. He would bring up a bad play on your part from last season to add fuel to his berating of you in the current moment. And the time Lance pretended like he couldn't hear me was no exception.

I still get a lazy eye just thinking about it.

A few weeks later, I opted not to go on a mission. But it was too late, as Majerus had already given out my scholarship and I couldn't simply walk on, having signed the letter of intent.

Yet as the season began in November, it was Coach's expectation that I be present at every practice, sitting in the stands, taking notes. Aside from a sick day or a test, I was present at every practice, dutifully watching and taking notes, which Coach would inspect every week to make sure I wasn't doodling. He was very complimentary and generous with his praise, and loved to take my notebook and show it off to recruits or boosters who were sitting in on practice. Watching longingly as the guys practiced, I gained a very eye-opening view of just how long and demanding Coach Majerus's practices were. But I wasn't deterred by this. I had set a goal, and I wanted to achieve it.

Toward the end of my gray-shirt year, it was announced that my mother would be the commencement speaker for the University of Utah's graduating class of the year 2000. It was quite a feeling to be attending school at the same time my mother was to be the graduation speaker. She gave a wonderful speech, and I was immensely proud of her. I wasn't so proud of Vanessa, though, for waving at the JumboTron when the camera panned to Mom's family during the speech.

Mom then enrolled in the University of Utah's special-education graduate program, to achieve her master's degree and finally receive certification as a teacher. Mom had been teaching at a unique school for nine years up to this point, without a college degree. She was incredible at her job, working with kids that others were ready to forsake. She dealt with teens that were on probation, addicted to drugs, schizophrenics, autistics, and sociopathic sex addicts. Yet my mother, through all of this, was able to keep her positive views on life. She never came home and played the weary victim of a long day of chaos, but instead always managed our lives flawlessly. She also tutored during this time to supplement her meager income. Mom soon had to turn down requests to tutor, as she just didn't have the time. And now, this forty-five-year-old mother of five was enrolling at the University of Utah to earn her master's. And she still made it to my basketball games.

And ironically, she would be enrolled in the special education program, learning the rules and standards that protect those with special needs, while her son, attending the same institution, would be enduring abuse and humiliation for his handicap at the hands of a school and state employee.

I'm proud of my mother. She is remarkable and has emerged as one of the finest and most astute minds in the state of Utah in the fields of autism and Asperger's syndrome.

Court came home from his mission shortly after Mom's commencement speech. He wasn't well. I hardly recognized him. He had been diagnosed with bipolar disorder. This news affirmed my decision not to go on a mission. Although I would never say that Court's mission caused his disorder, I know that being away from everything he knew didn't help him. He was no longer the Court I knew, the Court I had grown up with. My big brother was gone, and in his place was a tortured soul whose mind was battling the conflicts of organized religion—a mind that had by now deteriorated to a state of chaos that not even I dared to explore.

The day finally came that following fall, in October 2000, when I was able to walk into the University of Utah locker room and find waiting for me my own jersey. I was the first one in the locker room, and I picked up my jersey and cried. I had waited for two years to wear this jersey and had worked and worked without much reward up to this point. I finally had a taste of it. I knew my place was low on the pole for playing time, but I was ready to play.

At that time, I thought I was much better than I actually was, but here is a news flash: every star in every profession gets to where they are by believing they're better than they actually are. You don't just wake up one day with a world of talent, skill, and experience and realize, Hey, I'm pretty *good.* Especially in the cutthroat, dog-eat-dog profession of basketball, where everyone is trying to get a piece of the pie, you have to be a little cocky. Because the minute you doubt yourself is the minute you lose. Many people will never know the pressures of a live game, with thousands watching and critiquing your every move. With that pressure, you have to guard yourself, and you do it by convincing yourself you're better than you are, because if you don't, you'll never have the courage to even step onto the floor.

To give you a sense of the kind of life we lived as Majerus athletes, I'll provide a diarylike summary of our days.

The Life of Lance Allred
During a Majerus Two-a-Day

Saturday, October 14, 2000

7:25 a.m.
After a haunting night filled with fear, insomnia, and cold-sweat dreams (I think I changed about six shirts over the course of the night), I'm awakened by a squealing high-pitched radio alarm and wonder where in the name of all that's holy that awful sound is coming from. Then after a second of reflection I realize someone left the radio tuned to 104.3 country. I condemn my alarm to the bloody bowels of hell and slap it off my dresser. I slump out of bed and try to stand, but a blanket is caught between my legs and takes one of my legs out from under me. I fall face flat on the floor. I then very gentlemanly lift myself up and proceed to curse my blankets to hell as well.

8:00 a.m.
I arrive at the Huntsman Center [the university's sports arena] and am the second player in the locker room. I find my own person-alized jersey in my own locker and have to sit down and let it soak in. I stare at my jersey and hold it and then realize it has all been worth it.

9:00 a.m.
All the players are out on the court warming up and getting loose for practice. An eerie darkness settles in, and the Empire theme from Star Wars begins to play as Majerus enters the arena, wearing his black shirt with a white EA Sports logo, which reminds me of an eight ball. Before he is even halfway down the steps, he is barking orders, and by the time he steps on the court, several drills

are going on at once. There is one drill station that isn't up and running. Coach sends that assistant coach on sprints (poor Jason Shelton).

9:15 a.m.
I realize that, no, it has not all been worthwhile. I realize this while my team and I are in the fifteenth sprint (down to the far baseline and back) because one of the junior college transfers decided to wear his earring this morning when he arrived at the Huntsman. All told, I think we hit twenty-two sprints.

9:45 a.m.
Coach Majerus talks to us for twenty minutes in the middle of practice and somehow times it perfectly for our legs to stiffen up; then in no time at all he has us running five more sprints. I'm panicking that my kneecap will randomly fall off due to stiffness.

10:05 a.m.
In a conversion defense drill, I fail to pick up the opposing point guard driving into the lane in good time, and Coach stops practice and begins to insult my character and then proceeds to insult my family name, and if that wasn't enough, he further insults my mother and her dignity.

10:07 a.m.
After being totally inconsolable for about two minutes, I realize *Hey, it could be worse, I could be a lanky deaf kid struggling to get by, oh wait . . .* I then am substituted back into the drill, and this time I succeed in accomplishing the previous wishes of Coach. But then he once again stops practice and begins to yell rather insulting one-liners in my general direction. Then I realize it's me he is talking to, and I have a puzzled look on my face. "Oh, don't throw that bail-out excuse that you can't hear me, Allred!" he yells. More difficult for me than being insulted is trying not to crack a smile in front of Coach. Luckily I succeed, but I now have tooth prints on my tongue.

10:35 a.m.
As I'm currently struggling to hold off Big Nate, our senior six-foot-eleven 270-pounder, I wonder in my mind what Mom will have cooked for me when I get home for lunch.

10:36 a.m.

I manage to hold off Nate. I get the rebound, sprint the fast break, and follow the shot with an offensive rebound put-back. Coach stops practice and begins to praise my "balls of steel."

10:47 a.m.

My "balls of steel" are violated as they're crushed by my teammate's knee on a rebounding collision.

11:00 a.m.

The women's team comes onto the floor, as they have been granted that time slot. Assuming practice is over, I begin to cry, "Hosanna!" Coach says, "All right, everybody up to the auxiliary gym." I then cry, "Dammit!"

11:02 a.m.

After sprinting up the tunnel to the gym, we're rather fatigued. We stretch a little. Coach comes barging in with a bagel in his mouth and cream cheese smeared over his cheek, and then decides to give us more sprints. I suddenly come to the realization that I have seen the face of Lucifer himself.

Tuesday, October 17, 2000

8:30 a.m.

I'm awakened by my biological clock as I have been the previous two mornings, probably because my senses are engulfed in fear and my body is counting the number of hours until practice begins today. Although I'm awake, I am somehow victim to a slight case of amnesia, for I can't remember who I am or where I am for at least twenty seconds. I start to panic, but then my memory comes back. I slowly begin to remember *I'm Lance Allred and I'm a Ute.* I'm calm. *Thank heavens!* I then remember that I'm still in the first week of Majerus preseason. I begin to panic again. *I'm Lance Allred and I'm a Ute.* Four hours to practice.

10:51 a.m.

I try, but I am weak and muster only a feeble attempt to stay awake and alert during my Intro to Psychology class.

Psychology, what a bunch of bullshit.*

Briefly I'm awakened and notice this hot chick across the aisle. She probably wants me. After dozing off again for about ten minutes I'm zapped awake by the professor when, during his boring *Ferris Bueller*–style lecture, he says the magic word *sex*.

To my dismay I realize he is only generalizing male and female. I slouch back down into my seat and doze off into never-never land, my only place of comfort, knowing that practice begins in only an hour and forty minutes.

12:15 p.m.
I'm tying on my basketball shoes when I have a powerful flashback, way back—oh, say, fifteen minutes ago: *I should've asked the girl for her number.*

12:16 p.m.
Why am I so lonely?

12:17 p.m.
As I walk onto the floor of the Huntsman, I stand on the out-of-bounds line. Then, before crossing that fine distinct line, I take a deep breath. I exhale. I then recite Psalms 23:4: "Yea, though I walk through the valley of the shadow of death, I will fear no evil: for thou art with me." I'm comforted.

12:31 p.m.
Coach walks onto the court and says, "Run ten sprints to get loose." Brilliant.

12:55 p.m.
During a drill of defensive conversion, I set a pick for my point guard and pop out to the three-point line for spacing. My man follows me up there to the three and ignores his duty of help-side defense. Coach stops practice and yells, "Phil! Why the hell would you hug Allred on the three? Is he going to shoot a three-point? Is he a threat?"

I mean, come on, people: who really wants to know about all these theories explaining and even justifying ludicrous behavior by obviously weak and inferior specimens? You know what I say: instead of society spending millions of dollars wasting time coming up with cock-and-bull ideas of the mind and bailing out all the self-pitying fools, I'd have them all come to the realization of my obvious genius. The genius is: tell the sulking bastards to get over it. (Funny, I said this then. . . .)

"If left open, yes, Coach."

"Bullshit! Allred, come shoot five threes."

I'm stunned and shocked. I step up to the line and make two out of five. (The other three—I kid you not—were in and out.)

"See, two out of five left open, that's horrible. Sure, he made two, but did you like those ones he made? I sure didn't."

I wonder what that was supposed to mean.

2:18 p.m.

During another session of conversion defense, I rebound a defensive board. Then my team breaks it up the court for offense, and my wing gets spaced for an open three and shoots it. It's missed, but alas, I'm there for the rebound. I rip the board down but am off balance and can't find an outlet bail-out pass. So I foolishly jump again and throw a prayer skip pass across the court to my guard, who in the first place should've come to me beforehand and helped me rather than just stand there. I knew as well as everyone else that it was a turnover as soon as I threw it. Immediately as it left my hands I saw the play I had predicted in my mind begin to form into reality. Rather than watching the rest of my apocalypse, I ran toward the baseline ready for the sprints that Coach was going to reward me with, for I knew well that I had performed one of the dumbest actions of my basketball tenure so far. But rather than just giving me the sprints, Coach had everyone come huddle around him.

"Sit down," Coach says to everyone. "Lance, that was just moronic; no, idiotic; no, I can't even begin to explain. I could've sworn you were a smart kid when I was recruiting you out of East, but maybe East has lower standards than everyone else. That was just ludicrous, idiotic. Mr. Idiot Man is the only thing I can call you to even grasp a glimpse of how stupid that was. Mr. Idiot Man is the only thing appropriate for this action. What a sad, sad thing: Mr. Idiot Man. Mr. Idiot Man." All the while Coach is talking to me, he has his right middle finger pointing at me in repetitious thrusts, just the way Dad changes the stations on his car radio with his middle finger. Thank you, Coach, I say to myself. Sprints would've sufficed, but this was just as satisfying.

2:31 p.m.

I fumble an outlet pass from my guard as I'm ahead of everyone else on a fast-break conversion drill, and the ball slips from my hands and out-of-bounds. "Well done, Mr. Idiot Man!" Coach hollers from across the floor. As I looked at him for that brief moment to listen to him from across the floor, I realize I have learned how to hate.

2:47 p.m.
Sweat gets into my ear canal, creating pressure between my eardrums and hearing aids, and I feel the incredible urge, nay need, to yawn. I do my best to refrain, but cannot. I yawn, and Coach sees me, drawing his undivided attention: "Am I boring you, Lance? Is this boring? I'm sorry. Let's make it more interesting. Five sprints. Go!"

What am I supposed to say? Coach, I have a funky inner-ear condition that's caused by the combination of my hearing aids and sweat. I have a yawning problem, people; however it isn't due to lack of oxygen, attention deficit, or lack of sleep.

As I run my sprints, Coach hollers at me from his seat behind one of the sideline hoops, "Up till late partying last night?"

Me? Party? Adding to the fact that my hearing impairment makes me pretty much a vegetable in large gatherings—as I cannot decipher what someone is saying to me if there's too much background noise or more than one person talking, because the tone shifts get tangled up and I lose the rhythm of how the person is speaking—is the fact that I'm also freakishly tall. Can you imagine what it's like to be six-eleven, go to a party or a club, and have people just stare at you and gawk or wait for you to do some circus trick? Yeah, it's no fun. No, Coach, I was at home reading a book last night. I remain silent.

3:07 p.m.
Twenty-three minutes till practice ends. I set a pick for my point guard and roll toward the lane. I receive a pass from him and am able to finish strongly with a dunk. "Hell of a play, Mr. Idiot Man!" comes Coach's voice. Don't know how to interpret, but don't care.

3:24 p.m.
Coach stops practice, has us all huddle around him, and gives us his thought of the day: "Allred, I hope this is your only day that you have to carry the title of Mr. Idiot Man. Hopefully, you never have that embarrassing title again. That would be tragic, Mr. Idiot Man." He shakes his head at me.

3:30 p.m.

Coach has a creed he lives by: The film never lies.

Coach and I are in his office. He is berating me for a missed block-out, one that I couldn't get to because of a defensive responsibility while covering for my teammate. He sees in my eyes that I want to attest my innocence. "Oh really?" he asks. "Should I have Eric come down and take you into the film room and show you? The film never lies. Are you sure? If I'm right, then you'll have double sprints."

Seeing that there is so much more to lose than to gain and that it isn't worth it, I decide to just accept my sprints, bitterly reflecting upon the injustice of it all but knowing that, inevitably, life in general isn't fair.

Coach sees that I'm still not happy and calls out, "Eric, bring down that last clip and show Lance what he did wrong and what I want from him next time. And when you two are done, Lance can run his ten sprints."

Coach Eric Jackson, affectionately referred to as Coach E or simply Eric, quickly obeys, takes the tape from one of two cameras that are always recording, and sprints down the steps. Why two camcorders? For this distinct purpose: while Eric and I are in the film room, another camcorder will be running unattended, and film from both camcorders will be edited, after practice, by Eric, who will then deliver the final copy to Coach at his hotel room, where Coach will watch practice from that day and pick up on any subtle things that he missed or overlooked, and then drill us about them the next day, usually before practice begins.

Coach E shows me the film, and I was right, but it's a lost cause. We walk back out to the court just in time to hear Coach holler, "In the film room." We filter in and take our seats, Coach in his padded reclining chair in the middle of the room, the rest of us seated on cold metal. Coach has milk and cookies awaiting us. This is his way of showing affection. He truly does love us.

I make the mistake of dipping an Oreo in my milk just as Coach singles me out in the film and asks, "What play is this, Lance?" And I have no idea, because my attention is singled in on the Oreo. It's a deadly game of indulgence versus discipline in the film room.

But the war of indulgences is never as hostile as the one between Coach and his laser lights. Today is no exception as Coach repeats the same routine he always does. "Where is the red thingy—you know, the pointer?" Coach calls out. He has never learned to call it a laser light.

Coach Strohm hands him the light over his shoulder. Coach fumbles with the light, and then gets irritated and hisses, "This doesn't work." That's because he is pointing it in the wrong direction, but no one dares say anything. He extends his arm toward the projector screen as though this will somehow help, but all he really needs to do is turn the light around.

Before he notices that the laser is pointing on his shirt, he impatiently tosses the device over his shoulder without looking: "Get me a new one." This time when Coach Strohm hands him the light he is holding it before Coach in a demonstration of how to properly handle it. It's all too reminiscent of a parent teaching a child how to hold a fork for the first time.

To make things even more painful, Coach Majerus is also narcoleptic. Since he stays up so late watching film, he loses out on much-needed sleep. As I look over from time to time in the dark film room, I can see his eyes rolling up in the back of his head, which is tilting back, slowly, slowly. It hits that point where it lobs, jerking Coach awake. He sits up stern and rigid, at immediate attention. "Who is this!" he calls out, shining the laser light onto the projector.

"That's me, Coach. Lance," I admit, always saying my name in the dark so he isn't confused.

"You see your stance here, Lance? You like it? Hmm? I don't. Do you?"

"No, Coach."

"That's why I can't play you."

Well, Coach, I think to myself, maybe if you hadn't been sleeping the last two minutes of film, you would've seen the great defensive play I made the sequence before.

Thursday, October 19, 2000

12:59 p.m.
"Jason! If any of the bigs take their eye off the ball, throw it at them!" Majerus barks as we run a team defense drill to protect a weak-side down-screen.

Jason Shelton, a great guy, naturally upbeat and positive, is in the precarious position of harming us and is hesitant to throw the ball whenever one of us turns our head.

"Throw it!" Majerus barks.

He flips a ball at me, and Majerus calls Jason's manhood into question and sends him, an assistant coach, on sprints.

1:02 p.m.
Jason is growing irritated that he is even in the position that he is, with Majerus barking at him from the other side of the court. His irritation soon turns to impatience, as he is no longer able to channel his anger and is now throwing rockets at us.

1:03 p.m.
Jason throws one at me, and I instinctively turn and catch it. Majerus tells me to now catch the ball and redo the drill. All fun and games until someone loses a hearing aid.

This time my head isn't turned completely away from the ball, but neither am I looking at Jason, only staring straight in front of me. *Whack!* The ball smashes right in my ear, perfectly, so that it compresses my hearing aid deep into my ear canal. I drop to the ground like a bag of potatoes and dig into my ear to yank my embedded hearing aid out.

1:04 p.m.
Practice has stopped, and Majerus barks from the other side of the court, sitting on the back weights of one of the side baskets, "What now?!"

Jason, holding a ball against his side, his other hand gesturing toward himself, sheepishly calls out, "This was my fault, Coach!" He kneels down to whisper to me, "Lance, I'm so sorry," his southern accent dragging the *sorry* out a good two seconds. I'm not mad at Jason, mostly because I'm too dazed. If anything, his error has gotten me out of this ridiculous drill.

It turned out I received a concussion from the hit, and my hearing aid was severely damaged. The university would in turn fund me a new set of hearing aids—my first-ever digital ones. They were so nice. They opened up a whole new world to me, a world of sounds that I never knew existed. The jump from analog to digital was euphoric. All it took was for me to take one in the noggin.

15

Following a preseason tournament in Puerto Rico, the team was called in for a meeting with Coach Majerus. He hobbled into the film room and sat on the table, wearing his usual cotton shorts, displaying his Kodiak calves, his knee wrapped up in an Ace bandage. He announced that his mother had cancer and he would be taking a leave of absence. Coach Hunsaker was to be the interim coach.

I didn't play much that year—sparingly at best, for maybe five minutes a game if at all. My best game that freshman year was against Washington State, when I scored eight points and fouled out in ten minutes. And I was OK with that most of the time, except for when Hunsaker would use me as motivation against my other teammates, threatening to bench them and play me, though he never did.*

Things got under way quickly in the off-season when Majerus returned. He had scheduled us for a European trip during the summer. Once finals were over, we were practicing, preparing for the trip. We practiced two times a day for ten straight days. On top of all of this, there were only eight players. And with eight players, it means more reps, more activity, fewer breaks.

I ended up herniating a disc in my lower back, the L5 vertebra, halfway through the training camp. I was undercut in a drill while going up for a rebound and landed on my butt, but the pain wasn't sudden. It was later in the night that I felt the swelling come. My whole left leg was numb, my pelvis was swollen, and my genitals ached constantly. I could neither lie, sit, nor stand.

---

*That's part of basketball, but try to imagine going to work every day and having your boss analyze your every move, always letting you know you can be replaced for even the slightest slipup. And you can visibly see your replacements waiting in line, peering over your boss's shoulder.

That final week of training camp, Chris Burgess's recurring back issues flared up as well. Even Majerus went down with a back problem. He was working all of us, even himself, too hard. It was quite strange to be lying on the table next to him in the rehab facility.

When it came time for us to pack up and leave, the doctors said my back might heal in time for me to at least play in the latter part of the European tour. I was relieved, as European history is my favorite field and I'd never been to Europe.*

Majerus didn't make the trip. Not only was his back bothering him, but he had suffered a large gash on his lower leg. Instead of risking serious infection to the wound while flying, Majerus opted to stay back, leaving Coach Hunsaker in charge once again. This time it ended up being quite a pleasant experience. I daresay that if Majerus had gone on the trip, we would've practiced more. Instead, we had a great time.

All that really needs to be said about the trip is that I won the karaoke contest at a local club in the Canary Islands one night with my rendition of Lionel Richie's "Say You, Say Me," and that I also had my first screwdriver.

There's a European custom that the hosting team will hold a banquet and feed the visiting team. After our game was over, we went to the banquet. The problem was that I was so thirsty and just dying for a drink, waiting impatiently for liquid to come out, and then *voilà!* A huge pitcher of orange juice! *Yay!* I ran up to it and poured myself a big glass and downed it like a camel. I quickly began to pour myself another, but then I slowly started to feel a tingle in my throat, which soon turned into a burning sensation, as though Bengay had just been stuffed down there. Thus I had my first screwdriver. I was nauseous the rest of the dinner.

Even if I wasn't LDS, I still wouldn't drink alcohol. I actually suffer from hyperhidrosis, which means that I sweat too much. I sweat from

---

*I especially love studying Europe in the Middle Ages. It was such an intricate chessboard of interdynastic family rivalries, all competing for power and the upper hand, with so much brutality and savagery, seemingly kept in check by the even more powerful Holy Roman Church, which was at the time a giant, scheming, money-laundering corporation, the living example of hypocrisy, trumping all other kings, dukes, and barons, with the threat of excommunication and interdict, while many of the supposed abstinent popes threw lavish weddings for their daughters. It was pure chaos and organized hierarchy all at once. The fact that Western civilization survived through all of this self-destructive and manipulative behavior is simply fascinating to me. Once again, I'm a dork.

my head and neck more than anyone I have ever met. I don't really sweat more in my armpits than the next person, but my head is a geyser. And with my lifestyle—always training, conditioning, and playing basketball—I sweat, and sweat some more. My shirt will be soaked when I'm done with a workout, and seven-eighths of it will be from my head, which I will wipe with my shirt. I'm getting lost in the gross details of my physiology here, but where I'm getting is that I get dehydrated very, very easily. And, being a big man at six-eleven, I need a lot to keep me hydrated.

I enjoyed my first European trip, but not so much the hepatitis I brought back with me.

A week after we returned from Europe, camp season began at the U. The dreaded Big Man–Guard Camp was coming up, and this would be my fifth straight year either attending or demonstrating. The mere thought of the camp inspired fear and a cold sweat in me. The camp was preceded during the week by a team camp, where various high school teams from across the country would come to gain tutelage from Majerus as well as gauge their own progress for the upcoming fall season. The only good news was that Coach Rupp had been hired onto the staff as an assistant coach. I was so thrilled to get to work with him again, but sadly, we really never saw a lot of each other, as Majerus usually had him busy with film or working out other guys.

The very first day of camp, Majerus was right on me. I actually appreciated it: as the saying went, "Coach Majerus rides hardest those he thinks will be good." Majerus walked out and called me out to the court.

"Post position, Lance. Arm bars high." I obeyed. "Throw him the ball. Call for it."

"Ball!" I yelled. I caught it, meeting it with two hands.

"Always meet the ball," Majerus said, turning to his audience. "Check over your shoulder to see what the defense and your other teammates are doing. Drop step." I obeyed. "Eyes not up soon enough. Five sprints. Go!"

I ran over to the sideline to begin my sprints as Majerus talked to his audience: "We run sprints here, down and back being one sprint, not only to help discipline, but as a form of conditioning as well, as we spend so much more time learning than we do running in the flow of practice. Lance will run them hard, or else he will run some more."

I finished, breathing hard for air, and jogged over to the post to resume the demonstration.

"Post position. Call for it. Meet it. Check your shoulder. Eyes up. Drop step. . . ." Majerus choreographed as I followed the beat. "Stop! Don't move." I froze as Majerus walked up to me, touched my lead leg, and pointed at my toes. "Toes are not pointed to the sideline," he explained to the audience. My toes were barely a few degrees shy of that, pointed to the corner. "Five sprints. Go!"

I ran over to the side and put in five more sprints. My co-demonstrator, Cameron Koford, then stepped up to fill in for me while I was running, only to be sent on his own set of sprints for not calling for the ball loud enough. The audience waited for me to finish my sprints as Koford joined me on the side.

We went through the motions again: Position. Call for it. Meet it. Check your shoulder. Eyes up. Drop step. What was hard was that we paused between every piece of the move to show the proper positioning, causing our legs to flare up with lactic acid and inducing incredible discomfort, not to mention killing any natural flow. "Lance will shoot a hook shot over his shoulder, with his arm raising up and releasing the ball between the 10 and 1 o'clock positions. Shoot it!"

My legs, having stood in a half-squat position, shaking and burning for nearly thirty seconds after having run so many sprints in just the first two minutes, tried to leap as I took my shot, only to barely lift up off the ground. I shot my hook between the 10 and 1 o'clock positions. I missed it as it careened off the front of the rim.

"Always aim at the back of the rim," Majerus immediately began to lecture. "Never miss it short. Five sprints!" I ran back over to my side and ran some more.

Koford filled in while I ran. I could never rely on Koford to give me a breather, as he always got sent on sprints much quicker than I ever did: "Post position. Call for it. Meet it. Check your shoulder. Eyes up. Drop step. Shoot it. Five sprints, Koford! For releasing the ball outside of the 10–1 o'clock position."

Koford rejoined me on the sideline. This went on for an hour. After our post demonstration, we were running a team defense demonstration. "Britton, toes not pointed to the rim!" Majerus chided as Britton

Johnson caught the ball at the three-point line. "Five sprints, go! Lance, fill in while Britton runs." I ran up and took my shirt off to go skin, as Britton had been a skin while demonstrating. "Lance, keep your shirt on. Go on the other team. Trace, go to the top." I ran over, picked up my shirt, and fumbled to put it back on. "Lance, too slow! Five sprints."

By the end of the first day I was exhausted. As I was eating dinner in the dorms with one of the high school teams, their coach came over to me and patted me on the back as he set his tray down next to mine. "I'm going to sit next to this guy," he told his team, "as Majerus is hardest on the players with most potential." And to me: "Let's see where you go."

I scoffed: "Careful what you wish for. You may be sent on sprints as well just for talking to me."

They thought I was joking. Most people didn't know that even coaches were not spared the sprints. I had seen Coach Strohm, Coach Shelton, and Scott Garson run sprints. I had even seen Coach Rupp, in his own gym at East High School, run sprints assigned by Majerus.

The week of team camp came to an end, only to usher in the Big Man–Guard Camp that weekend, where we simply pushed the reset button and repeated the cycle: Position. Arm bars high. Call for it. Meet it. Check shoulder. Drop step, stay low. . . . It was a forty-eight-hour camp, but it always felt like it lasted a week, as the two mornings always came early at six.

The last hour on the last day I'm sure I set some sort of record for sprints in an hour. We recapped everything we had gone over in the last two days. But on this day, Koford went down with pain, leaving me as the lone guinea pig. I demonstrated and ran, and ran and demonstrated. Toward the very end of the final hour, Majerus was talking to the audience while my soaked shirt leaked sweat all over the baseline: "Lance is now going to catch the ball, then outlet and follow, and then . . ." For whatever reason, whether from sheer fatigue or because he was turned away from me, I didn't understand what it was that he said or was ordering me to do. I gave him a quizzical look, and he noticed it.

"Lance, you look confused."

I shrugged and stammered.

"It's OK if you're confused, just tell me." He looked to his audience, smiling at himself, showing them his magnanimity.

"Yeah. I don't understand, Coach."

He sighed and shook his head. "Twenty sprints!"

I blinked in disbelief and looked to Coach Strohm, who was covering his mouth, disguising his laugh as he pretended to be rubbing his 5 o'clock shadow. I really think Majerus was trying to show his benevolent, caring side but had not expected me to accept it and admit my confusion—putting him in a bind. He was such an impatient man, he had not the motivation to follow through.

When camp was over and the kids filtered out, all of my teammates gathered in the film room, waiting for Coach to come in and outline the rest of the summer and his expectations for us as a whole and individually. Scott handed us our handwritten checks, and Chris, who was seated next to me and had worked during the camps but not demonstrated due to his back problems, looked at my check and then did a double take on his.

"How come you got so much more than me?" he asked.

Without skipping a beat, I responded matter-of-factly, "I got a dollar for every sprint I ran more than you."

When school started, Coach Majerus felt that we were all soft and not tough enough. He had the idea that we should take boxing lessons as a form of both conditioning and toughening—two birds with one stone. I ignorantly at first thought that all boxers just stood there and punched. It wasn't like they had to run and jump. I have since learned proper humility. I now have the utmost respect for boxers, because not only is it ridiculously tiring; you're also getting punched in the head and stomach while at it.

The first day of boxing lessons came after we'd lifted weights and were already tired. For the first two weeks we shadowboxed, working on simple jabs and hooks, progressing to combos as time went on. That first day, as we jabbed the air and jabbed some more, my shoulders burned like hot coals.

After two weeks, we were finally taught how to wrap our knuckles, which took some of the gents about twenty minutes to figure out. We then were handed gloves and told to simply shadowbox each other. I was paired up with Koford, who was seven feet tall, with a seven-foot-three-inch wingspan. Even he didn't understand and respect his reach. As the whistle blew, I gave Koford a couple of air jabs, clear away from his face. Koford then bared his teeth, shrilling like Chewbacca, and countered with his own air jab. The next thing I knew I was on my back, staring up at the many stars circling the blazing midday sun, which was piercing through my blackout.

"Koford, what the hell are you doing?!" Jason Veltkamp, our strength coach, screamed from across the turf field.

Koford held up his hands in genuine confusion: "I was just boxing. I didn't mean to hit him." I sat up, not noticing the blood that was gushing down my nose. Koford could never do anything right.

A week later, the kid gloves came off and we were unleashed. Jason even had a tournament pool allowing bets to be placed on us. Trace Caton, the team heartthrob, and Chris Burgess were paired up one day. It didn't last very long. On first glance, you placed money on Chris, due to his size. But Jason knew to put money on Trace and was videotaping the fight.

Chris went for a full hip-powered hook on Trace, who ducked and uppercut Chris right in the gut. Chris immediately hunched over in reflex, allowing Trace to follow with his strong hand and power-punch Chris right in the head. Even though they were wearing helmets, it really made no difference, as Chris dropped like a bag of potatoes. It took twenty minutes for Chris to come to and walk out on his own. Once Chris was able to give a thumbs-up to signal he was OK, which proved quite difficult for him, such was his daze, Jason immediately took his video camera to his office and replayed the fight, and replayed it some more, until his whole office was packed with football players narrating the force of the crushing blow inflicted upon Chris: "*Oh! Ah! Bam!*" Coach Majerus even requested a copy when he heard about it from Scott and Strohm, who laughed themselves silly upon seeing it. Everyone thought it hilarious except for Chris, of course.

16

Sophomore season began in November, and it went as expected, with all the usual name-calling and degrading insults one would expect. Usually I was referred to as "Cunt Extraordinaire," or else Coach would finger-spell "cunt" to me to make sure there was "no miscommunication between us." Why was coach being so mean? Coach was irritated with me because I had been instructed by our trainer not to practice in the tail-end section of two-a-day practices to keep my back from flaring up again.

Coach loved his two-a-days. Every weekend, on Saturday and Sunday, for the first three weekends of the season, Coach had two-a-days. He would've had two-a-days every day were it not for school. Coach loved his practices. He got to listen to himself talk for three hours every day without interruption as we stood there on the baseline like bowling pins.

After a late night where Coach kept us up until 2 a.m. watching film, we had to pack our bags and be at the airport by 6 a.m. to fly to Alabama. As a program, the University of Utah men's basketball team was the epitome of logic in action.

That morning, dazed and confused, I walked through the security checkpoint—my first time doing so since 9/11. I moseyed about looking for something to eat. I was minding my own business, just looking for a damn smoothie, when I heard Coach, with a McDonald's breakfast sandwich stuffed in his mouth, say, "Lance, we're meeting back in the security room to watch film! Just go—" He stopped and swallowed his food, his face growing red with irritation at me even though I had done nothing wrong, nor had I said anything. I knew full well we were meeting for film, which wasn't for another ten minutes, more than enough time to get myself a smoothie. Sometimes I just need a smoothie.

"You know what? You're not going to set me off today, Lance." He said this as though it was more for himself—an empowerment mantra. "Strohm!" Coach beckoned, and like Louis XIV, he waved me off. "Take Lance away."

I don't know what surprised me more: the fact that I inadvertently required Coach to begin positive self-affirmation or that Coach was able to secure a security room to watch something as trivial as a basketball game on some security monitor so soon after 9/11. Either way, the smoothie would have to wait, although Coach still allowed himself enough time to eat his food.

After watching film we got on the plane and flew to Alabama. During practice that day, Coach hurled obscenities at anyone who entered the arena, even a lowly janitorial assistant with Down syndrome. In Coach's defense, his tirade began to lose wind once he realized that Jimmy the Janitor was special.

The next night I scored ten points and grabbed five rebounds, even though we got a nice shellacking. I made my first bucket, but I totally traveled and luckily wasn't called for it. It was the only field goal I attempted that game, and I made all eight of my free throws, much to Coach's surprise. He had previously written me off as someone who couldn't shoot the ball well and had allowed me to shoot only layups. There's such a thing as overcoaching, and at some you point you just have to go out and play basketball.

Toward the end of the game, after I made a great defensive play, blocking a dunk, Coach pulled me to the side in the huddle and said, "You really are a warrior." It was to me, and only to me. There was no sarcasm, no showmanship, no audience. It was just me and Coach. And when he coached like that, he could be the most inspiring coach to play for. I'd have done anything he asked of me in that moment. If only he could have remained that way all the time.

I was in Coach's good graces for the next two days, as he recalled my toughness throughout the next few practices and the size of my testicles, metaphorically speaking. Coach was so complimentary toward me that my teammates began to tease me in the locker room. I was fine with that. It was nice being on top of the world, knowing that Coach was pleased. And yet I feared so much that I would let him down. I in no way thought I had arrived. I feared I'd lose it. And I did, the next game, against Arizona State.

In the first sequence that I was subbed in for Chris, there was a loose ball on the floor, and we were on defense. I was the one nearest the ball, and I saw my teammate Jeff Johnson leaking out for a layup. I quickly tried to pick it up and lob it to him, going for the home-run play. Instead, an opposing player dove between my feet to knock the ball away into his teammate's hands for an easy layup. Coach was livid. Had I made the play, I would've been a hero. But because I was a nanosecond too late, and the other guy dove for it and I didn't, I came away looking the weak part. I'm not afraid to dive on the floor for loose balls, trust me. But if I see a quick two points for my team I'll always go for them before I'll go for a possibility of points from a quick hustle. Hustle points don't count on a scoreboard, just like brownie points don't really get you into heaven.

When I dejectedly inbounded the ball, Coach was standing at the half-court line, hollering for my attention: "Lance . . . Lance . . . you pussy!" It was a quiet gym, and everyone heard it. And I died inside. I wanted to hide. As I had feared, I lost Coach's favor in just one game. The very next play, an opponent jumped up over me, over my block-out, and scored a layup off the offensive rebound. I was then immediately subbed out. "Are they too tough for you, Lance?" Coach asked sarcasti- cally as he escorted me to my seat. "That's what I get for trying to be positive with you. You thought you arrived, didn't you?" For the rest of the year, Coach would commonly recall that play, referring to it as the play "Lance pussed out of, too scared to dive on the floor."

No one stays at the top forever. What goes up must come down.

In December of my sophomore season Chris Burgess tore the plantar fascia in his foot. I became the default center. It was finally my time to play. I could hardly sleep those first few nights before my start, tossing and turning, obsessing about what-ifs. My obsessions would become self-fulfilling prophecies as I worked my mind into a state of cathartic attrition. My very first start, against lowly Stony Brook, was a disaster. I was terrible. I missed dunks, layups, bricked shots, and free throws. My hands were pasted with Crisco, as I couldn't bring down any rebounds. And I was so worried about blocking out that I took myself out of re-bound position.

Yes, blocking out is important, but sometimes you have to abandon the block-out and just nut up and go get the damn thing. A good coach once told me, "Good rebounders block out. Great rebounders just go get the ball." I'd never dare to go get the ball, so terrified was I of giving up an offensive rebound and drawing Coach's ire. My lack of confidence and Coach's bullying nature were just a poor combination. It was like pouring gasoline over hot coals. I was a poor rebounder at Utah because I played scared, never risking, always playing it safe, just settling for a block-out, happy that my man didn't get the offensive rebound.

After that Titanic of a first start, I was sitting at my locker with my head in my hands when Coach Rupp came up to me and said, "Lance, Coach wants to see you in his locker room."

I obeyed and entered Coach's locker room to see him standing naked in his shower stall. He motioned for me to come closer. "Lance," he began, as though it was perfectly normal for me to stand there in my clothes while he showered, "Gordon Monson, whose work I don't care for, wants to interview you, and I answered for you and said no. He only wants to interview you because you're deaf, not because you're a good basketball player, which you're not. It would be like him wanting to interview me because I'm fat, not because of my coaching ability."

Good talk, Coach. Good talk.

Gordon Monson was a sportswriter for the *Salt Lake Tribune*. After his request to interview me, Coach's hostility toward me increased. I'd comically tell my family, "Gordon Monson was the man that ruined my life." My relationship with Majerus continued to deteriorate rapidly. "You're a cunt, Allred," he'd say. "And go ahead and give me that blank stupid stare like you always do. If that doesn't motivate you to grow a pair, then I don't know what will. Go ahead and give me that stoic look and then go home and cry to Mommy."

I'd never go home and tell my parents of the abuse I endured. I didn't tell anyone about what I saw each day. Instead I just went home and sat in silent recollection of the day's practice, dreading the one that would inevitably come tomorrow. While a piece of me stayed true to myself, most of me began to at least entertain the notion that I wasn't worth much, and I slowly began to fade away from my family and friends. I was a zombie, a dead man among the living.

Stereotypes are stereotypes for a reason: because they are, for the most part, true. History repeats itself, and when people are unable to learn vicariously from the mistakes of others and repeat those same mistakes, a stereotype results. I have had to battle many stereotypes in the basket-ball world.

A final paper was due at the end of the semester in one of my history classes, and I presented a well-researched ten-page paper. Three days later I checked my grades online and saw all the grades I expected except for:

Middle East Hist: Incomplete

I began to panic, because I had never received an incomplete before. The professor didn't answer at his office. It was only three blocks away from my house, so I typed up a letter, walked it up to his office, and slid it under his doorway. I didn't hear from him for another two days, all the while fretting and obsessing about my grade.

I walked up to his office one more time, and this time I was fortunate enough to find him there.

"Ah, Lance, come in." His raspy voice faded off before it could even reach me. He motioned for me to sit down, and I complied.

"Professor, I saw that I had an incomplete, and I was hoping to learn why so I could address it and have it resolved."

"Yes, yes. About that. Your paper. It's a bit long, and it seemed suspi-cious. I doubted its credibility and suspected plagiarism."

"Plagiarism?"

"Yes. I must admit that I was in the wrong here, as I didn't believe an athlete could present such a fine paper. I have been teaching for many years now, and I have never had a basketball player write such an elo-quent paper."

"Um. I can assure you professor, it's mine. My own work."

"Yes, after I read your letter under the doorway and saw another proof of your writing style and evidence that you understand the "i-t-apostrophe-s" rule, I have determined that your writing was genuine. I have called the disciplinary office to ask them to remove my claim from the file. And I offer you my apologies."

I didn't know which affronted me more: that he thought I was in-capable of writing a coherent paper or that he doubted that I could understand the "i-t-apostrophe-s" rule: that contractions are unaccept-able in formal papers and therefore *it is* should never be written in con-tracted form (*it's*); and that plural references to the pronoun *it* are never apostrophized. A simple grammar rule that, sadly, many people don't understand.

I accepted the professor's apology and downplayed his embarrass-ment over his erroneous assumptions, without much offense, because

I love stereotypes myself and found it all very humorous. After all, my father did raise me on Helen Keller jokes.

Instead of being offended when people stereotype me, I enjoy the challenge of overcoming them. I love proving people wrong, making them eat their words. Success is the sweetest revenge. Yet through my vengeance, I can still laugh at myself. Stereotypes are stereotypes for a reason—because they're often, if not generally, true.

I walked home proudly, having debunked yet another stereotype that I have had to overcome in the basketball world. To congratulate myself on a job well done, that night I got stoned and engaged in reckless, unprotected sex with multiple partners at once. And then later I angrily fired off several rounds into the midnight air from my unregistered Glock and poured a couple for my homies as I slurred about drunkenly without any T-shirt on, displaying the "Thug" tattoo across my stomach. It was only after I had read some French literature into the wee hours of dawn that I finally slept.

There comes a day in certain young men's lives that they look forward to with much curiosity and trepidation—the day when they can finally determine whether or not they have a learning disability. That day came for me during my sophomore year of college.

Coach Majerus was growing impatient with my stuttering whenever he spoke to me, and irritated with my frantic mind that would over-analyze everything to the point where I'd forget even the most simple of plays. I could no longer hide in the back behind my teammates when Majerus went on his tirades, as I was now front and center, in the starring role.

One day, Coach had an epiphany: "Lance, I'm sincerely beginning to believe that you have a learning disability. And I mean that with all kindness. I'm going to have you tested." This was a strange conclusion, considering that I had the highest GPA on the team and that only a month earlier Coach had kept me from leaving practice early to make it to a study group for a final, as he wasn't worried about my grades.

It became his new favorite mantra for two weeks: "Lance, I'm going to speak slowly to you, since I believe you have a learning disability"; or "Don't worry, Lance. I'm arranging to have you tested for a learning disability. Help is on the way."

Coach Rupp came up to me the evening before my big day. He had a hard time not rolling his eyes, with an "I can't believe I have to waste my time with this" look on his face. "I finally booked you for a testing down at the Bennion Center," he told me. "It's tomorrow at eleven." He looked at me and saw the tired frustration in my eyes. "I know," he said. "Just go do it, so Coach will stop hounding me . . . you as well."

That next morning I walked slowly to the Bennion Center, taking in the stupidity of it all: I had earned, for three straight semesters, Academic All-Conference Awards and had the highest GPA on the team—and not with a cupcake major like communications. Yet here I was, about to be tested for a learning disability.

I entered the office that said "Human Resources" and gave the receptionist my name. I sat for a second and looked at all the motivational posters lining the office walls:

"Failure is an event, never a person."

"While most are dreaming of success, winners wake up and achieve it."

"The achievement of your goal is assured the moment you commit to it."

I never hated those tacky posters so much in my life as I did at that moment.

My name was called, and I sauntered in. I shook hands with the tiny lady.

"So, Lance, I read that you're here to get tested for a learning disability?"

"Yes," I said curtly.

"Well, there are several types of learning disabilities, and there are many ways to test, but not many ways to deduce."

"Yes," I said once again, unable to hide my discomfort.

"Well, why don't you tell me a little about yourself." I began to sum up my life: my hearing, my speech therapy—the works. After hearing me speak and noting the words I chose to use, she seemed entirely confused.

"I see. So you have struggled in school?"

"No."

"Do you get bored in school?"

"Sometimes."

"Are you frustrated often because you don't understand the material?"

"No."

She scribbled a note. "What are your grades like now?"

"I have a 3.8 GPA."

She raised her eyebrows. "I daresay that's probably one of the highest on your team."

"Yes."

She attempted to make another note, but then sighed. She dropped her pen and removed her eyeglasses as she sat back in her reclining office chair and began to rub the bridge of her nose. "Explain to me again. . . . Why are you here?"

"My coach wants to humiliate me," I said matter-of-factly.

She nodded. "I see. Well, I can assure you, you're a bright and articulate young man, and even if you were even just a tad bit slower, making you an 'average' person of intelligence, I wouldn't have the time to work with you, as there are other people who are in more dire need of the resources here than someone like yourself."

"Sounds great."

"But, let me say one thing. You don't have to put up with it."

I nodded. "How do I tell him that I'm thinking too much? It sounds arrogant."

"You'll know when the time comes."

I left the office, walked back up to the Huntsman Center, and handed Coach Rupp my clean bill of health—a pink slip with a written assessment that I had no learning disability, at least not one yet known of. Rupp looked at and placed it on his desk, sighing at the exercise in futility.

I asked, in my best deadpan way, "Do you need to keep it, or can I place it on my fridge at home?"

17

Say what you want about sticks and stones, but when you hear day in and day out about your flaws and are being told that you're not good enough, after a while, even though you may not entirely believe what is being said about you, it's nearly impossible to not entertain the thought or at least question it, especially after three years of it in your face. When Coach Majerus would tell me day after day, week after week, that I had to have a learning disability and was stupid, it wasn't that I believed him and believed that I was stupid, but I allowed it to enter into discussion with my inner thoughts.

Still, for the most part I was getting by. But that began to change on January 6, 2002. We were in the Bay Area, practicing at Saint Mary's College, getting ready for a game the next day. One of my teammates made a mistake during practice, a bad pass or something trivial, as all things basketball are trivial when compared with real-life issues.

Coach Majerus stopped practice and had us all line up on the baseline as he paced back and forth, going up the line, taking turns with each of us like ducks in row, calling out our deficiencies, flaws, and weaknesses. We stood there and took it, as we always did. Usually you tried not to laugh when Coach was talking and humiliating another teammate, not because you liked seeing your teammate humiliated, but rather because you knew your teammate and knew what they were about; and the things that Coach Majerus would say to them were so ridiculous that they were almost comical. It wasn't, however, comical when he was speaking to you.

After Coach had ripped into Britton Johnson, making crude references about his girlfriend, he looked at me, even though I had done nothing in this particular instance.

"You know, Lance, you're the worst of all. You use your hearing as an excuse to weasel your way through life. You're a disgrace to cripples, and if I were in a wheelchair and saw you play basketball, I'd shoot myself."

This was in front of everyone—the entire team, the coaches, and Coach Rupp. Many of these witnesses, if you ask them, will tell you that this happened—and many have, although some chose to remain anonymous.

I said nothing, which only made Majerus more angry, as he could never get a reaction out of me.

But inside, it ruined me. Here was a man that I had dedicated three years of my life to, that I had idolized, that I had sweated and labored to play for since I was sixteen. He had turned against me and betrayed me. Had I never met the man, or had he meant little to me, I would've laughed at what he had just said.

But this was a man I had entrusted my entire future to. How could I muster up the courage or even the passion to go out and play for this man anymore, knowing that no matter what I did, he would get the glory? Conversely, any shortcoming of mine would be mine and mine alone. Majerus let it be known loud and clear that it was my fault if something went wrong. And I believed it when he said it, because I was already prone to do so.

Basketball had been something that had allowed me to feel normal, to fit in, and yet Majerus, like so many before him, isolated me because of my disability. He didn't discriminate against me. If he had not played me because I was deaf, that would've been discrimination. Instead, he simply used my hearing impairment as a means to humiliate me. Sexual harassment isn't discrimination; it is, however, against the law. Humiliating someone in the professional workplace because of a disability isn't discrimination, nor is it against the law. But does that make it right?

When I called my mother from the hotel later that day to wish her a happy birthday, I didn't tell her about what happened. I didn't tell anyone about what happened until Mom and Dad heard from Britton and Jeff Johnson's parents about it. My parents sat me down and confronted me. I remained removed and aloof, which was the only way I knew how to be at this point, until I finally broke down and admitted what had happened. Why didn't I tell them earlier? Because, as when I was a boy, I wanted to deal with it myself. I didn't want my parents to fight my battles for me. But more than that, I was too ashamed to tell them. *Mom, Dad, Coach was mean to me today. Boo-hoo.* Cleverly, Majerus always challenged me at the end of a berating by saying, "You can go cry to your mommy now." Basic bullying tactics that I bought into.

My mom was a threat in Majerus's mind, as he was aware she held a lot of esteem on campus, especially after she gave the commencement speech. He did a good job of putting up a psychological barrier between me and my mother by often bringing her up during his many soliloquies, daring me to go whine to her. And I felt I had to prove him wrong—that I didn't need my mommy.

I finally told Mom and Dad about all the things that were going on, and how I had been tested for a learning disability. They were enraged. But I asked them not to do anything and just let me finish the season quietly. I was committed to my teammates. I loved my teammates, and I loved Coach Rupp. I have never quit on a team, and I never will.

I had hidden myself in basketball, allowing my obsessive-compulsive tendencies to channel through the sport. No longer was I praying compulsively, questioning whether I was gay or whether I had failed this or that test. I could instead obsess about missed shots or bad passes I had made. But my brutal self-criticism combined with Coach Majerus's was a recipe for disaster. All of my emotional walls were crumbling around me, and I had become a zombie. I didn't talk to anyone anymore, because I was so vulnerable and unstable. I flirted with suicidal thoughts every night as I'd watch the clock and count down the hours until the next practice. Ten hours and thirty-seven minutes until I have to see Coach Majerus again. I feared, loathed, and despised him so much that I really did want to kill myself some nights, just so I wouldn't have to see him again and reflect on my failures and shortcomings. No one knew I was thinking these thoughts.

Many nights I contemplated suicide versus quitting. Quitting meant I'd leave in the middle of the season and the community that had invested so much in me would look at me as a failure. Many, due to my past actions and arrogant facade, would say I was a spoiled brat. Suicide, on the other hand, meant no more practices, no more disappointed faces—no more pity, either. But both avenues meant quitting, and that's why I never chose either. I'm not a quitter.

The last straw came on my birthday, February 2. We were playing Colorado State, and it was a late-night game broadcast on ESPN. Coach had said to me during practice the day before the game, "Lance, if you make a mistake or embarrass me, you'll come out and go to the bench for a long time, and I'm speaking not in terms of a single game."

What was I going to do? Play a perfect game? Of course not. The game is under way, and a few minutes in Jeff Johnson is trying to throw me a lob pass, and I'm shaking my head, mouthing, "No." My mind is saying, Please don't throw it, please don't throw *it.*. . . Jeff throws it. Please don't drop it, please don't drop *it.* . . . And what do I do? Of course I drop it, and the ball goes out of bounds.

Majerus immediately subbed me out, and I didn't step back onto the court during a game for over a month. While being banished to the bench was the final blow to my nearly flatlined confidence, at the same time I actually welcomed the exile, because while I wasn't playing I was also free from persecution during film viewing and practice. Majerus ignored me at that point. Given the circumstances, isolation was much more to my liking than daily degradation.

But Majerus didn't just bench me. I could've handled that. Right after he benched me for dropping the pass, the commentators were discussing why I was no longer playing. One said, "Well, Majerus says Lance has to learn that there's no 'I' in team."

Had Majerus just said, "I choose not to play Lance," that would've been fine. But he chose to publicly justify his decision by slandering my character. This was the greatest insult, and a false statement to boot, as my teammates were the only reason I even chose to stay and continue to deal with the man.

I sat for two months, not seeing the floor for the next ten games. I finally entered a game, my very last for Utah, where we lost to the University of Indiana in the first round of the NCAA tournament. By then I didn't care about how I played. I just went out and got a couple of rebounds, hit a few free throws, and told myself, "Hey, I'm here playing in the NCAA tournament, and I'm never playing for Rick Majerus ever again. Just go out there and have fun." And I did.

After the game was over and we were back at our hotel, I found Coach Rupp in the restaurant. We went into the conference room that the team had reserved for the tournament and sat down in the dark. I looked at Coach Rupp as stoically as I could, but I could barely get the words out of my mouth before I started to cry: "I need out."

"I know," Rupp said quickly. "I'm sorry. I want out, too. Had I known this is the way it really is, I'd never have let you come here. Heck, he fooled me, too. Go somewhere and play. You deserve it. I might go back to East, but I think I'm going to stick this out for a few more years, just to give myself a chance to move on up somewhere else."

"I'm sorry I let you down, Coach. I know you put your neck and reputation on the line, vouching for me and defending me."

"There isn't a thing you could do to let me down, Lance. I'm proud of you. I have no sons, only daughters, but you're one of my sons. Let people on the fringes say what they want to say, but you and I—and most importantly, you—know what you have been through and endured, and there's no shame in that."

When I announced my decision to leave the following Monday, Coach Majerus granted my request. I went to say good-bye. I took one last walk around the Huntsman Center, walked into the basketball offices one last time, and said good-bye to all the secretaries and coaches. I walked past all the trophy cases and then out onto the dark Huntsman floor. No one will know how much I loved that place, and how much it meant to me growing up as a kid, seeing the dome from various places around the valley, telling myself in silence, "I will play there someday." Though I achieved that dream, it turned into a nightmare.

I was alone. I stared up at the jerseys that I had hoped one day would carry my name, but now I knew they never would. I smiled at the side of the court—my preferred side of the court, where I opted to run my sprints. I then looked at it all and asked the darkness, "Why?"

The years I played for him, I saw Majerus's shortcomings and brutality, as well as his good, generous side. However, my shortcomings at the University of Utah were mine and mine alone. I cannot blame him for my lack of development and performance. I take full accountability for my disappointment. As I put no blame on Majerus for my subpar development, I give him no credit for my future success. I went into a program that had been in place for over a decade, and I was treated no more or less cruelly than dozens before me. So why should I be any different than the rest of them? Why should I believe I was special and should've been treated more tenderly? It does not work that way, and so the fault lies with me.

I walked back up the steps I had walked so many times before, and looked back down to the floor, imagining the band's songs that rang out come game time, and the rush I felt so many times when the crowds roared. I did love that place.

Then the voices in my head came and cackled at me, telling me the crowd had never cheered for me and that I, like my time at the University of Utah, was full of sound and fury, signifying nothing.

18

"Laaaaance, this is Joe Cravens, coach at Weber State." I have always wondered how a man from Indiana, a state bordering the Great Lakes, somehow managed to have a southern drawl. Coach Cravens in the early 1990s had been an assistant for Coach Majerus at the University of Utah and had a number of horror stories to share with me. He wanted me to play for him, but I was concerned about the fact that Weber State University was only thirty minutes from the University of Utah, and from Coach Majerus.

I wanted to be far away from my problems and ignore them, somehow believing that if I ignored them long enough, they'd go away. I was emotionally unwell and traumatized, and I felt that some change, albeit just a change in proximity to home, would help me escape some of the demons in my head. I didn't know yet that it makes no difference, as it's all in your head and your head goes with you wherever you do, as far as Timbuktu.

I visited Weber a few times and played pickup with the team. I played well when I was there, and my strengths worked well with the strengths of the other guys there. But I made an effort to push these things out of my mind, propelled by my irrational thoughts that I needed to be far, far away.

In my effort to run away from my troubles, I thought about going to the University of Montana, Dad's alma mater. I wanted to move back up there, live with Pax and Sam, and be far away from Utah. But the coach of Montana didn't think I was worthy of a scholarship.

One night when Andy Jenson, the assistant coach at Weber, called me just to check in, I panicked and "dumped" him: with my wits gone, I insanely told him that I was turning down their scholarship—the only Division 1 scholarship that was being offered to me—to pay my own way and walk on at Montana. It was a ridiculous decision, one that only an unstable and unhealthy person like me would have made.

Mom and Dad held their breath as I hung up the phone. I walked out of their house sobbing, knowing it was the wrong choice. But I was terrified of going to Weber because it was only a half hour away from the U. From Coach Majerus.

I drove to a friend's apartment, and just as I arrived, Coach Rupp called me on my new cell phone—my very first cell, which I had bought on impulse; I had no idea how I was going to finance it once my scholarship checks ended.

"Lance," he said sternly, without any intro. "You need to go to Weber. Your parents just called me and told me you turned down the scholarship. They're a good school, a good team. And they want you. And you'll play. And you'll play a lot. Get back on the phone, call them, and accept the scholarship."

He hung up, and I, forever his soldier, complied.

"'Bout damn time," Coach Cravens said with his southern drawl.

I never filed a complaint of discrimination or a lawsuit against Rick Majerus. And although some people have reported otherwise, Majerus was never absolved of his treatment toward me; he was only cleared of any wrongdoing.

As I mentioned earlier, my mother was getting her master's in special education, learning about the rights and laws protecting those with disabilities. This led her to file a letter of complaint with the U about Majerus's behavior. She took this action apart from me. I chose to not have any part in the process. I wanted to stay far away from Majerus, as I had studied enough history to know that coups d'état rarely succeed if you try to carry them off in-house, relying on the processes of the very institution that is supporting the ruler.

Mom even mailed a copy of the letter to Jon Huntsman, the generous philanthropist whose very name adorned the arena I played in at the U. Jon Huntsman has a son who is challenged in many ways. His name is Markey, a great guy. He is very active and has a lot of hobbies. He holds down a job and is very responsible, considering his challenges. The fact that Jon Huntsman, who had a son who has battled and overcome limitations throughout his life, would have a friend in Rick Majerus, who belittled one of his own players to hide his own deficiencies, was too much for my parents. When the whole incident erupted, Huntsman's silence, as Mom said in her letter to him, was deafening.

Word was spreading around that summer and early fall as I prepared to go to Weber about some of the things that had been said and done to me, by people in the know. Despite several interview requests, I kept my silence.

The athletic director at the U, after receiving my mother's letter of complaint, invited my parents up to his office. He said he understood and empathized with my mother and her plight, and that he was sad to see me go. But the truth of the matter was that Majerus won basketball games. As long as the team won, most of the fans were happy and didn't want to concern themselves with the tactics he used to get those wins.

Within my first month at Weber State, I received a phone call from the investigative committee at the University of Utah in regard to possible harassment and discrimination. After all the rumors going around, the university wanted to officially put it behind them.

I at first refrained from answering any inquiries, but finally Coach Cravens agreed to accompany me and I decided to see the investigator. I answered her questions.

I never expected anything to be done, because it wasn't an investigation into Majerus or his actions, as they knew what he was like. It was an investigation to see whether the school was liable for a lawsuit. It was farcical to say the least—*apocryphal* would be more like it—and very well crafted. The university's fears of liability allayed, the athletic department could release a statement, to whoever might ask about the incident, that Majerus was "cleared of any wrongdoing." He was by no means absolved of misconduct.

It was insulting, really, that the university thought I didn't know what they were doing. But they were not the first, nor the last, in this world to pass me off as a naive deaf jock.

Shortly after I committed to Weber, I was invited to take part in the World Deaf Olympics in Athens, Greece. Coach Cravens felt it was a good idea, since I was ineligible to play the next season and would have to sit it out as a redshirt, due to NCAA rules about transfers.* I finally

---

*Even though this was my fourth year in college, having another red shirt year meant I would ultimately graduate after six years in college: three at Utah and three at Weber.

agreed to go to Greece, being the historian that I am, intrigued by the possibility of seeing Athens. Because I could speak and read lips properly enough to survive in the mainstream, I was unsure how this group of deaf athletes would accept me, as most of them depended on sign language to communicate—something I wasn't gifted at.

But six-foot-eleven transcends language and culture barriers; they were happy to have me on the team. They helped make me comfortable and kept telling me to just relax, that I would pick up on all the sign language eventually, which I did. So much so that I stopped wearing my hearing aids after the second day.

It was so liberating not to have to wear my hearing aids or wonder whether someone was speaking to me or if I heard them properly. Instead, I could sit in my natural state of silence and just read the body language of my teammates and coaches. Of all languages, body language is the greatest form of communication, whether people realize it or not. Living in silence, I learned to read people and their body language. People will tell you a whole story without saying a word if you just watch them.

It was a whole new experience to just stare down at my hearing aids in the morning and spitefully leave them behind when I walked out the hotel door. I spent my days happily letting things happen around me. For the first time in a long while I was able to sleep easy, free from anxiety. I hadn't realized just how much each of my days, even a simple one, was a big stress inducer for me. Just having to put my hearing aids in, and daring to interpret the verbal world, was a huge source of fear and stress. I was so used to it that I no longer recognized it as such. Now that I do, I better understand why I struggle with insomnia and the fear of another day on the morrow.

We held the best record going into tournament play, and for the first time in a long time, I was enjoying playing basketball again.

Then I tore my medial collateral ligament, or MCL.

It was hot and humid in Greece, and there was no air-conditioning in the gyms. While I was blocking out a guy on the Lithuanian team, he pulled me back and we both fell to the floor. My teammate got the rebound, and my team began running to the other end of the floor. I quickly got up and turned to pivot, my foot stepping on the wet spot my opponent and I had just created on the court.

You can imagine what happened next. As I put all my weight on my back foot to launch out on a sprint, my foot slipped on the wet spot, sending all my weight onto my knee. It buckled, and I felt it tear. I screamed but then got up to finish the play and actually scored on a lob pass for a layup. Right after, I had to call a time-out as my knee was burning with searing pain unlike any I had ever felt. I had been privileged up to this point to have never had, aside from your basic jumper's knee, an injury to my knees.

The next day I tried to stretch and warm up the leg, and the trainer tried various taping jobs to alleviate the pain or channel the weight elsewhere. None of her methods worked. When game time came I couldn't run or jump, no matter what I put on my knee. And so with teary eyes I watched my teammates lose to Greece by four points. I sobbed as I took the silver medal on the stand. I had let my new friends down.

We flew home in coach, my bad knee locked up in the corner against the window. I didn't even have the comfort of sitting in an exit-row (not aisle) seat, as it seems there are always other people who have the luxury of having nothing more to do with their time than arrive at the airport early enough to assure they have these roomy seats. The Ace bandage did a little to help, but the knee finally went numb and blue with the swelling and the change in cabin pressure, sending my leg to sleep.

The team doctors at Weber State evaluated my knee and graded it a high level-two MCL sprain—nearly, but not quite, needing surgery. For, as much as I sprain my ankles and other joints, I'm blessed in that for some reason I heal very quickly. But I have not healed from the sorrow of not sharing a gold medal with my friends.

19

My redshirt year at Weber State was one of the most productive years in my basketball career. Coach Cravens sat me down at the beginning of the year and said, "I'm not going to say one word to you the entire season. You have been overcoached to the point where you don't know how to play anymore. Just have fun each day, work hard, and teach yourself how to play again. Since you can't play in any games, as you're redshirting, make each practice your game, and just have fun."

And I did just that. I enjoyed going to the Dee Events Center for practice each day, shooting any shot I felt like shooting without consequence. Launching up three-pointers, even one from half court in a defensive conversion/ fast-break drill, because I damn well felt like it. On game days Coach Cravens would have shooting competitions and games that only those who were playing that night could participate in. This didn't hurt my feelings, as I'd sneak into the tiny weight room down the tunnel and get in a quick lift. Fifteen minutes later I'd be back and the games would still be going. I completed my shoot-around session by walking over to the bench, having myself a seat while reading *USA Today,* catching up on current events.

"What's going on, Easy Money?" Coach Cravens would say as he looked over at me, observing my casualness. To which I only shrugged and continued reading.

When it wasn't game day was when I came to play.

Weber ran the table in conference, winning seventeen straight.

Coach Cravens was named the coach of the year.

During this year, my obsessive-compulsive disorder began to leak out away from the basketball court. I saw a counselor on campus for a few visits and was diagnosed with post-traumatic stress disorder. Certain words or phrases that Coach Majerus liked to use would trigger panic attacks. Plus, I was having recurring dreams, mostly of being late for practice, missing a game, or being left alone in a room with him. When I awoke in a cold sweat, I'd sit up and breathe heavily in the dark, counting to ten. I'm now at Weber State, I told myself. I play for Joe Cravens. At first this little mantra would suffice in calming me in that moment of awakening. But the dreams became more frequent, more intense, with each passing day. I had the dreams two, three, even four times a night, each time awakening and repeating, I'm now at Weber State. I play for Joe Cravens.

By January it was a full-blown disease, rotting away my mind. If I dared to sleep, by the second or third recurring dream in a night I'd wake up, repeat my feeble mantra, and break down in tears. I was exhausted. I was so tired that I wished I could just sleep for a thousand years.

In addition, Coach Cravens wasn't nearly as demanding or time-consuming as Majerus, and I found myself with so much free time that I didn't know what to do with myself. I was used to Majerus being the center of my life, this man on a pedestal whom I had to please.

When I arrived at Weber, instead of restructuring my life, I simply looked for a replacement. I found it in the form of women. I would quickly place a girl on a pedestal and overwhelm her with my insecurities and how much I needed her approval. But for the most part, these were the wrong kind of girls—with year-round tans and baggage from past relationships that I could in no way handle.

I was such a wreck that even if I had found a girl who was emotionally stable, she wouldn't have been able to help me. I assumed a passive-aggressive role when dating women, intentionally overwhelming them in hopes that they'd dump me so I could stop thinking about what I needed to do to make the relationship work.

I'd call a girl or send her a text, and when I didn't immediately hear back from her I'd start to obsess: Should I not have called? Did I leave a bad message? Should I have left a message? Was it too short? Too long? Why hasn't she called me back? Is she screening my calls? Do I need to call back and correct the last message? Did I do something wrong? Did I do something wrong by not doing anything at all?

One girl I was dating had called and left me a message late at night. She said she was sad, that she missed me and was going to bed. I called her back; she didn't answer. Was she sleeping? Yes, most likely. But my mind would begin to churn. Is she mad at me for not answering the phone? Is she screening my calls? I knew I was being ridiculous but couldn't stop thinking about it. To calm myself, willing to risk it all for peace of mind, I went over to her house, which was dark, and woke her up by ringing the doorbell, only after I had tried throwing pennies at her window lest I wake her roommates. It scared her.

I analyzed these situations to the nth degree, burying myself in a hole of scenarios and subscenarios that would make any normal person crazy with overload. I'd stay up all night running these scenarios in my head, recapping them and checking them again, over and over, to make sure that for every possible scenario that could go wrong, I had an out to correct it. I even drew out maps of scenario webs and kept them in folders in my closet, learning from the Russell Crowe film *A Beautiful Mind* that you should never leave your schemes up for anyone to see. Interesting that this was the lesson I took from the movie and not the obvious one—that if you start drawing up schemes and conspiracies, you really should get some help.

I was so used to everything being my fault at Utah that I was stumped while at Weber when I didn't have a problem to fix. I looked for problems that weren't even there. As I tried to fix a problem after I had created it, I did everything within my power to solve it, to the point of lying and telling little tales that were not even worth telling and led only to a self-fulfilling prophecy.

When I was dating a girl, I wrote down scenarios of how the relationship could go, and like a stage director, I chose the script I wanted, the dialogue, the setting. It's creepy to me now as I look back and see how nearly perfectly I manipulated poor, unfortunate girls into a setting that I had drawn up. So many times it went according to plan. I had a solution for everything.

I hope you can appreciate my honesty at this moment, as it isn't easy for me to describe just how sick and manipulative I had become. It gives me chills to realize just how effective a puppeteer I can be.

I sank lower and lower into this world of self-inflicted perfectionism, seeking problems to fix. I began telling little lies to my family and friends. When my mom asked me what I had done that day, I, not wanting her to know I was thinking about a girl or had spent the afternoon plotting and scheming how I could single-handedly make this relationship work, would instead tell her I had gone to the store. If she then asked if I remembered to get some random thing she needed, I'd say, "Oh, yeah! It's in my car. Just a second."

I'd run out to my car, race to the store, and buy whatever it was Mom was asking about. I often stopped in the middle of these episodes and just shook my head. I was finding myself in these ridiculous situations too often, because I was so paranoid that I felt I had to lie about anything and everything I was doing. I wasn't well.

I was exhausted mentally at practice, and my teammates, especially John Hamilton, would tell me to chill out, as I'd spaz over the slightest mistake and wouldn't move past it. They thought I was just super-intense when I was truly mentally ill.

Schoolwork was another issue. I obsessed about making my papers perfect and would look at them and see all their flaws and finally give up, trashing them altogether. I would willingly trash a paper simply because it was never going to be perfect. Even though I knew there was no such thing as a perfect paper, that it was all in the eye of the beholder, I knew it wasn't perfect in my eyes. And rather than receiving criticism on it, which I couldn't handle emotionally, I opted to have no criticism at all and instead take an F.

I knew I was being irrational, that the scheming and plotting were ridiculous, but I couldn't stop. Why could I not stop? Because what if I did stop and it led to something disastrous, or what if she was the one? What if? What if? I'd rather cover all the bases and view every scenario in my head than allow the what-ifs to haunt me at night. Even when logic seized the day, the impulse to lie, plot, and scheme, or just obsess, was far stronger than the logic in my mind. Why did I have to obsess? The answer is, simply, because I had to.

Finally, right before my twenty-second birthday, I called up Raphael, sobbing on the phone, sitting in my room in the dark, holed up away from human contact.

"Hello?" she said as she answered the phone.

"Hi, Raph," I said weakly, trying not to vomit as I sniffed and wiped away tears with my hands, more vulnerable than I had ever been before. I had never told anyone about these thoughts that were torturing me. The walls were down, and I was just a younger brother with no ego or will to hide behind, calling his older sister for help.

"Lance, what is wrong?"

"I'm sick."

"What do you mean? Are you hurt?" She thought I was referring to a physical sickness.

"No. I'm ill."

She paused. "I know," she said simply. I had been deteriorating over the last year to the degree that all the family could see it. I was pale, sleep deprived, reclusive, and angry. "We all have known. But we could only wait until you were ready, when you were ready to hear us."

The next day I went on medication. Two days later I walked back into the office of my old childhood psychologist. He was able to help me break down my thinking patterns and program my mind to be more positive in self-reflection.

I will probably be on medication all of my life. And that's OK. People mistakenly view mental medication as a sign of weakness, but trust me: the inability to admit you have an illness is the greatest weakness of all.

The great mistake many people make is assuming that medication will fix their problems and make them all better. This isn't true by any means. Medication simply slows down the brain and allows the chemicals to balance. After that it's up to the person to alter their thinking patterns, to restructure their routines, thoughts, and inner dialogue. It's up to them to push themselves past the pain and discomfort of accountability toward emotional health, no longer allowing themselves to be the victim.

People always ask me how I have overcome OCD. First off, I have not overcome it; I have harnessed it. It will be with me all my life, and I must work with it. But at the same time, I don't refer to it in the present tense. I don't let it define me. I will say, "I have had my battles with OCD," not "I'm OCD" or "I suffer from OCD." I will never let it define me.

Along with putting my hearing aids in every day, I must take a loony pill as well. At first I was ashamed, just as I was ashamed of my hearing impairment. But then Coach Cravens said one day, "You taking that pill is just the same as Brad taking his insulin shot every day for his diabetes."

I'm not ashamed of those pills anymore. I'm proud of them, as they remind me of the hard path of acceptance I have had to embrace.

By accepting my weaknesses and accountability for my actions, I'm able to delight in and appreciate my accomplishments in turn. It's more than a fair trade.

20

At the beginning of my junior year, I finally moved out of my parents' house. I turned to the path that many of my teammates were walking: low-income housing. Several of my teammates were taking advantage of the option, as our scholarships were not considered a source of income and thus we were classified as at the poverty level, making us eligible for government housing.

That summer, I also got a puppy, a Scottish terrier. I named him MacMurrin, in honor of my Scottish ancestry. He has traveled the world with me. He is my friend and companion. When I moved into government housing, Mac was able to come with me, as with my hearing impairment I was able to have him certified as my hearing-assistance dog. Although it may seem that I was pulling the Handicapped Andy card here, I wasn't, as I was by myself and Mac did help me, letting me know if someone was at the door, or if my phone was ringing by bringing it to me. Somehow he knew that his job was to be on alert. He brought me my phone only when we lived in that apartment, though. Since then, as we have house-hopped through my vagabond days of professional basketball, he has totally slacked off.

My junior season introduced a few new teammates into my life. There was a walk-on named Jack. Jack was a big ex-marine coming to school on the GI Bill. He was twenty-eight or so at the time, had a few kids, and was about six-foot-nine and close to 290 pounds. He told the coaches he wanted to walk on, and they had no objection to it, seeing as how he was a big body. During pickup in the preseason, I accidentally hit him in the shin with my shoe and cracked his tibia. As he limped off the floor, I turned to him, out of breath, and asked, "Are you OK?"

He began to cuss me out. Apparently, the tone I asked him in had sounded sarcastic or mocking. This happens to me a lot. I cannot hear what I say as well as others do. And if I'm breathing for air because of my asthma and try to say something, it comes out sounding a bit different than what I aimed for, and the tone is wrongly interpreted. Even when I'm not playing, I try to catch the right rhythm in speaking, sometimes adjusting the pitch in a sentence to try to match the tone of the conversation, going from memory as to what that tone is supposed to sound like. It has gotten me into trouble often, the incident with Jack being one of many such events.

Jack kept telling me and everyone else on the team that he was going to get back at me when he was healthy. By the time I went to apologize to him a second time, I was already his enemy. He just said, "Don't worry about me, man, I will see you back on the court," and then looked down to the cast on his leg. You can't really rationalize with crazy.

When Jack came back, within the first week he got even. We were playing a drill in practice, and he intentionally swung his elbow into my face, splitting my chin. Pat Danley walked over to help me up as Jack looked down at me and said, "Payback."

I said nothing as I pressed the skin against my chin, taking Pat's helping hand. John Hamilton looked at Jack and said, "Idiot."

Incidentally, Jack would later be involved in an on-campus paintball fracas and consequently was with us for only one season.

The new teammate I was most excited about was Troy Goodell, a junior college transfer from Snow College. He was a smart, hardworking kid out of Layton, Utah. I could write pages about how good a guy Troy is, but all you really need to know is that our senior year, Coach Cravens would label Troy and me as two of the best senior captains he ever coached. Troy wasn't vocal by any means. He had a surfer-dude mentality, and he shaved his legs. He might be the only guy that has ever shaved his legs who I actually deign to call my friend. Troy had more nicknames than anyone else I ever knew, but "Frenchman" stuck over time. Troy had the long European nose that typifies the Frenchman. We even called him French Onion Soup from time to time.

In my very first game for Weber State University, wearing the purple of the Wildcats, I scored twenty-seven points.

Utah winters kill me. The inversion-induced smog that settles in the valleys during the winter plays hell with my sinuses and lungs. Every winter I have an annual bout with bronchitis as well as countless sinus infections. The bronchitis hit me early my junior year, right after Thanksgiving.

I chose to continue to practice through it, having some coughing and hacking fits on the side but making it through the day.

In December we went down to play Southern Utah and won a good game. Afterward, I coughed up some blood in the sink. My lungs and airway were not doing so well. We then flew to the Missouri Valley State tournament . . . and lost in a not-so-impressive game. I should've taken time off after this, as I'd be up late at night with coughing fits hunched over a boiling pot of water, breathing in the humid air to help break the layer of mucus blocking my windpipe.

I coughed so hard that blood came out of my throat, but then so did much of the mucus. I finally got to bed at 4 a.m. When I arrived at the Dee for practice the next day, Coach Cravens was in a bad mood because we had lost and was feeling it was time to give things a bit of an overhaul. He decided to run a little drill with the bigs; that meant we had to play post defense for however long he wanted us to. If we gave up a catch in the post, we had to run a sprint.

It was during about the twelfth subsequent sprint that I finally noticed that something wasn't right. A heavy pressure was building in my chest, but seemingly on the outside of the lungs, forcing them to collapse, as I couldn't take a deep breath. If I fought it, a choking sensation would squeeze my windpipe. It was very painful, and I was growing light-headed and very irritated. And my inhaler wasn't helping. The next play, I was up. Coach threw a lob over my head, and I blocked Anthony Jackson's shot from behind, still knowing I was going to be running, since Anthony had caught it in the first place. I ripped the ball from Tony's hands and gave it a good boot into the nosebleed section of the Dee.

"OK, Lance. Here's another one," Coach said sarcastically as he rolled a new ball to me. "You wanna kick that one, too?" I wasn't going to say no, so I took the second ball and gave it a good boot as well. "Good job, Lance. Now you can go up and get the two balls."

I jogged the steps of the Dee, each step causing a burning not only in my legs but in my chest as well. Something was wrong, but what was I going to say? *"Coach, I can't breathe"*? That was the oldest trick in the book, but also the last one you want to use, as it tells a basketball coach one thing only—that you're out of shape. And I wasn't.

Retrieving the two balls, I ran back down to the court, where the group was waiting for me. If I was going to die, I wanted my last act to be a defiant one.

Before Coach could even say a word, Anthony threw the ball in the stands himself and began yelling in my face. To top it off, he began to shove me—right in the chest, right where it hurt. He was hitting the pressure point, making me nearly keel over in submission as he cussed me out. "You think I like doing this stupid drill? Huh?" he yelled, pushing me again. "Grow up!" He berated and reprimanded me for a good twenty seconds, but I was too short of breath to even respond. But that was Anthony; he always meant well.

Practice finally ended, and I went home to my apartment. I got Mac and drove home to Salt Lake, as I knew something was wrong. When I got to Mom and Dad's, I tried lying down for a while, but that actually made the pain worse. Mom finally took me to the ER. Three hours and seven bleeding drunk idiots later, my X-rays revealed that I had torn a hole in my windpipe, or rather I had coughed a hole in my windpipe. The mucus buildup had been so strong and thick that my skin and muscle were easier to rip through than the mucus. The X-ray showed air pockets surrounding the lungs, which explained the pressure that was pushing down on them, bringing them near to collapse.

The doctor said I'd be out for three weeks. But the doctor didn't know me and my stubborn inaneness.

For a week I slept in Mom and Dad's guest room, working on my senior. Even though I was a junior athletically, the combined inac- tive gray and redshirt years allowed me to be well ahead of schedule to graduate before my NCAA eligibility expired.

One week is all I'd sit out, not wanting to let my teammates down. Mom wasn't happy, but she acknowledged by this point that I was a twenty-two-year-old man and could make my own choices. "Just be careful," she said, as though I was running around with a pair of scissors, not a broken windpipe.

I walked into the locker room and gave all my teammates a hug. The next game up was against BYU in Provo. Slobodan Ocokoljic ended up sitting out with the flu, while I played with a punctured windpipe. The game was close at first, but thanks to me and a couple of bonehead turnovers early in the second half, BYU pulled away. I should not have come back so soon. I was seeing stars for most of the game, and I recall it only as a blur.

I mostly remember just getting a whole lot of elbow in my throat and face from their starting center, Rafael Araújo. Now, don't get me wrong: Haffa, as he is called, has a decent shooting touch and runs the floor very well for his size. But he got away with some pretty dirty stuff because he was a star and the Mountain West Conference was banking on him being an NBA draft pick. In fact, they let him get away with murder.*

Araújo was allowed to camp in the key and just stand there. It was their home court and their officials. To my frustration, and apparently unnoticed by the officials, Araújo would seal me above him and wait in the key for a lob to be thrown to him, placing his forearm in my throat, giving me an all-too-close view of his many charming tattoos, most of them of Japanese markings; I'm sure he had no clue as to what they meant but thought they looked pretty. He would then push against my throat, catch the pass, score the layup, and run back down to the other end, pounding his chest in a fit of excited 'roid rage as the BYU faithful cheered and the angels of heaven blew their trumpets. Hooray, Jesus!

The next day in practice Coach Cravens had us sit down in the film room and drew up a stat on the board: "33–1."

"What is this, Lance?" he asked.

I shrugged.

"This is how many minutes you played," he said, pointing to the *33*. "This is how many rebounds you had." He pointed to the *1*. He then punched the whiteboard and spoke a few unkind words, after which he announced I'd be coming off the bench and would no longer be starting. I sat there and didn't say a word. I could've whined about how I was playing in pain, but I never want to be that guy. So much for trying to come back early with a broken windpipe. I should've stayed in bed like Slobodan.

No one likes a hero.

If you want the glory, you have to be ready to accept the blame.

That January, the University of Utah came up to play us. As I walked into the Dee, luck had it that Coach Majerus and I would cross paths, alone, in an empty hallway.

"Hello, Coach."

*I must admit that I'm mostly picking on Haffa because of the institution he played for—Brigham Young University. No alcohol, shorts above the knees, premarital sex, or tattoos allowed, unless of course you're an athlete. BYU loves their athletes, and they love being Team *Jesus*, displaying their talent for all the world, showing all how the Lord has blessed them, even if that means compromising their values and standards, allowing athletes such as Rafael Araújo, who is covered in tats, to represent them. It's safe to say that the BYU athletics program is a living enactment of hypocrisy that would make even Billy Graham scratch his head in bewilderment.

"Hello, Lance."

The game came and I wasn't starting, as Cravens feared I'd try to do too much. Utah jumped out to an early 12–4 lead before Coach put me in. A few of my old teammates at Utah—Nick Jacobson, Tim Frost, and "Big Red" Chris Jackson—greeted me as I stepped onto the floor. My first bucket was a three-pointer from the top, one that Majerus would never have allowed me to shoot and furthermore didn't believe I could shoot. I ended with ten points at the half, and we were down by only four. The second half, Utah's defense shifted priorities and I was no longer so free to score. It was a hard-fought game, but when the Utes got a lead, it was hard to crack it. They slammed on the brakes to slow down the game and wear the clock thin, limiting our opportunities to catch up the score.

When it was over, my old teammates at Utah gave me a hug and congratulated me on the good game. Eric Jackson and Scott Garson were all there at the end to pat me on the back, and Coach Rupp hugged me and told me he was proud of me. I quickly walked off the floor. Majerus shook no hands.

I went to my locker and cried—mostly out of relief. It was over. My ghosts were silenced.

When I came out of the locker room, Dad and Mom were talking with Chris Jackson's parents.

"Lance! Great game! I didn't know you could shoot like that. You do so many things!" Mr. Jackson said, barely concealing his amazement.

I smiled. "There are a lot of things I can do, I just wasn't allowed to do them."

He gave me a knowing smile and shook my hand good-bye.

Two days later I was told that Gordon Monson, the *Salt Lake Tribune* sportswriter who had wanted to interview me when I was playing for Majerus, wanted to do an interview with me. And this time my coach wouldn't be saying no to block the interview.

But I was nervous. I was terrified of the long-term ramifications that telling my story would have, not only on me, but on my family, as Mom and Tara were still in school at the U. I called Dad and told him the situation.

"What should I do, Dad?"

"What do you think you should do?"

"Well, I'm happy now. I've moved on, and I have a nice life here in Ogden. So I don't know if there's really any point in telling my story anymore. I don't want to ruin anything for the family."

Dad asked one more question, and it was all I needed.

"Lance," he said, and then paused. "What do you think is the right thing to do?"

Two hours before practice, I walked into the Dee and met Gordon Monson for the first time: "Gordon Monson, the man who ruined my life. Nice to finally meet you."

He gave me a confused look, and when we were at last alone in the Wildcat club room, he sat down and took out his pad and pen. "OK, well, first things first: What do you mean, I 'ruined' your life?" he asked worriedly.

I laughed. "When you wanted to interview me two years ago, Majerus answered for me and told me I could not."

"I was told you declined the interview."

"Nope. Coach answered for me, and for some reason decided to make my life hell after that."

Gordon smiled and said, "Well, I apologize. Please know that wasn't my intention."

I then told Gordon my story. I told him of the verbal abuse; of the day, January 6, 2002, my mother's birthday; the practice in the Saint Mary's gym in California, where Majerus called me a disgrace to cripples. Gordon was blown away by the material I was giving him. "Lance, is there anyone, anyone at all, that can confirm these allegations?"

I gave him the names of friends and teammates who were there, who I knew would confirm my story, either because they, too, wanted to see the truth come out, or simply because they were good people who wouldn't tell a lie.

On Friday, January 18, 2004, while I was in Bozeman, Montana, where we were to play Montana State, Mom and Dad woke me up at my hotel to tell me that I was not only on the front page of the sports section of the *Salt Lake Tribune,* but on the front page of the entire paper as well. Apparently the talk-radio shows were being bombarded with phone calls while I was out of town, many questioning me or outright denouncing me as a liar. Gordon Monson, at the time of the printing, wrote that two former teammates of mine confirmed the story. But later that day he received confirming phone calls from other former teammates who wished to remain anonymous.

When asked on television about the chaos he had created, Gordon simply stated, "I could go on and on about the anonymous confirmations, but I have been doing this long enough to know when someone is lying to me, and Lance Allred wasn't a liar on that day."

Ten days later, Majerus resigned from the University of Utah. Due to health reasons.

Telling my story was the right thing to do. But right isn't always popular. Even now, when I walk onto the Utah campus to visit the library that I love, people will give me a stare. I have even been confronted at times: "You have a lot of nerve showing up here" or "Are you happy with what you did?" I could get defensive or engage in a debate with them, but how could I truly hold a grudge against them for speaking on an issue that they have no true concept of? I may as well be angry at a five-year-old for not understanding the impact of Maximilien Robespierre and the irony of the Ninth of Thermidor in the French Revolution.

Telling the truth was the right thing to do. Maybe not the popular thing, but the right thing, regardless of the effect it had on next season's win/loss column.

Coach Rupp assumed head coaching duties after Majerus resigned, and he led Utah to the NCAA tournament after winning the Mountain West Conference Tournament, something Majerus never did. When the season was over and Utah was looking for a new coach, Coach Rupp wasn't considered for the job, against the voices of his players. Majerus liked to tell people that Coach Rupp couldn't recruit—even though Coach Rupp was the one that flew to Australia and got Andrew Bogut to commit to Utah. To this day, Coach Rupp and Bogut are friends. Majerus and Bogut are not.

When the newly hired coach, Ray Giacoletti, came to Utah, he didn't ask Coach Rupp to stay, not wanting any tension or imagined competition for the job. He feared that the loyalty the Utah players had for Coach Rupp would not work in his favor, and so Coach Rupp had to find work elsewhere.

Coach Cravens continued on at Weber, unfazed by all the hoopla. We were finally able to right the ship toward the end of our season, winning our last seven games in conference, until we fell to Eastern Washington in the conference tournament semifinals. Seeing that the Big Sky was a small conference, the only way a team was going to earn a spot at the NCAA tournament was by winning the conference tournament. At-large bids are not an option.

The season was over, and I was now prepared to assume the leadership role as a senior. I gained thirty pounds that off-season, wanting to give myself the best possible senior year. And I got it.

21

Before my senior year started, I decided to tag along with my friend Josh Lund one summer and volunteer at a weeklong muscular-dystrophy camp. Each camper was paired with a counselor. There were two campers assigned to each two-bed room, while the volunteers slept on the floor.

I was afraid that while I was sleeping I wouldn't hear my camper in the middle of the night if he needed assistance, and so I wanted Josh, who understood my hearing impairment, to be with me. He was happy to arrange it so that he and I would be roommates, as he had enough clout with the higher-ups to arrange it. Plus, he was dating a girl who could make the switch. Yes, there are politics even at MDA—Muscular Dystrophy Association—camp.

I had a camper named J.D., who was confined to a wheelchair. A very somber and quiet kid, J.D. was interested in Lord of the Rings, Dungeons & Dragons, and other various board games. He wasn't the biggest socialite and neither was I, so we did well together. Josh, on the other hand, had a camper named Abram, who was eighteen and who, because of age limitations, would be making this his last camp experience.

Abram thus used the week to his fullest potential, squeezing every ounce of socializing that he could from any situation. His main MO was to take his stereo out into the hall during our long afternoon breaks and listen to Depeche Mode, setting a little trap that would create conversation with anyone who walked by. Josh, meanwhile, would sit beside him, saying nary a word. It was, during these breaks that I'd take a nap as J.D. happily watched TV. It became a routine, and on most days, while Abram was organizing his playlist of songs for that day's hall mingling, I would turn to J.D. and ask, "J.D., what do you want to do? Watch TV?" J.D. would grunt, "Yeah," and then I'd give a silent fist pump in relief, hand him the remote, and lay myself down to sleep.

Despite nap time, camp was hard work. Josh and I had to wake up early to take a shower and then give our campers showers and get them ready for the day. And, concerned about not being able to hear J.D. at night while I was asleep on the floor, I had the brilliant idea of tying a string from J.D.'s hand to mine before we got ready for bed; I figured that that way, I'd be awakened if he needed my assistance. The system didn't last very long. Either the string would break or J.D. wouldn't give a strong enough pull on my arm. Either way, I'd be awakened in the middle of the night by Josh turning on the light as he stood over J.D. The first few times, I'd get up and put my hearing aids in while J.D. would mumble something incoherently. I had no idea what he was trying to say and neither did Josh, and so our default response was just to roll him over on his other side so he wouldn't get bedsores. That usually did the trick. Eventually, after J.D. had cried wolf a number of times, I'd sit up when Josh turned the light on and ask, "J.D., are you OK?" And before he could whimper a response, I'd say, "OK, cool," and lie back down, leaving Josh to attend to my camper. I essentially was asking Josh to pull a triple shift at nighttime and to be a volunteer not only for his assigned camper but for J.D. as well—and, furthermore, for me. Josh Lund, my little soldier.

Abram had an assistance dog named Icon. Icon was a well-trained dog, stoic like a German housewife, always on guard. But all I had to do was say, "Oh ya boo! Oh ya boo boo, doo doo!" and Icon, like a guard at Buckingham palace, would do his best not to show emotion— in his case, not wag his tail. But every time, I'd get him: his tail would lightly twitch. And Abram, feeling his dominion over his dog threatened, and appalled that anyone could trump his authority, would shout, "No, Icon." A shamed look would come over Icon's face as he returned to attention. At the end of the day Abram would let Icon off duty and the yellow lab would jump up on my bed and cuddle with me while I scratched his feet, which he loved. The love triangle reached its greatest degree of tension when Icon chose to sleep with me rather than on his assigned blanket.

Along with charitable events such as MDA camp come pretty girls. There were lots of them. Often when J.D. and I were out and about at the zoo or the atrium and pretty girls were walking by with their female campers, I'd say to J.D., "OK, bud, help me look good." J.D. knew his role. I'd pull out some sunscreen and dot a little on his nose, and when I finished I'd give J.D. a little pinch on his cheek and then casually look up, like what I had done was no big thing, like I was hoping no one had noticed how altruistic I was being. But of course I wasn't hoping that at all. I was cheating at solitaire. In a setting where it wasn't about me but about my camper, I proved to myself that true altruism isn't possible.

Even if a volunteer isn't there to impress members of the opposite sex or gain praise, there are some people who put their volunteer work with the MDA or other societies on their résumés, which defeats the purpose. And there are some who keep their deeds entirely secret. But even those who don't put their deeds on their résumés, like my friend Josh, still feel the intrinsic reward of knowing they did something good, something charitable, something selfless. Now, does that warm, fuzzy feeling they get when they recall their good, altruistic deeds rob those deeds of any altruism in some way, seeing as how those folks are rewarding themselves with a boost of self-worth?

The argument about whether altruism is possible is synonymous with the question of whether it's possible to be a selfless Christian. Even if we're silent in our charitable deeds, are we not, as Christians, still hoping that God is watching us and that he will reward us, thus making our actions indeed selfish? I believe there's a God who loves me, but I don't plan on that making a difference. I don't plan on being rewarded in heaven, as I feel this helps my deeds be more altruistic. Planning on a heaven leads to expectations, and expectations lead to a sense of entitlement.

Charity and altruism come with a catch–22. Whether you have a deck of cards that you're memorizing before you play, like my father, or you're blindly convincing yourself that you're indeed being totally altruistic—either way, we're always cheating at solitaire.

Having graduated at the end of my junior season and having received Academic All-America honors, I decided that after all that hard work, with an athletic year to spare, I was going to take pass/fail courses with those of my favorite professors who knew of my situation.

The season was under way. I was in good shape and feeling good about the direction things were going. But then I received one of the stupidest, most painful injuries of my life.

We were two weeks into the season, preparing for our first game against Utah Valley State, and Coach Hunsaker, now with the Wolverines. The game was three days away, and before practice I decided to get in a lift in the weight facility. I was doing bench presses, and when I had completed them I began stripping the platges off the bar. I reached for the last plate on the bar, a forty-five-pounder, and began sliding it off. But stopped in the process, leaving the plate on the bar, to wipe away a drop of sweat that was close to landing in my hearing aid. Seeing as how hearing aids are so valuable, I protect them whenever I feel sweat or water coming near them. Thing is, the plate came off the bar.

It fell four feet and thudded, standing upright, onto my big toe. It remained there for a split second before tilting off of my foot and plopping onto the ground. I stood there in complete shock. The wave of pain was so strong that it actually didn't register up to my brain, instead sending me into shock. Your toes and fingers are a rich source of nerve endings, and the signal to my brain, alerting it of pain, crashed from the huge flux of data. Quicker than I have ever seen before, sweat started to form around my hair and brow and just poured down my face.

I looked around to see if anyone had seen my ridiculous error. The weight room was empty. (It's amazing how my impulse to make sure I had not embarrassed myself trumped my impulse to ask for help.)

I took a step over to a bench to have a seat, but my foot wouldn't fire. The muscles were in total shutdown. I instead hopped over to the bench on one leg and untied my shoe. When I pulled my foot out, my sock was already red and dripping with blood. I pulled off my sock to see that my big toe looked like a waffle. The weight plate had not landed on the toenail, but just beneath it, at the joint. The blow of the landing had created so much pressure that it had forced the entire nail, including the nail bed, to erupt out of its place, tearing through the flesh around it. I grabbed the base of the big toe and squeezed the life out of it. I didn't move for ten minutes. I just sat there, choking the life out of my toe until it was blue with lack of blood. The flowing stream had stopped, and instead, a clear, yellowish ooze began to pour from the nail bed.

Coach Hohn finally came in and saw me sitting down. He walked over, about to ask why I had stopped working, but then went white upon seeing all the blood. "What the hell did you do?"

"Oh . . . I just dropped the plate on my toe," I said matter-of-factly.

He went across the lot to get a trainer, who came in and awkwardly dabbed at my toe and bandaged it with gauze. I then hopped across the parking lot toward the training room, where I lay on the ground and propped my foot up against the trainer counter, sighing at the release of pressure. I was still in shock, but trust me, I still felt pain. So much pain that I was high and woozy. I drifted in and out of consciousness as people came and went from the training room, looking over at me and wondering what on earth I was doing lying in the middle of the floor, taking up all that space. I waited for a half hour for Joel Bass to get to the training room.

Joel was a hard-ass. He was as rustic and hardened as they come. But he is squeamish around blood, which is odd for an athletic trainer. When he came into the room, he dropped his equipment bag, short breath, and walked over to me.

"What the hell did you do?"

Sounding drunk, and using a lot of hand gestures, I slurred out as best as I could the story of what had happened.

Joel had me get up on the counter, where he hesitantly unwrapped the initial gauze job, tilting his head away as though he was changing a dirty diaper. He kept one eye on the toe as he faced the wall, talking to another person to help him deal with the crisis. He dried and dabbed my toe as though it were diseased.

He called the team doctor, who recommended a hand surgeon. But the surgeon was currently in surgery, and so I had to wait. Why I was seeing a hand surgeon and not a foot surgeon is call for speculation, but the hand surgeon was a specialist in repairing damaged nail beds, and what does it matter whether it's a big toe or an index finger you're repairing in the grand scheme of things? While I was waiting for him to be available, I had to go get the toe X-rayed.

When I stood up to walk to my car, the pressure all went back down to my foot, and I nearly began to cry right there in the training room. But I wasn't going to cry in front of all the pretty female athletes. I quickly limped out of the room, leaving a trail of bloody toe prints on the carpet and in the hallway, thanks to the ooze from the cowardly, half-assed taping job that Joel had given me.

Thankfully, the plate had landed on my left foot, so I could still drive, pushing gas and brake pedals with ease. A pool of blood formed on the floorboard beneath the gas pedal as I zoomed over to the hospital. I walked in with only one shoe on, my bare foot sloshing blood with each step. The receptionist at the desk gave me a look that said *We don't serve your kind here* as she forced a smile. She pointed me to an office, where I was quickly serviced with an X-ray. I was sitting in the office, keeping my foot up, pinching the arch as hard as I could, when the radiologist walked in with a pitying smile.

"You did quite a number on yourself," he said as he pulled up the X-ray. "You made mashed potatoes." He showed me where I had broken the bone in my big toe in two separate places.

All I could think about was the season.

"How long am I going to be out?"

"These take some time to heal. But it's all up to you really, and how much pain you can tolerate." He was a good doctor, allowing me to envision my own timetable. He knew I was nuts and had a high threshold for pain, as I had just driven myself to the hospital. The booster part of the doctor knew I was the team's senior and returning leader in scoring and rebounding, and he was thinking about Weber State, not just me.

He continued: "The thing we have to ensure is that the bone does not get infected. The skin that you have ripped and torn around your nail bed is so close to the bone that it runs a high risk of infection. And if your bone does catch infection, then we're looking at a six-month absence." He was very stern about this, and I filed the information in my head.

I sloshed out of the office, following my bloody footprints back out of the hospital. Two hours later it was time to go back to the hospital and meet the surgeon. Opting for a local anesthetic, I gracefully handled the large needles of Novocain squeaking in and between the joints of my toe. Metal sliding through the cartilage of your joint isn't a pleasant feeling.

He asked me if I wanted to repair the nail bed or remove it entirely. Looking back, I wish I had asked him to remove it entirely. But the vanity in me couldn't imagine my having a nailless big toe, and so I asked him to repair it. He warned me that it would most likely grow back mutated and defective, which it did, and to this day it irritates my foot when I play. Why do we even have toenails? Can anyone really say? If evolution is a true concept, then by now—given our present-day dependence on shoes—the human race should've evolved to the point where toenails no longer exist. The only thing toenails are good for, for me at least, is pain and discomfort. I've lost count of the many toenails of mine that have been mangled by people stepping on them. I often contemplate having surgery to have all my toenails removed. No kidding.

The doctor took the nail bed and sewed it back in. He then clipped off what used to be my toenail and made a little shield with it to protect the damaged skin. He took the flaps of torn skin that were still salvageable and wrapped them around the nail shield to keep it down. Yes, I'm trying to gross you out.

I went home to Salt Lake City that night and slept. I woke up on Mom and Dad's couch in the middle of the night screaming, as the local anesthetic had worn off and my body was no longer in shock. That was the rawest, most cruel pain I have ever felt, yet it was superficial pain. What is a broken toe and nail in the grand scheme of things? Nothing— but man, does it hurt! I couldn't put my toe in ice water, which is my favorite painkiller: the stitches couldn't get wet, lest they come loose and carry bacteria down beneath the skin, increasing the risk of the real worry, which was infection to the bone. I had to make do with a bag of cold vegetables, which hurt because of their weight on the toe. It was just miserable.

A week later, I laced up my shoes and walked onto the floor of the Dee Events Center, ready to play Southern Utah. A week into an estimated six-week timetable of recovery, I was back out on the court. People have called me a lot of things and will continue to do so, but no one who knows me can call me soft. Crazy maybe, but not soft.

I had eighteen points and seventeen rebounds that night, but to no avail, as we lost. It was a hard and humiliating defeat. Coach Cravens came into the locker room and chucked a whiteboard eraser to the back of the locker room, near Danko Barisic, who, having grown up in what is no longer Yugoslavia, instinctively flinched and covered his head. Yet the terrified look on Danko's face said he was anything but war-hardened.

By late December, we were on a terrible losing streak. The only bright spot at the time was the national attention I was getting for leading the NCAA in rebounding. Andrew Bogut, who was at my former school, the University of Utah, and I put on an interesting show for the world to see. Throughout the season Bogut and I battled for the national rebounding title, going back and forth in a seesawing race. When we played head-to-head I came in with twenty and he had twenty-two. But he had seventeen rebounds that game and I had only seven. It was a pretty frustrating game, as their team scouted us well and knew we always sent two guards back on defense immediately when the shot was taken. So his teammates at the guard spots would come and block me out on either side, and Bogut chased down the rebound. I was inclined to dislike Bogut, but I knew he and Coach Rupp had a good relationship. If he was a friend of Rupp's, he was a friend of mine.

How often does the basketball world get to see two big men, at universities only a half hour from one another, battling for an NCAA rebounding title? Not often. It was a special year.

As the regular season ended, I held the rebounding title at 12.4 rebounds per game. We had pulled off a great turnaround at the end of the season, winning our last seven conference games.

The next game, my second to last, was against tournament host Portland State. I got into quick foul trouble with two terrible calls. Terrible. I have the film to prove it. I was sent to the bench in the first two minutes of the game, where I sat and watched as my team destroyed Portland State. I ended up with three rebounds that game, and played only a few minutes. Coach and I agreed it was best that I sit out and watch, to spare my energy for the championship game the next day. For the sake of my team, hoping to better our chances of winning the tournament, I risked my rebounding title.

I lost both.

We played the University of Montana in the championship game. It was televised nationally on ESPN. We came out strong and led at halftime by ten, by which time I had also secured my twenty-first double-double of the season, with twelve points and ten rebounds at the half.

We lost by two. Jamaal Jenkins missed a last-chance Hail Mary from thirty-five feet out. I finished with twenty-four and twelve in my final collegiate game.

I went into the locker room and sobbed. My collegiate career was now over. Six long years. I was twenty-four years old.

I loved my teammates at Weber. But I was also glad to move on. Six long years of collegiate basketball, with coaches monitoring my actions 24/7, holding my hand and walking me to class, evaluating and judging everything I did, giving their two cents on each and every issue, whether I asked for it or not.

But I also knew that with it I'd be losing that camaraderie in the locker room, that rapport with my teammates. Since then, I have traveled around the globe with no team or home to call my own.

Many of the locker rooms I have occupied since college have been empty and cold. They can be like morgues, rusty, dripping faucets making the only noise as we all lace our shoes up in silence, with nothing to talk of or share other than the common denominator of money. No longer would I be laughing and mocking the coaches and those on the outside looking into the locker room. No longer would I be posting pictures of look-alike celebrities above the lockers of my teammates. No longer would I arm-wrestle on the floor as teammates wagered bets. No longer would I smile with my friends and peers—a team of men who committed and sacrificed for a game they love, without hope of pay or financial reward. Money didn't talk in that locker at Weber. Only we talked.

The locker room, as I was warned so many times, is what I miss the most of my college days. We thought we were men, and we were, but we were also innocent.

22

The last month of my senior season, I was flooded with phone calls from agents looking to represent me. I ultimately went with an agent out of San Francisco- Dave.

Dave flew me out to Southern California to work with a personal trainer to help prepare me for the Portsmouth Invitational Tournament, which was the first of two NBA pre-draft camps. Portsmouth was for seniors only, those who had completed their collegiate careers. Sixty-eight players were invited. I was glad to be invited, but at the same time I had hoped to skip over the tournament and just attend the Chicago pre-draft camp, which was much more prestigious and more likely to further a player's chances of being selected in the draft.

Portsmouth was a "damned if you do, damned if you don't" situation. When you're invited to Portsmouth, it means you're not a lock to be drafted but are at least considered to be a prospect, though not a high enough prospect for the Orlando and Chicago pre-draft camps. If you chose not to attend Portsmouth, it told the scouts that either you thought you were better than you were or you were afraid: both were bad impressions.

Dave recommended I put on some weight for Portsmouth that I had lost throughout the course of the season. I fired up the Lance Weight Gain 2004 program once again, and after two weeks with my trainer, Andre, I bloated up from 255 to 275.

This was a mistake. While I was doing strength and conditioning drills with Andre, I wasn't playing a lot of basketball. And the best way to get in basketball shape is to just play a lot of basketball. I showed up at Portsmouth a burly and cut 275, but it was the first time I had played a full-court game since losing to Montana a month earlier. Two trips down the court and I was winded, unused to the extra weight. What good was I as a rebounder if I couldn't even get to the other end of the floor?

Rather than hunting my shots, I tried to be a good team player and move the ball around and defend as well as I could. I ended with five points and seven rebounds in sixteen minutes in that first game. The scouts were not impressed. I wasn't athletic enough or talented enough, they said.

My second game was even worse.

Portsmouth is a catch-22. If you're athletic and hog the ball and try to dazzle your way out of the gym, the scouts will pass you off as not being a team player. If you try to play it simple and pass it, and get your teammates involved, the scouts will pass you off as not athletic or talented enough. For a guy like me, who has been well coached on how to properly play basketball, I need structure. I play team basketball. I'm not a baller. I'm not a track star. I'm merely a basketball player—nothing more, nothing less.

Portsmouth was a setting where they just threw the ball out and told us to play, structure be damned. I wasn't going to outjump anyone. But if you give me smart teammates in a structured format, I'm the antithesis of pickup ball. At Portsmouth I was thrown into an environment that I had not been groomed for, and I paid the price for it. Only one senior who attended Portsmouth was drafted: Jason Maxiell, by the Detroit Pistons. Out of a total of sixty-eight who attended Portsmouth that year, one senior was drafted. It was an exercise in futility.

It was an uphill battle coming from the Big Sky Conference, where, I was continually reminded by the scouts, I had been playing with poor competition. In the eyes of many at Portsmouth, I was just another Mormon boy who had done well in a small-time conference; I had reached my potential and could grow no more, as my ceiling of talent stretched only so high.

Basketball is a business of first impressions. If you go to a restaurant and are unimpressed with it, you'll be hesitant to give it a second look. And when an assessment, especially a negative one, has been made about you, you have to go through hell and high water to overcome it. There are millions of people in the world who want to play basketball. With so much ground to cover, GMs and scouts rarely have the time to give people second looks, especially if they were not impressed the first time. Their job is to find the next superstar, and if someone beats them to it or finds that diamond in the rough they may have overlooked, they will have to answer to their team owner. It's a cutthroat, survivalist league, where loyalty comes second to self-preservation.

I was now a vagabond. As much as I wanted to cling to the hope that I could still make it to the Chicago pre-draft camp and redeem myself, and possibly still be drafted, instinct told me that I was done for and I was in for a long road ahead.

Ending up in third for the national rebounding title earned me the right to have one pre-draft workout with an NBA team. And it was with the Utah Jazz. I was thrilled. I had watched Utah Jazz games since I first moved to Utah as a kid. Growing up in the Stockton and Malone era, I saw how basketball was supposed to be played. I experienced the pain and disappointment of the playoffs for so many years. I cried when the Jazz lost to Houston in '95, when it was supposed to be "our year," after Jordan had retired, or so we thought. I watched as Jordan came back and ruined the party, two years in a row: in '97 and '98. I loved the Jazz, and I was ecstatic for the opportunity to meet Coach Sloan.

I was scheduled to work out with Charlie Villanueva and P.J. I knew Villanueva from watching him play for UConn, but I had no idea who P.J. was. I did some research on him and saw that as a senior he had played in NAIA Division II and averaged something like twenty points and seven rebounds. I also saw that he had a shady past, with a criminal record, but I'm not writing this to crucify him. I mention this only as I thought that there was no way the Jazz—and Jerry Sloan, with his no-nonsense attitude—would really be interested in a guy with such a past.

Coach Sloan came out with his head assistant, Phil Johnson, who came up to me, shook my hand, and said, "You had a nice career up there." Back in the late 1960s, Johnson had coached Weber State.

"You too," I remarked.

Practice began, and Ty "the Milkman" Corbin, one of my all-time favorite supporting cast members in the Stockton-Malone era, led the workout. All things considered, I had a great workout. I shot the ball well, completed the drills in time, and did everything they asked me to do. When I completed the last conditioning drill in good time, I went over to the garbage can and threw up. Nerves.

After having been deceived by Majerus, I always swore I'd never get starstruck again. But I did with Coach Sloan. This was a different case, though. He never gave me the illusion that he was anything but grouchy and demanding. What you saw with Coach Sloan is what you got.

The media came out onto the floor, and I gave an interview with many familiar faces of the media that had covered me throughout my college career. They asked me what I expected would happen or where I expected to go. I had no clue.

"I'm not a freak. I'm not the type of player you spend a draft pick on. I'm the type that will make a team through the back door, so to speak. Wherever I go, you'll see me again," I told them, with as much confidence as I could muster. But I was lying. I was terrified.

I then had an interview with the Jazz front office, with Coach Sloan and his staff sitting in on the meeting.

When I sat down they asked me, "Why should the Jazz draft Lance Allred?"

I sat there for a moment, and then said, "Lots of reasons. One, I'm the hometown kid that everyone knows. That Mormon boy they have watched grow and develop since he was just a teenager. Two,"—I turned to Coach Sloan—"... no one will work harder than me. People may work as hard as me, but no will ever work harder than me. Coach Sloan, if I may be so blunt, I'm your archetype player. This meeting alone means so much to me. That I get to sit here . . ." I began to choke up.

I felt it had been a great interview, and I walked away proud, knowing I did the best I possibly could.

Draft night came, and some friends held a barbecue at their place to watch it. I really didn't want to go. I wanted to be far away. But I went, and Mom and Dad and all of my friends gathered. I watched Andrew Bogut selected first in the draft. The Jazz took Deron Williams at three. Charlie Villanueva went to Toronto at number eight. And then I watched as the Jazz took P.J. in the second round.

I was heartbroken. I sat there graciously as all of my loved ones, unsure if I wanted their sympathy, sat and idled for a while and then slowly began to trickle out. I wanted to just get up and leave, and drive far, far away. I didn't want anyone to see how bad it hurt. Instead I had to sit there stoically until it was finally time for me to leave. I thanked my friends, went out to my car, and wept. I cried at the wheel for two hours.

Why were all of these kids being rewarded for their talent and potential and not their production, when I had produced? Why were all of these terrible European kids with stat lines resembling a final soccer score being given all of this free money?

I had no answers to these questions, and Dave couldn't give me any.

As I had my entire life, I tried to objectively and logically understand it all. But I couldn't, because there's no objectivity to it. It's an arbitrary process. The more I tried to understand, the more it hurt as I sat there in my beat-up old Nissan, which I now knew I'd be keeping much longer than I had been expecting. As I tried to evaluate what had happened, logic could find me no answers. It led only to more pain. The only thing I could make of it was the doubt creeping in my mind, telling me I was of very little worth. I was a basketball player, and not a desired one. If I wasn't a basketball player who was valued, what was I?

Looking back now, I see and understand so much of the draft process that I didn't then. What is talent? What is potential? These are relative terms that are completely at the behest of the beholder.

At that time, I didn't understand that European kids are often drafted by an NBA team that does not have any roster space. They draft the young European kid knowing they will maintain his rights while he stays overseas and continues to play and develop; hopefully a few years down the road the kid may be able to come to the NBA ready to help, when the team has need of him. Whereas, if they take an American college player in the first round, they're obligated to give said kid guaranteed money. While they're not required to pay an American kid if they draft him in the second round, if they choose to keep his rights they don't have as much control over his development overseas as they do with a European kid. Economics.

I couldn't see at the time that it was all economics; I could see only that it was personal, and I wasn't valued as much as these other players.

I'm one of thousands that have come and gone, suffering the cold shoulder of the NBA. I was no exception. There were others in my class, hundreds before and since, just as good as or better than me, who, too, were at the raw end of the deal.

Most of it, just as life, is luck and timing. Many of my teammates will tell you it was simply their time, when they were fortunate enough to be drafted or to sign to a lucrative contract. Aside from the obvious superstars, there's such a thin, fine line that divides a man from being a reserve player on an NBA team and being a star in the Development League. The line is nearly invisible, if it isn't entirely. Timing—being in the right place at the right time—determines to such a great extent who will reap what they have sown.

When the lights and glamour of the draft die down and the night is done, the race is still on. The draft isn't a finish line; it's simply a dog-and-pony show. And anyone else who sits in an NBA locker will tell you the same.

I sat in my car until 2 a.m., and then went to my old church gym and laced up my shoes.

A week later, I was invited to an NBA summer camp, which is where several teams gather in a setting to play their teams of young players, draft picks, or free agents so that they can evaluate what they have. I joined the L.A. Clippers, who kept true to their word when they said if I averaged ten rebounds a game my senior year, they'd invite me to their camp.

I was nervous and worried up till the time I arrived in Las Vegas. Rory White, Mike Dunleavy's assistant, was the summer coach. He liked me and was very complimentary of my efforts. He even pulled me aside one day and said, "You're doing such a great job with your attitude and your effort. And I'm hesitant to tell you this, because I can't guarantee you anything, but people have been asking around about you."

I was playing behind Chris Kaman, their center out of central Michigan that they drafted the year before. Chris Kaman is a heck of player. I'm a big fan of his. I appreciate it when a big man can score with either hand, which is a rarity these days. Chris has it mastered to an art. I actually spent time in college watching film of him, just to study how he did what he did to get drafted.

Chris played most of the game, and I'd come in and give him a breather. The Clippers were investing a lot of money in him, and so they were going to see him develop as much as he could before next season. I wasn't high on their priorities. But they all complimented me on how I made the best use of the time I was given. In one game against Sacramento, I scored six points in four *seconds.* Top that.

When camp was over, I shook hands with the coaches and they congratulated me on a job well done, but they all had a look in their eye that sadly said, "Good luck. Your place isn't here with us, but may you find fortune elsewhere."

I flew home that day with no regret. I had very little hope that I'd get a call from the Clippers inviting me to fall preseason camp. I knew that playing in Europe was a foregone conclusion. But I wasn't worried. Let's not forget, I'm a European history major. I love that stuff!

Part Four

Vagabond

23

"Lance?" the deep voice asked over the phone.

"Yes."

"John Greig, man."

"Oh, hi. What's going on?"

John Greig was Jermain Boyette's agent, and Boyette was the senior who led Weber to an undefeated year in conference play during my red-shirt year in '03. Coach Cravens and John Greig had a long-standing relationship and considered each other good friends. Coach had held John off from contacting me about representation when John wanted to do so during my junior year.

When Coach Cravens finally let John in on the race for me, he was well behind, as I was already picking out my selection of suitors. Seeing that he came in so late, and not knowing the full story about how Coach Cravens had respectfully asked him to hold off, I never gave John ample time to recruit me, believing that Dave had been the first to want to work with me.

At Portsmouth, John had introduced himself to me and my dad. And at the Vegas summer camp, while I was with the Clippers, John came up to me toward the end and once again just checked on me and congratulated me. And now, two weeks later, here I was on the phone with him.

"Just calling to check on you. Coach Cravens asked me to look in on your situation and see how things were going. What's the word? What are you hearing?"

"Nothing."

"Nothing?"

"Nothing at all."

"You haven't had any offers yet overseas?"

"No."

"You're kidding!"

"No."

"Wow."

"I know. I'm close to firing Dave. We don't communicate well. But I'm afraid of a lawsuit."

"What are you talking about?" John asked, befuddled.

"I don't want to go through a lawsuit if I fire Dave."

"What?! It doesn't work like that. All you do is mail him a ten-day termination notice, and after that it's done with. People fire agents all the time."

"Oh. OK."

John told me what I needed to do, but he also took the reigns that day and began making phone calls to Italy, where he himself had played and where he had a good rapport.

I called Dave and fired him, at which point he confessed, without much remorse, "Well, I have to admit, this is a weight off of my shoulders." It was best for both of us.

John Greig called me the next day with options.

When you call John Greig and get his voice mail, you're greeted with a low, deep voice saying, "Hello and thank you for calling Sports Talent." An image of a disc jockey for a soft-jazz radio station, solitarily sitting in a dark, smoky room, as a half-burned cigarette smolders in an ashtray, comes to mind. On his résumé John Greig notes that he has worked in the record industry, producing Kenny G. How cool is that?* He sounds mean and black. In fact, many people mistake his race. John was hired to play for a club in France, and when he arrived and they saw that he was white, they sent him home. John Greig has lost many potential clients because they thought he was black, me being one of them. I didn't give him a chance at first because I thought he was black and was afraid I might not have enough things in common with a black agent. I didn't know if he would be relatable. Conversely, because of this prejudicial folly he has won some clients who otherwise might never have considered him in the first place. When John finally showed up to meet Jermaine Boyette in Gary, Indiana, Jermaine's father asked where John Greig was and why he had sent his assistant.

When you finally meet John, the voice does not match the man, as you see a gangly six-foot-nine white guy who wears Jordans with his cargo shorts and polo shirt, with some midcalf socks to seal the deal.

---

*And John is now a literary agent, thanks to yours truly.

Sometimes he will be wearing denim shorts instead of khaki. He drives a Ford F-250 as he listens to country music while driving his black clients around.

Currently based out of Seattle, John Greig grew up in Oregon and played at the U of O before joining the Seattle Supersonics in the early eighties and then finishing his career overseas, playing in Switzerland, France, and Italy. Being well traveled gives him a foot up on so many other agents, as he knows the tricks of the trade on both sides of the pond. He knows the markets of all the countries, and the budgets of the clubs within those countries. He knows his stuff.

John Greig is as smooth a talker as they come; he could sell ice to an Eskimo. But what he has that most agents don't is brutal honesty. When he told me, when I was narrowing down my list of agents, that I had very little chance of being drafted, I checked him off as someone who had little faith in me. He really was just being honest. John hated it when, in his days as a player, his agents would get his hopes up on jobs or salaries that were mere speculation—which, of course, led only to disappointment. He hated it so much that he swore he would never do it to any of his players. He tells them the cold, hard truth, letting them deal with the hurt up front rather than down the road. "Hope for the best, plan for the worst" is his motto.

"What is the plan?" he asks whenever I'm sifting through options. He won't take the first job available for his client, nor will he take the highest-paying job if it isn't the best situation for his client in the long run. He will give you a preference or his advice, but he will do his best to line up as many options as he can and then let you make the final call. He may disagree with it and will let you know if he does, but in the end he will let you choose your own fate. And if your decision, which he advised against, turns into a disaster, he will be there to help you out of it.

John Greig has never made me sign a contract with him. We work together in trust, our word and oath as strong as our bond. In this arbitrary, unforgiving world of basketball, John Greig has become my second father, and I'm a son that he never had.

John does not have many clients in the NBA, because he does not go after just anyone. He prefers working with players who attended all four years of college and graduated with a degree. He won't go after the prima donnas, because he has no desire to babysit egos, because he does not need the money. In this business loaded with wealth, egos, and politics, John comes as close to being altruistic as anyone possibly can.

He has stuck with me through thick and thin. Through depression, anger, and injury. He has encouraged me when I have needed it, as well as disciplining and reprimanding me when the moment has called for it. Like so many others before him, John Greig gave me his guiding hand, without which I wouldn't be where I am today.

Shortly after I hired John, Dave called to inform me that a team in Turkey that he had been working with was offering me a contract.

The original contract was for $80,000. While I was excited to actually have an offer on the table, word carried far and wide that Turkey was an unstable market. There was money to be made in Turkey, but it came with a risk. There was no player's union in Turkey, and thus no job security for the player if a team decided to cut him, regardless of contract.

I talked to John about my concerns. He didn't recommend I accept the offer. Though it was near the end of August, he told me to remain calm, as the season wouldn't officially begin until October. The months of August and September are for conditioning and training, or so it is claimed. But John informed me that what goes on during those two months is really just a glorified tryout. The team in Turkey wanted me to go out there as soon as possible so they could evaluate me. If they didn't want me, they'd have time to send me back—in spite of a signed contract—and look for another player.

A contract in America means a bound agreement. I'd learn that in Turkey it's simply a batch of papers with some abstract numbers that leave cause for interpretation. I'd learn that when a team signs you for a contract, the number you see on your contract means only that that's the most you'll make.

After listening to John's concerns, Galatasaray, the Turkish sports organization that was interested in me, raised the offer to $90,000 tax free, with $20,000 of it due to me upon arrival and my passing of a physical. The offer caused us to reevaluate the situation. If they invested twenty thousand in me up front, they'd be slow to cut their losses if they had an inkling to waive me. I told myself that the deal was a solid option, but I could never bring myself to feel good about it. My gut told me it was all wrong, that it was a farce.

John was very hesitant about the job. "I won't lie," he said. "For a rookie, this is a very nice contract in a very nice league, with a lot of money to be made in the future if you do well. But that's best-case scenario. It's a high-risk situation."

Things were tight financially for my parents. Along with all the traveling they did during my senior year to support me, they were also helping with Court's bills and trying to find the funds for Tara's wedding in September.

That summer when I came home from camp with the Clippers, I had no money to stay anywhere other than on Mom and Dad's couch. All of my immediate possessions were in that living room. I was crowding Mom and Dad's space, but not nearly so much as the elephant named *disappointment* that sat in the middle of it all. I could feel the tension between me and Dad every day. He loved me, but he was also very frustrated—not with me specifically, but with life.

One day in August, while I was sitting in the kitchen stewing over the offer from Galatasaray, Dad finally blew up and began to rant at me about how I was lazy, didn't clean up after myself, was in his space, and didn't do anything to help around the house. Most of these accusations were true. I was busy trying to stay out of the house, shooting hoops or running or staying at Josh's, because I couldn't bear the tension that lingered at Mom and Dad's. It was a no-win situation either way: if I stayed at home and cleaned up around the house, I was still in Dad's way and would be a constant, visible reminder of failed expectations. If I left the house and tried to stay out of Dad's way, I wouldn't be around to help.

I began to hide away, doing my best to avoid people and their questioning: So where are you going? Have you heard anything? What about the Jazz? Do you really think you could handle overseas?

With each fielded question came another painful reminder that I had failed. I wasn't a collegiate big shot anymore. I had no team, no place to call my own. In my mind, I could deduce that I was no better than the old hacks who play at the community center trying to recapture their glory days. I became agoraphobic. I didn't want people to look at me, let alone talk to me. I didn't want their eyes, filled with either pity or spiteful amusement, boring into me. I wanted to be forgotten.

Dad's tirade ended with how boneheaded I was being, not able to see how fortunate I was to have a $90,000 tax-free contract waiting for me. With all the financial struggle he was going through and the sacrifices he had made to help me get this far, he couldn't understand why I was so hesitant to take the money.

I went into the living room, packed up what little things I had, and left to stay in Vanessa's apartment with her and her husband, Nathan.

I then called John and, against his warning, told him I wanted to take the Galatasaray job.

"OK. Again, just look at the positive angle. This is a really nice contract for a rookie. Let's go from there." John did his best to assuage my fears.

The next day I signed the contract and faxed it to John.

I was going to Istanbul, the old capital of the Eastern Roman Empire, where the Hagia Sofia and the Blue Mosque resided.

John called my dad to give him the full details of the job and the risks involved with taking it. Dad drove over to see me and pleaded with me to not take the job just because of the money. He said that he had been wrong and that he wanted me to go where I felt it would be best for me.

But he had been right to confront me. I was useless that summer. I had no worth. I wanted to leave. I wanted to be out of that house, out from under the eye of the family as well as my community, which had invested so much in me, to no avail.

When Mom came home from Montana, where she had been for a week, she quickly came up to me and, with tears in her eyes, asked, "Are you sure you want to do this? Don't make this choice if it does not feel right. Don't make it just for the money. Are you sure?"

"Yes," I said, knowing I was making a mistake. It took great effort to ignore my gut instinct, which told me this was all wrong. For as logical and rational as I claim to be, I had a hard time rationalizing this decision, even to myself. It was a decision made on pure emotion. I wanted to disappear.

She strained to say, "I need to know . . . that you're OK."

I did my best to reassure my mother with a smile. "I'm fine," I lied.

And she knew I was lying.

Upon the completion of the contract from all ends, I took out a $10,000 loan against it. I gave it all to my parents—not as a loan, but as a gift—so that they could help contribute to Tara's wedding. I was grateful for what they had done for me. I wanted to give them more, so much more. But I couldn't say it in words because I was so ashamed. I could only give them a check. I know my parents didn't invest in me expecting a financial return. They invested in me because they loved me and wanted me to succeed and be happy. But even though I knew this, when I saw my parents struggling financially, mostly to provide for their children—me especially—I couldn't help but feel remorse. But I had never asked them to come follow me on the road. They chose to. It was where they found their joy.

I wanted to buy my parents land in Driggs, Idaho, where they could build a home, one last time. I wanted to give my mother so many things that she deserved, that this world has not given her. All I could do was give them a check, with a sad smile on my face, as I got on the plane and left my family behind to travel to the other side of the world.

24

Before I landed in Istanbul, I had never seen a three-lane highway accommodate six lanes of cars. Common logic says that if you simply let the cars go every other one and merge into the lanes politely, traffic will go as fast as it can. Whereas in Istanbul, common sense is nowhere to be found. Cars will hug the guardrails, even scrape them—paint jobs be damned—en route to wherever they feel it's so important to go. Bumpers will tap and side-view mirrors will collide and drivers will look straight ahead pretending that nothing happened.

I was taken to a tiny hotel, with tiny rooms and tiny beds, in the middle of the mass urbanization that was the crossroads of the world. The next day I was escorted on foot to the practice facility, which was only a few minutes away. Erbil, the team manager, came knocking on my door and said in his broken English, "Lance, . . . I take you to practice now. Understand?"

My first morning at the gym, I met Coach Oner. He was an older man and had said this would be his last year coaching. He was very welcoming. He was also totally Mafia. He had six separate businesses that he ran on the side and would often show up for practice an hour late, have us do a few drills, and then go back up to his office, where he conducted his other enterprises. He had a chauffeur escort him around town in his Jaguar and had the same setup for his son, who was on the junior team.

Later that day while riding in a taxi, I just stared out the window in awe at the endless ocean of concrete with beautiful towering mosques rising up over the hills. I had never seen anything like it.

The following Monday, I passed the physical exam, and I was paid a week later upon final certification from the doctors. I received my $20,000 advance up front—in cash. That's when I knew something was wrong. They gave me some big spiel about how it was wise to always take your money in cash, to make sure that it was all there, and how there were often typos and failed payments with wire transactions. A receipt for a wire transaction was just as good as cash—I knew that much. They were just paying me under the table to avoid taxes.

For two weeks I lingered in the tiny hotel in the sweltering humid heat. I listened to books on tape to pass the time while I wasn't at practice. I had not yet received the car that I was due, nor had I been moved into an apartment. They were stalling, and I already knew, within that first week, that I was in for a ride.

The training coach walked us through a warm-up drill every day and then ushered us into the weight room before practice. We did the same lifts every day. If you had any questions about what lifts you should be doing, you were to just recall from memory what you had done the day before and you were golden. We did bench presses, squats, biceps curls, dead lifts, and hang cleans every day. Every day. I'm no certified trainer, but even I could tell you, from trial and error, that if you don't give your muscles a day to recover, they will never get stronger. For the first two weeks I was there, we did the same lifts at the same weight every day. No one went up in strength. No one. It was stupid. And if you tried to venture off and do your own lift, even after you completed the regimen, the strength coach would give you a no-no look and tell you to stick with his routine. What could I say? It was their house, their rules, and their stupidity.

After weights we had practice with Coach Oner's two assistants, who smoked as they coached us, awkwardly, through drills. When they picked up a ball, you could tell it didn't feel natural in their hands. They were probably old soccer coaches whose time had come, who had no other livelihood, and so took up a job coaching basketball, even though they had no clue what they were doing. When they shot the ball, they proved your assumptions correct.

In our first preseason game I had twenty-five points and fourteen rebounds, surprising everyone. Coach Oner came up to me, gave me a kiss on the cheek, and said, "You're a steal!" implying that I was well worth the $90,000 they had bid for me. They even called John Greig several times just to reiterate how pleased they were. "You don't play like a rookie," Oner said to me while offering me a ride in his car.

"Probably because I'm much older than your normal rookie," I said, referring to the six years I spent in college basketball.

This conversation could've been a great one had the circumstances been less awkward. I was riding in Coach Oner's car with the $20,000 they had paid me in cash. For a week I had been walking around Istanbul with all of this money in my pocket, trying to figure out how to get it into my bank account back home in Salt Lake. Because of the heightened security measures around the world after 9/11, I couldn't open a bank account in Turkey without a Turkish social security number. And they wouldn't blindly transfer it in faith, either. The only way I could get it out of Istanbul was to carry it out. I didn't want to be hiding this money in my hotel room any longer, so I asked Coach Oner to stash it away for me in his bank account. I trusted him, and he liked me, and he was honest with me, always.

I could've held on to the money and carried it with me on the plane when I flew back to the States a week later for Tara's wedding, but I just didn't like the idea of carrying that much cash on me and the hassle of reporting it to customs. I had faith that Coach Oner would transfer the money for me through his own private bank account.

Coach Oner took me to my first-ever European soccer game. It was Galatasaray playing Ankara. I had never seen anything like it. I hardly watched the game. I just watched the crowd. It was amazing to see these thousands of people in different parts of the stadium who would carry through rally cries, cheers, and chants in harmonious timing, each section playing its part in the orchestra. Incredible. We don't have fans like that in America, for any sport. I have never seen such tradition choreographed through the masses. Galatasaray won the game, and I got food poisoning. I had to be taken to the hospital because I had been vomiting every twenty minutes for eight hours straight through the night. Don't get lamb kebabs from a vendor at a Turkish soccer game.

When the time came for me to fly back home for a few days for Tara's wedding, the team was worried about letting me go, as they feared I might not come back or might weasel my way out of the contract and try to sign on with someone better for more money. But I told them they could trust me, even though my first paycheck was past due by four days at this point.

"You'll have it when you get back," the secretary assured me.

Eighteen hours is how long it takes to fly from Istanbul to Salt Lake City. I arrived in time to make the rehearsal dinner for Tara's wedding, thanks to a little subterfuge on my part, when I snuck through security at O'Hare to make it to onto the plane just before it departed the gate. The door had already been shut. I may have violated international laws, but it didn't weigh on my conscience, as I don't buy into that speculative threat-level-red fear mongering. All I know is that I made it to the rehearsal dinner in one piece.

The wedding was the next day. It was a splendid event, and I was pleased to see that Tara, who had battled through reactive, self-destructive behavior, had found and was about to settle down with a high-quality guy such as John Greene. I got to see all my friends and loved ones and happily tell them about the situation in Istanbul, which by this point had exceeded my expectations.

I had invited Court to come with me when I first decided to go to Turkey. He loves traveling the world, experiencing new cultures, and is very good with languages. I wanted someone to come with me, as the idea of learning a new language, with my hearing impairment, was overwhelming. Plus, I wanted to take Mac, my dog, with me, and I needed someone to watch over him when I was gone on away games. Court had made up his mind to fly back with me.

The day after Tara's wedding, I was startled to realize that Court had not yet packed or moved out of his apartment.

"Why haven't you moved out?"

"Because I had no one to help me," he said defensively, as though that absolved him of any wrongdoing, which it didn't. Court also wanted to be bring his cat, Tommy. If it were not for the fact that Mac loves cats and was very good friends with Tommy, I wouldn't have agreed to let the cat come. Tommy was a thorn in my side. He had nothing but total disregard for human authority and would openly challenge you for your food, jumping on the table right in front of you, racing to eat as much of it as possible before you could throw him off. No matter how many times you flicked or spanked him, or even threw him against a wall, he would never relent. His one redeeming quality was that he was best buds with Mac.

When we arrived in Istanbul with our pets in tow, the first thing Court noticed was the women. Turkish women are incredibly beautiful. And Court is obsessed with women. We took a taxi to my apartment, a three-bedroom flat. I also finally had my very own car: a beat-up used minivan. But I wasn't complaining. I actually prefer to be assigned used beaters; that way, if you happen to ding them or wreck them, no one loses sleep over it.

I couldn't stay in the apartment with Court for long, as one of the team managers was there waiting. He and I were going to take a ferry across the sea to the Asian side of Turkey, where we were to meet up with the team for a preseason tournament.

When I arrived, I met the new players on the team. Malik Dixon was an American point guard, and Malik spelled the end for me. He was a good guy. But he was a shoot-first point guard. And Coach Oner was giving Malik the green light to shoot whenever he wanted. I'm the type of big man who's only as good as his point guard lets him be. The tournament lasted three days, and I didn't play well. The team was used to me scoring twenty and ten before I left for the wedding and before Malik arrived. All I really scored that tournament was a set of stitches in my cheek.

Borak, the team captain, was back from an injury. He was a Turkish All-Star, and he was going to shoot it every chance he got. With Malik and Borak, there simply weren't enough shots for anyone else. And then there was Hussein. This guy was trouble for me. He arrived late to the team for reasons I don't know; I think there was a buyout with another team and Galatasaray quickly bought him. Hussein knew I was the obstacle standing in his way to starting and making more money in the future. So in practice, while taking it easy on the other guys, he would cheap-shot me and then initiate an altercation. Because he was such good friends with all the other guys and spoke Turkish, they gave him the benefit of the doubt, and they all began to think I was a just another whiny American. Hussein validated John's warnings about the possibility that a teammate would try to make me look bad.

Even in games, Hussein would throw me difficult passes that were just out of reach or had too much heat on them. Or he would purposely miss my pass, so that I looked the part of the ass, giving me a turnover, and Coach Oner would take me out.

With change in offensive schemes, Malik and Borak now carrying the weight of the offense, the team owners began to pressure Oner to bring in a more shot-blocking-minded center. The owners kept saying that I was a rookie and would eventually crack, that with so little experience I'd never be able to make it through the wear and tear of the long season. Plus, they wanted to make a real push for the championship this year and felt they truly needed to invest in a more experienced center, at least one that could block shots.

The revolving door was gaining inertia. Every week, for three weeks, the team brought in two new big guys, Americans, either veterans or shot blockers. They'd have them practice against me, believing that the next one would be the one who was better than me. Yet they kept sending all of them home because I was outplaying and outworking all of them in practice. This went on for three weeks. By now it was October, and aside from the $20,000 advance that I received upon arrival in August, I had not yet received a paycheck. We were coming up on the third payday, the previous two still unpaid.

As far as the advance, I had yet to see that safe in my bank account. Coach Oner kept messing up the transaction information, or maybe he was just holding on to it; I don't know. It was lost somewhere in cyberspace. After six weeks of employment with Galatasaray, I had received not a dime for my work.

My gut instinct had proved true. I was now in the situation I had feared.

After practices, to ease my mind of the financial stress and the politics, Court and I went out into Istanbul and visited the sites. The Hagia Sofia is immaculate. To think that man, fifteen hundred years ago, created such a powerful structure is awe inspiring. The notion that Court thought he could possibly convince the guards, who spoke no English, to clean up the pigeon shit that had accrued on the walls of this famous piece of architecture, one that they took for granted, was inspiring in and of itself. They simply looked at him like all Europeans do: There goes another American thinking he rules the world.

In Istanbul, you don't have to be wary of the enticements of harlots. Rather, you must be on the lookout for rug sellers. It's illegal to solicit in public in most of Istanbul, but when you emerge from a taxi or car in the bazaars of the city's old district, you find people waiting, whistling and whispering into you ear. Public solicitation is legal here.

First they'll whistle lightly under their tongue, like prostitutes calling their johns: "Hey..." Then, in a throaty voice that bespeaks years of cigarette-smoke intake, they'll ask, "You want to buy a rug?"

The first time we were accosted, Court and I were flattered, as we had visions of pimping out our apartment with a nice handmade Persian rug but hadn't known where to look for one. To our delight, one came looking for us—or rather, the seller of one. We followed him. He spoke to us in good yet broken English: "You chose right. Stay with me. Buy only from me. Trust no one. No one else. Just me, Hassan. Trust no one." He reiterated this point several times as he took us to a shop in the back alleyway.

"You play for Galatasaray? That's my team!" Hassan erupted, opening his jacket to display his Galatasaray shirt.

His partner supported the Fenerbahçe team, a rival club. "At Fenerbahçe, we at least pay our players on time," he remarked, which, ironically, led me to explain my monetary situation.

"I have no cash right now. I'm sorry," I told them.

"That's OK."

"I will come back when I have cash."

"No worries," Hassan said. "Take it now, come back and pay later. Trust no one."

An image of my hand being held in a blender to pay off a debt while Court was plunged into ice water with a potato sack over his head flashed across my eyes. "Um. . . . Thanks, that's really nice of you. But I prefer to pay as I go. Really. I'd feel too bad. But I promise when I get the money, I will come back to you. I love these rugs," I said, panning over the rugs one last time. I really did love those rugs. I never broke my promise, because I never did receive my money.

It all became abundantly clear that my time with Galatasaray had come to an end the morning I showed up with the team to travel to the season opening tournament. When I showed up at 1100 hours for the bus, as the manager had told me, I was the only one there. The bus had departed two hours earlier.

The timing couldn't have been more impeccable: as I was standing there at the chain-locked doors of the clubhouse, Coach Oner sent me a text: "I'm sorry, Lance. You're my friend. I'm your friend. I'm sorry."

"Lance, I just talked to Yaman. He has received the $20,000 that Coach Oner has been holding for you, and he will get it to you tonight. And it has to be tonight, as you and your brother are on a plane to France tomorrow."

"OK, John. I got it. What is the name of the team in France?"

"Rouen. It's a two-month contract, to fill in for an injury. They need help, and you'll be playing. It's a good league, and you'll have the playing time to get the visibility you need. But right now, just worry about getting the money. Meet Yaman wherever he tells you to meet him."

I hung up with John and then called Yaman, the Turkish counterpart to John. "Lance, I cannot be there tonight," he told me, "but my assistant will meet you at the Atrium, where he will give you your money."

The Atrium is always busy, people coming and going in the capitalistic-driven culture that is Istanbul. Honking cars and taxis drive up on the curbs and sidewalks to cheat their way past traffic that is often held up by a special someone who thinks they are important enough to park in the middle of the street and walk into the coffee shop to buy themselves a latte. In their defense, they turn on their hazard lights. Hazard lights make everything all better. They absolve idiots of any accountability. They really do.

It was the heart of Ramadan, the monthlong equivalent of Christmas in the Muslim world. People were racing home for their supper before evening fell and the Taraweeh, the evening prayer service, was read. Court and I walked up to the Atrium, only a few blocks from our apartment. We stood on the steps of the shopping mall waiting for whoever Yaman's assistant was to find me, as I had no idea what he looked like.

Like the sounds of an orchestra setting the scene in a movie, the Taraweeh began to blast from the speakers of the toweringmosque beside the Atrium, a gleaming crescent moon atop its towering spire. In the Taraweeh, one-thirtieth of the Koran is read each night of the month of Ramadan: Allahumma innaka afuwwun kareemun tuhib-bul af-wa fa-afo anni. . . .

Those lacking in faith continue on with their shopping and day-to-day routine, but for the most part, everyone stops. Taxi drivers pull up on the curb, lay a towel out on the sidewalk, and humbly kneel to join in prayer with the rest of their world.

Modern men who don't believe in such superstitious ways—Allah be damned along with Santa—stand and smoke at the steps of the Atrium, their unnaturally blond wives happily skipping out with full shopping bags spilling with shiny things. Money talks, while Muhammad does not. Staghfirullah hallazi la-ila-ha illa huwal Hayyul Qayyumo wa atu-bu ilaihe. . . .

A man, cigarette in mouth, approaches me. "Lance?" he asks.

"Yes."

"I work for Yaman. Here is your money." Without caution or worry—even with total disregard—he pulls out an envelope and removes $20,000 in cash. Two men with long black ponytails, standing only a few feet from us, immediately see green and look over at me, eyeing all the Ben Franklins. One nudges the other and hints with a nod toward me. They begin to whisper. Court nudges me, hinting at them. The damage is done. Seeing no point in chiding Yaman's assistant for his folly, I quickly take the money. "*Tsekkur,*" I say as we part ways.

Hoping to become lost in the crowd, Court and I quickly walk into the busy Atrium—a pointless exercise, as I stick out like a sore thumb with my blond hair. Being six-foot-eleven might have something to do with it, too. We walk toward the McDonald's, finding solace in our American friend Ronald—the only time I have ever appreciated the sight of a clown; I hate clowns. I look over my shoulder to see the greased ponytails walking into the Atrium, eyeing us.

"Here, Court, take the envelope," I say, giving it to him but leaving the cash in my pocket. "Go downstairs and exit through the grocery store, and I will keep walking out and exit the north side. Run back to the apartment, but make sure they're not following you. I will meet you back there."

We split and I continue down the busy corridor of the hexagon-shaped building. They stand and look at both me and Court as he rides down the escalator and I continue on. When I turn the corner, out of eyeshot, I take off in a dead sprint past the salon and candy shop and plow through the revolving door like a lineman.

"Inna anzalnahu fee lailatul Qadr, Wa maa adraka maa lailatul Qadr." Words of the Koran bellow through the dusk of Istanbul as though they had been waiting for me, the infidel, to come back outside. My heart is beating. I turn a corner, and an elderly lady screams in fright as I—a giant of a man—dart past her. I awkwardly apologize in poor Turkish, "*Uzgunum,*" and continue on down the sidewalk toward another corner, where I dart behind a high wall of shrubs.

I'm now in a back alleyway, the walls on either side obscuring me from vision. I pause for a minute to peer around the corner from where I had just come. No one. I rocket down toward my apartment. Homeless dogs and cats prowling through trash cower out of my way. Pigeons disband and take flight, scattering in my wake. "Inna anzalnahu fee lailatul Qadr, Wa maa adraka maa lailatul Qadr!"

At this moment I think of Montana. I miss her. How did I, once merely a deaf polygamist kid and nothing more, find myself here at this very moment: on the other side of the world in a culture unlike any I have ever known, being followed by thugs, with $20,000 in my pocket and no place to put it?

"*Salaamun heya hatta matla-il fajr. . . .*"

It's a shame my first 20k marathon was of a different sort.

Court and I arrived at the airport to fly to Paris the following day. As I sat there waiting for our flight, confident thoughts of rising above adversity mixed and matched with thoughts of self-doubt: Am I really not that good? Am I overrated? Was I really just a big fish in a little pond in the Big Sky Conference. Yes, yes, these may be true, but I'm more than that. I'm more than that. I wish I could say that this pep talk I had with myself at Istanbul's Atatürk International Airport was the only one I needed to give myself, but that would be lying. There was worse to come.

Court and I landed in Paris that night, October 16, 2005. We let our animals out of their cages to relieve themselves and then loaded them and our bags into the taxi van that promptly took us to Rouen, a forty-five-minute drive north of Paris, where we were met by Coach Michel and Pascal, the team manager. I knew enough about Rouen to know that at one point it had been the old capital of British Normandy and that both Henry II and his son were buried at Rouen Cathedral, and that Joan of Arc was burned at the stake in the very same city as well. I was actually very excited to visit Rouen and was looking forward to getting to know the city and its culture.

Monday practice came. Coach Michel walked me through the set plays a few times and asked if I had it. "Yes," I answered, remembering most of the plays, as they were your basic elementary sets of wheel actions and all-American box plays.

Things were going along splendidly in practice until I mixed up one play. Michel, in a Jekyll and Hyde manner, blew his whistle and went red as he got in my face: "You said you knew the plays!"

Kenny Whitehead, a veteran American, gave Coach a stunned look and then turned to me and shrugged: "I have never seen Coach do that before. What did you do?"

"I forgot a play . . . on my first day."

"Must be because you're a rookie and he thinks he can mess with you," Kenny observed, walking back to his spot on the floor.

It was then that I knew this was trouble.

Life in France was unlike anything we had experienced.

"Lance, dude! I just got back from breakfast," Court says as he enters the room of our residential hotel, unloading the armful of *pains* and croissants he has absconded with. "I walked down there this morning and there was porn on the TV as everyone was just sitting around eating their breakfast as though it was some normal thing."

"Porn?"

"Yeah!"

"Like cable porn or hardcore?"

"Hardcore!"

"People are just having porn for breakfast?"

"Yeah. I walked in and just stared at the TV, and the manager lady noticed the shock on my face and she smiled and shrugged. 'France,' she said, as though it explained everything."

Skeptical of such a story, I take a bite from a croissant as I get up from the counter and head out the door—you know, not because I like porn; I'd never think of it. I just wanted to see if people were really dipping their croissants in their coffee with some DP action going on behind them on the television.

I enter the breakfast commons, and much to my disappointment there's only a homely-looking weather man mumbling something in French on the TV screen. Either it had just been a hardcore intermission or the channel had changed. Oh well. I take another *pain* from the basket and leave for Paris, as I have a busy day ahead.

The assistant coach misplaced my passport a few days ago, and I have to go to the American embassy in Paris to replace it. I walk up to the car and wince again at the sight of the top of it, which was badly scraped by Court last week when he decided to race the garage door rather than just wait for it to close and then push the remote again. No. It would've taken an extra twenty seconds—too long to just sit there and wait. There goes my five-hundred-dollar car deposit.

I leave Rouen and enjoy the green scenery and the fog that creeps through the woods of Normandy. I really love this place. Too bad my coach is unbearable. And too bad there are toll booths every ten kilometers on the French expressways. Nothing discourages me more from driving than toll booths. I reach the outskirts of Paris, where traffic is being held up thirty kilometers outside of the city center. I sit there in the car and creep for two hours at a snail's pace. Graffiti lines every available surface that can be plagued: expressways, billboards, lampposts, buildings, and windows. Nothing is sacred, not even cathedrals. As I drive into Paris, I feel as though I'm back in Istanbul. I realize that all big cities are the same, no matter where you are on the globe. When you have seen one, you have seen them all. To Paris's credit, the wide boulevards that were constructed in the Second Empire, during the reign of Napoleon III, as a riot deterrent are a unique characteristic. By widening the boulevards, the city planners made the rioting mobs who were either marching or trying to block off a portion of the city more vulnerable to open cannon fire and much easier to disperse. Silly French: baseball is America's pastime, while revolting is France's. *Vive la révolution!*

I stop at several different shops and markets trying to find directions to the U.S. embassy. A few times the directions were just lost in translation, I'm sure. But I know for a fact that a couple of times the Parisians I talked to felt humorous messing with an American and sent me clear out to the other side of the city. Had I had boobs, no matter what my nationality the Frenchman in the cigar shop would've been more than eager to help me and would've taken my hand and kissed and then stroked my hair: *"Ooh la la, ma chérie!"* But because he felt threatened by the handsome, towering, boobless John Wayne in his shop, he sent me to the hinterlands.

I finally arrive at the embassy and wait in line for two more hours before I'm able to get my photo taken. By this time, it's two forty-five and practice starts at four. I race out to my car and zoom out of Paris, taking a quick look at the Eiffel Tower across the courtyard and the Louvre, and consider my first and final trip to Paris to have been a sufficient one.

Pulling into the parking lot at the gym, I have ten minutes before practice starts and I'm starving. I can't very well practice on an empty stomach. I race to the delicatessen and order myself a sandwich. I race into the team office, where everyone is seated and waiting for me as I am just in time, with only a minute to spare. But Coach Michel, feeling that a rookie should not be the last one in, does not like that I wasn't there ten minutes earlier. His disapproving stare turns into outright offense as I begin to snarl at my sandwich, eating it as though it would be my last. Michel stands there in silence, folding his arms in front of the projector like an idiot, acting as though he doesn't mind that the projector is blinding him because he is so tough. Then he speaks: "This is very unprofessional, Lance. Do you think you could maybe wait to eat your sandwich after film?" Without a word I drop my sandy and sit back all professional-like, letting him know I'm ready to be a better basketball player today.

We're now on the practice floor, ready to better ourselves as professionals.

"Conduisez la boule par les cônes et marquez un seau . . ." Coach Michel rambles off, pointing at all the cute traffic cones he has laid out on the basketball court. He then begins to translate: "I say, you'll drive the ball through the cones . . ." I nod my head, not needing an explanation of things, as common sense would articulate what the drill is— a stupid drill.

I play at being excited as I rip the ball from a teammate's hands and am the first to run up to the drill line. "Let's go! Let's do this!" I holler, which is my own way of pumping myself up when I'm about to do something I don't want to do. Today would be no exception as I stare down these petty little cones spread out in a fashion that recalls memories of Little League soccer practice, which was more productive than what I'm about to do. At first Coach Michel thought I was just an energetic little rookie who was eager to learn. But over time he has come to see that he has nothing to teach me and that I'm mocking him.

I stand, ball in hand, ready to master this prepubescent drill that Michel has devised as though he knows something that we don't. Michel gives me his glare—which has, since my arrival, begun to trigger a twitch in his eye. He leans over to Alexis, the unofficial translator, and whispers into his ear. Alexis tries not to smile as Coach Michel looks away and begins to clean out his whistle as though he is above all of this.

"Coach said for me to tell you to shut up."

I take the first dribble and intentionally, but pretending it's by accident, kick the first traffic cone out of the way. Then I start to play but trip and fall on the floor. In the glum of December, this floor is so hard and cold it could pass for an ice-hockey rink. I reach for my kneecap and begin to rub it. This is no charade. I actually hurt this knee a week earlier in practice when someone fell on the ground and rolled onto my foot, blocking my path forward. When the knee popped back, I told myself it was just a simple hyperextension, and I kept playing on it. It was my rookie year, and I felt I needed to salvage my reputation after the debacle in Turkey. I didn't want to be known as injury-prone.

Massaging my kneecap, I struggle to stand, but everyone around me thinks I'm still playacting. The silence covering the gym is broken periodically by the sound of my ball, which is far, far away on the other side of the sprawling gym, which seats 334 people at maximum occupancy. My teammates do their best to contain their snickering as Michel stands there caught between shock and anger at what has just happened— a mutinous ridiculing of his authority.

He raises his hands incredulously in the typical European soccer way, as though he is a victim and has done nothing to deserve this. He looks around and sees the rest of my teammates red with muffled laughter. He then decides that this farce has gone on long enough and blows his whistle in a well-timed fashion—except that it's ten seconds too late.

"What is our attitude?!" Michel yells.

I stare at him, stoic and mute. I think of a few answers but choose to remain silent. My two months with this man have been long and unpleasant. I have only one week left on my contract before I fly home for Christmas.

"Well! What is it?! Why do you not answer?! Why do you Americans think you rule the world?"

He set himself up so perfectly that I cannot resist. I rationalize that this is the last week of my contract and that I thus have nothing to lose. I take a long, savoring breath, cherishing what is about to come as I make eye contact with this coach and answer, "Why do the French think they have a say in anything at all?"

Michel screams something in French, looking like he is about to cry, but it's just the French tongue and how they facially express their feelings. He walks away from me and blows his pacifier once again, and the rest of the team starts dribbling through the cones.

The drill finally ends, and we move on into half-court defense. The very first play of the drill, Jean-Emmanuel Le Brun, the team captain and a guy I really enjoy, accidentally head-butts me. Jean-Emmanuel shaves his big skull, and it's very big, so there's no hair padding the impact as my lip splits and my teeth puncture the skin. Michel laughs. I'm sure because it looks funny, but also because he is happy to see me hurt. His traffic cones shall not be mocked!

Playing for Rouen was a joy because there was no trainer handy, let alone a team doctor. Pascal escorts me to the doctor's house, where he will stitch my lip.

The black cat purrs, in French, as it weaves through my legs. The scent of crepes lingers in the air. I salivate, tilt my head back, and clench my teeth as the doctor needles my lower lip. No local anesthetic needed—more important, no anesthetic available—as I sit at the MD's dinner table while he applies two stitches. Never taking his eyes from my mouth, he speaks to his wife in the kitchen while his two children, one on crutches, shout back and forth across the house. The cat, the doctor, his wife, their kids—I'm surrounded by the French tongue.

Seven thousand miles away from home, having surgery performed in a dining room, with what looks like a fishhook gutting my lip, I calmly remind myself it's all part of the European experience.

When we part for the last time, Michel and I say nothing. We simply shake hands and lay down our arms.

25

It was hard to enjoy the Christmas break once I got home, as I had no idea where I was going next. John had hinted that I might be headed to Boise to play with the Idaho Stampede of the CBA (Continental Basketball Association). And so I waited. And waited some more, just doing my best to stay in shape while I was home, watching some movies, unable to get a job because no one would hire me knowing that I could leave at any moment. And it was the dead of winter, so there was no lawn work available.

When I finally fetched a job application in late January at a nearby 7–Eleven, John called to tell me I was headed back to France, once again for an injury replacement. The team was JL Bourg, in the tiny town of Bourg-en-Bresse, about an hour west of Geneva and the Swiss border.

When they signed me for a month, Bourg was in third place in the league standings. John admitted he didn't know how much I'd be playing, as they were a good team and had good chemistry as it was. Seeing this, I approached the job as a job, telling myself that I wasn't going to be much more than a practice player. But hey, it was a $5,000 paycheck for a month's work.

As I packed to fly back to France, Mac hid behind the door, peeking out slightly, revealing one eye to let me know he knew I was leaving and that he was pouting. Court stayed home and got a new job. I flew back to France and left Mac with Mom and Dad. I was picked up in Paris and met Coach Frédérique Sarre.

Oh, Sarre. How do I describe him? He looked like a fifty-year-old Mr. Burns from *The Simpsons*. He spoke English well, but he was incredibly intense, and everything had to be done his way. He had full control of his team, and there was no discussion. He ran the show, and his players respected him or feared him, or both. In his defense, he knew the game. He was the best coach I had in Europe in terms of knowledge of the game. He knew what he was talking about when drawing up the *X*s and *O*s of the floor, and he held everyone accountable. He had no favorites. It was nice to be on a team again where everyone had their job and everyone was held to the same standard and treated equally, albeit harshly.

The next morning, I had the haunting realization that I was indeed playing for a sadomasochist. He handed me the week's schedule. I thought maybe he had mistakenly handed me an old copy of the fall preseason practice schedule when I saw that there were two-a-days for the entire week until game day. *Unreal.* I began to panic.

I turned to Kelvin Torbert, a fellow rookie who had played at Michigan State: "Kelvin, is this normal? All of these two-a-days?"

"Yeah, man," he said without passion or life, all of the joy of basketball sucked from his veins.

The gym we played and practiced in had without a doubt the hardest floor I ever played on. It was the coldest time of year, as we practiced in the dead of January and February, and the tiny town was perched on the plains of France, with no mountain range to block the wind chill. It was so damn cold. Just running up and down on the floor for warm-ups, you felt like your kneecap was going to fall off.

As expected, I didn't play much for Bourg; I was mostly there just to make sure they had ten bodies for practice. If I did get in, it wasn't for much more than five minutes. In practice I had a hard time not smiling at Coach Sarre when he would suddenly burst up from the sideline, resting on his haunches, and yell, "What the shit!" when someone made a bad play. It was the first time I had ever heard *shit* used in that syntax: in the place of either *fuck* or *hell.* Since my time with Sarre, "What the shit?" has become my favorite turn of phrase when expressing my own incredulity.

Whenever I tried not to smile, I'd bite my lip or try to cover my mouth with my hands. "Look at me when I'm speaking, Lance," Frédérique would bark. He soon figured I was looking away because I was trying not to smile. Whenever he caught me, he would make the official referee's hand signal of a substitution, and while all ten of us stood there in silence, he would walk over, grab me by the arm, and then escort me to the sideline: "You're done. Have a sit until I call you."

Had I not been so worried about my long-term prospects and career, I might have enjoyed my time in Bourg more. Instead, I just went back to my hotel and worried over what this was all for, pondering different options and scenarios. I began considering just going back to America and becoming a schoolteacher and high school basketball coach.

I began to have these doubts again not only because of the uncertainty burning me out, the lack of play and the two-a-days, but because my knee was in pain. When I injured it in Rouen, I thought it would heal with time and rest over Christmas break. But it didn't. Over time in Bourg, after the grueling two-a-days, it was beginning to be quite painful. It got to the point where my knee hurt whenever I would jump, slide, or even walk. But since I was simply there as an extra to have a functioning practice and was there only for a month, would it make sense for me, an injury replacement, to sit out of practice with an injury? Sarre would just look at my knee and say, "You can run, right?"

"Yes."

"Then I'm sure it's fine."

Before the last game in Bourg, John called to tell me he had found a job for me in Spain that would last until the end of the season. I was hesitant to tell John my knee wasn't doing well, because I needed the money. I went to Valencia.

People often ask if I took time to learn the language in these various countries. I did. I really did try. But with my hearing impairment it took me fifteen years to learn to speak proper English, a process in which I would read a word, then watch how someone pronounced it with their mouth, and then have the sound corrected for me by a speech therapist. Picking up a new language and its rhythms isn't easy for me. The guys in Spain at least appreciated my effort to try to learn their language. I knew how to count to ten and order from a menu. And that was a lot more than most Americans even attempt to learn.

My first game with my new team was recorded without benefit of a scoreboard or clock due to complications at the scorer's table. It's a frustrating experience—playing a game when you have no idea of the time or the score. All we could do was play our little hearts out and wait for the judge's results at the end of the game, as though it were a boxing match. We lost. I had eighteen rebounds. The owners were pleased with the performance but not with the coach. He was released the following day, and the team hired a new coach, giving me my fifth coach in five months.

Five coaches in five months. Five different schemes and strategies to learn or take in and adapt to. Five different coaches who talked to me like I was a rookie who had no idea what he was doing, despite the fact that I had played six years of college basketball with some of the best minds on the planet.

My knee continued to get worse. It hurt so bad I could no longer dunk the ball. I couldn't even walk up the two flights of stairs to my apartment and had to use the slow elevator to beam me up. The Spanish physical therapist, like the PTs in France, simply said it was tendonitis. But I knew something was seriously wrong. My kneecap burned at the top and underneath. The quad muscles reaching to either side of the knee were in constant tension no matter what position I put my leg in. They wouldn't relax. And the inner side of my knee snapped and popped when I flexed it. But in order to protect my reputation, I kept playing and practicing.

I went to physical therapy every day. But the therapist knew that because I wasn't a citizen of Spain, I wasn't covered by the government health-care system, and the team didn't have the funds to pay for an MRI or surgery for me. There was only one month left in the season, and they simply wanted to keep me up and running and intact for as long as they could and then wrap me up in duct tape and send me home, leaving someone else to deal with my injury.

I hold no grudge toward them and how they handled my knee. They were a poor club and money was tight, and yet they always paid me on time.

I loved Spain. It was my favorite country of all the ones I visited that year in Europe. The landscape is unlike anything I ever saw growing up in America. Sure, I was used to big rocky mountains, but with smooth valleys and basins between them due to glacier formations. But in Spain there's no rhyme or reason to the geography. You can be at sea level, and then before you know it you're staring at towering, snowcapped peaks with valleys and orchards nestled away in their far confines. You'll be traveling through valleys and orchards of gold and green and then will be driving through the thick, beautiful hills of León, above Portugal. It's a beautiful place.

And the Spanish know how to relax. ¿Que pasa, Lance? Relájate, me amigo. I can't tell you how frustrating it was to have two-a-day practices with Coach Fede—to come home after the morning practice, take a nap, and then wake up, wanting some lunch, only to realize there isn't a thing open in the afternoon. Nothing. In Spain, between the hours of 1200 and 1400, you have a better chance of becoming pope than you do of getting a meal. These guys take so much time off to just chill and *relájese* that you can't help but understand why Spain is now no longer simply "the sick man of Europe" but the rotting corpse. At least once a week they have a national holiday. Each day I had a one-in-seven chance of popping my head out the window to see a little parade or carnival coming down my street with poppers being set off, children in gay splendor tossing firecrackers into crowds as their parents smiled at them proudly for their demonstrative patriotism.

When I flew home, Mom, Dad, and Mac met me at the airport. My knee ended up requiring surgery—arthroscopic debridement, as the cartilage on the back of my kneecap had ripped away and some of it had floated into the joint, blocking the knee and pinching the meniscus. The knee had been in this state for seven months. For seven months I ran around with floating cartilage blocking my knee, pinching the tendons and nerves—all because I feared for my reputation.

Although Dr. Cooley would perform surgery on me free of charge, the HMOs would still get their fee, depleting what little funds I had accrued during that long and tumultuous rookie campaign. I paid to have my knee fixed, using the very same money I had earned playing on that very same bad knee. I'd like to say it was a wash, but in truth it wasn't, as I was now well in debt.

I spent the next month recovering on Mom and Dad's couch, unable to move anywhere without crutches, passing the time by finally deigning to read the Harry Potter books. I devoured them all in one week.

I never would have predicted I'd end my first year of professional basketball in the red column. No one tells you these stories as they fill your head with fantasies of the fame and fortune that await you at the next stage. No one cares to tell you these stories, because basketball is fun. It must be fun as we run around putting a ball in a hoop while happy and merry fans applaud us for our boyish endeavors. It must be fun to be suicide machines that feel no pain. It must be so much fun to just play basketball, and not to have to worry about anything else.

I'm sure it is.

26

It was six weeks before I could run on my knee again. The healing process was painful and slow, as so many of the muscles had atrophied pre- and postsurgery to a point where it felt like I was learning to walk all over again. I had no insurance, so I could only wing my own physical therapy as best as I could and forced myself through the pain, knowing that it was mostly just the superficial pain of tearing scar tissue.

John flew me up to Seattle for a week to play with some of his clients to help me get back in the groove of playing. He put me up in an apartment and fed me for ten days, paying all of my expenses, as he knew I had no funds.

When I came back from Seattle it was late July. John told me to hang in there and that he had some things cooking overseas. But he warned me that it was going to be difficult with the résumé I had accrued the season before, unable to play for one team the entire year, combined with my recent knee surgery. Add to that the fact that the Eurobasket Web site listed that I was deaf and had played in the Deaf World Championships back in 2002. This little fact would rob me of several jobs, and John eventually asked the Web site to remove that information. The year before, the site had not posted that I was hearing-impaired, and this had not been an issue. Then Eurobasket found out about my impairment, thought it was a neat story, and posted it.

One overseas coach told John that he couldn't take the risk. He felt that my hearing impairment would only add to the language barrier, despite the fact that during my entire rookie season this issue never arose. Basketball terminology is universal. Because it's a relatively new sport in the world, many of the coaches were either coached by an American or attended American camps, where they learned the terminology. Most of basketball is simply body language and reading cues from your opponents and teammates. At least that's the way I taught myself how to play it, and I had been doing pretty well up to that point.

When you're in a gym and the crowd is on their feet, roaring and stomping, everyone is deaf. We all have been in a noisy gym, cheering on our team, where we cannot even hear ourselves yelling. When the JumboTrons and sound systems are blaring Metallica and fans are rooting for the home team, I'm on an equal playing field with everyone else. In the land of temporary deafness, the permanently deaf man is king.

I was living on the generous faith of a remaining few who still believed in me. October came, and John, too, was growing frustrated. I wasn't angry with John, because if I hadn't gone against his advice a year earlier when I signed with Galatasaray, the story could've been completely different. I chose my fate when I knowingly made the mistake of signing with Galatasaray. I was now paying for it.

Finally in mid-October, John called to tell me that the Idaho Stampede, a CBA team in Boise, was joining the NBA Development League (D-League) and that the new coach, Bryan Gates, wanted me to join his team. Bryan Gates was the understudy of Rory White, my summer coach with the Clippers from the year before. Rory had told Gates to take the leap and get me on his team. Coach Gates trusted Rory and took him at his word. Gates called John asking if I was available. Although he was interested in me and would attempt to have me allocated as a local player to Boise, I still had to go through the draft.

Because the NBA D-League was still in its early stages and looking for fanfare, it had a system where it allowed a team to pick up nearby college players so that they could draw more fans. Otherwise, if you signed a D-League contract, your name was put in a pool where you were up for grabs, with any team free to select you. I didn't want to sign a D-League contract and end up Bismarck, North Dakota. You went through the draft process only once in that if you were drafted by Idaho and played with them, they retained your rights if you returned to the D-League the following season.

The idea of playing in Boise, only five hours from Salt Lake and a nice halfway point between home and my sisters in Oregon, was a very welcoming idea. It went through. I signed a rookie contract for the gross pay of $12,000 for the season.

It blows your mind how ridiculous the pay is in relation to the pay scale of the NBA, which the D-League is affiliated with. The D-League is comparable to baseball's minor-league farm system. The disparity of pay is unlike that of any other sport. In one day of a road trip, the average NBA team will spend more money than it takes to budget a D-League roster for an entire season.

But that's the price you pay, and you know this when you sign on with the D-League. You willingly make a choice to sacrifice more money overseas for more visibility at home in America. NBA scouts and GMs keep a close eye on the D-League because many NBA players are assigned to the league throughout the season. Each D-League team is affiliated with at least one NBA team. Idaho was affiliated with both Utah and Seattle at the time I signed. NBA teams can send a player down to receive more playing time only to their designated affiliate, but a D-League player like me—a free agent, so to speak—can be called up by any team, not just Utah or Seattle.

In the back of my mind, as no jobs were coming my way from overseas, I knew the D-League was my last chance at a career—my last chance at my dream of making it to the NBA. When I signed the contract, I knew it was all on the line.

When I showed up at training camp, there were four players with NBA experience, and many other well-known names from the college circuit. It was a bona fide tryout. Idaho had invited sixteen men to camp. The fact that you sign a D-League contract does not mean you're on the team. It means only that they own your rights. You still have to make the team.

I showed up in Boise and met Coach Gates for the first time. Upon first seeing him, with his long, droopy dog face and beak for a nose, you wouldn't think he knew even the slightest thing about basketball. Gates started off as a team bus boy for the Idaho Stampede, working for free for several years, climbing his way up the ladder to eventually become an assistant coach under Rory White. He then spent time coaching in Lebanon and was now back in America, with his first-ever position as a head coach. He was a purist. He held everyone else to the same standard—that the game should always be respected and that giving anything less than your best was only cheating yourself.

You can say what you want about Bryan Gates as an "X and O" coach. That's all relative. But there's one thing you cannot dispute: he is a brilliant personnel director. He understands chemistry. He takes hard work over talent. He knows which guys to put on a team, figuring in the traits and tendencies of his players. He does his homework early, creates a machine, and then just sits back and watches the creature he's created work on its own.

The NBA Development League is a cutthroat environment, where you have players with NBA experience or talent and skill competing like rabid dogs over table scraps for the chance to be seen by NBA eyes. Starvation brings out the animal in all of us. People tend to shrug off the D-League because they make the mistake of assuming that our talent matches the level of our pay. When people see NBA players making millions, that's their point of reference. So they judge every other player according to that standard, and when they see me making $12,000, they assume I must not be very good.

If I could change one thing in the D-League, I really would raise the pay to at least seventy thousand dollars minimum, because the average Joe fan will say, "$70,000? He must be halfway decent. Let's go see if he's worth it." They will be more inclined to go to a game and see if the player can earn his keep. But if they know a player is making only $12,000 to $25,000 dollars, they can all too easily assume it will be a poor showing. If you want to make money, you have to spend it.

It really is no small feat to make the roster of a D-League team. In the NBA you have guaranteed contracts, and the players can relax and just play and do their jobs without the angst of wondering if they will be cut tomorrow. An NBA training camp will usually have twelve or thirteen guys already protected under guaranteed contract, with the remaining three places up for grabs between guys who are on the outside looking in. In the D-League, nothing is secure and nothing guaranteed. The level of intensity and awareness, the panic and worry lying just beneath the hardwood waiting to erupt—it's all enough to make you want to quit right then and there. When I stepped onto the practice floor in Boise for the first time, I nearly vomited. The tension was fogging the windows as each of us players cautiously introduced ourselves, knowing we were all enemies, gunning for the other's job.

Coach Gates warned us all that no one was safe and that it was going to be ten days of hell full of two-a-days until the very last moment, when he would have to cut the roster down to ten men. He told us not to get hurt or injured, because if we did, we were going home. It just depended on who wanted it the most. Even though I was allocated locally, and held a lowly rookie contract, I knew I wasn't secure in my positioning. The D-League has only so many men at so many pay rates. There are A, B, C, D, and rookie contracts. Each team must have at least two rookies, and they have to be receiving rookie pay at all times. The fact that I was coming cheap didn't make my future any more secure than the rest of the guys'.

I walked onto the floor and laced up the same shoes I had been wearing since I was in France the season before. They were worn and tattered. I couldn't afford new ones, as I was completely broke. I was asking these shoes, which had carried me through the end of Spain, through my knee surgery, to carry me just a bit further through this training camp, whereupon I'd receive team-endorsed Adidas shoes. As much as I was hoping for the job, I was hoping for a new pair of shoes.

They did their best, but they couldn't last. During the very first practice, while I was doing defensive slides, the skin on the ball of my right foot ripped off without even blistering. And then the entire toe print on my big left toe ripped off. When practice was over and I walked over to the bench and took my shoes off, my socks were caked with blood. The calluses that had formed over the years on my well-worn feet simply ripped without warning. The rips were deep. They took a month to fully heal. Coach Gates came and looked over at my feet and then immediately turned away as he grew squeamish.

I duckwalked to the locker room, where I took a shower and did my best not to scream as the water stung the exposed flesh of my feet. Blood flowed, with the soapsuds, down the gutters of the shower stall. Kevin Taylor, our trainer, awkwardly worked on my feet, doing his best to patch up what was nearly irreparable. I went back to the hotel, where I soaked my feet in Epsom salts. That evening practice, with only Band-Aids to protect my feet, I laced up the old shoes again and went back out on the floor. Gates had warned us to not be injured, and I wasn't going to sit out of practice because of flayed flesh on my feet when my future depended on it.

There wasn't anything else waiting for me. It was either Boise or bust. I had resigned myself to the fact that if I didn't make the team, I'd be hanging my shoes up for good, and moving on. Seeing that this was my last chance, my last-ditch effort along the path toward my dream, I wasn't going to step off the floor with any regrets. If I was going to retire, or be forced into retirement, I was going to do it on my terms, knowing I had done everything I possibly could to achieve my goal. I wouldn't let what-ifs haunt me for the rest of my days.

I stepped out onto the floor and practiced and ran and sprinted, cursing the pain in my feet until the sensory overload shut down the nerve passages, sending my feet into a state of numbness. When practice was over, I took the shoes off to see blood crystallizing with the salt of sweat. This time the pain was so unbearable that I silently cried in the shower and bit down on the washcloth. I was safe to do so, as my tears disappeared with the bloody shower water.

The next day I received my per diem: $30. I put aside 10 of it for food and then bought a pair of basketball shoes for the other twenty at an outlet store. The shoes were a hit with the rest of the team. There were junk and looked like junk, but at least they were not tearing up my feet anymore. The next day Coach Gates took pity on me and gave me a new pair of Adidas shoes, even though he wasn't supposed to until the final roster cut.

On each of those ten days of camp, I drove to my bank and put 20 of my daily $30 in my checking account, allowing myself to eat for the day on only a $10 budget. I was able to make that month's bills without any overdraft fee, with $5 to spare.

Coach Gates was still unsure whether he could keep me. In practice I wasn't doing too well, because Jeff Graves and Pete Ramos were bruisers who believed they had never committed a foul in their life. Jeff and Pete were much stronger than I was and would just manhandle me in practice, where I had no one to uphold the standards of the game or at least protect me.

Then in the very first exhibition game Gates saw what I could do in a structured environment. I scored eleven points in eight minutes in the first half. Gates saw that I wasn't the strongest, nor the most athletic. I didn't have the biggest wingspan or freakish hops. I wasn't a baller or a gangster.

I was merely a basketball player. Nothing more.

I made the final cut and was the lone token white guy on the team.

27

My point guard, Randy Livingston, became my close friend—maybe the closest friend I have made in my basketball travels. Born and raised in Louisiana, Randy Livingston has become my brother from another world. We speak a different dialect and have nothing in common but basketball, yet we have only absolute love and respect for each other, because we both love and respect the game and try our best to play it as it should be played—with heart.

Randy was a grizzled point guard, well traveled, having hopped around through various NBA teams throughout his career, setting the record for most call-ups to the NBA from the minor-league systems of the CBA and D-League. He was originally drafted by the Houston Rockets out of LSU in the mid-1990s, but several devastating knee injuries would wipe out the freakish athleticism he had originally been known for. You can always find Randy in an airport, as he is the guy who is waddling around like a duck.

Randy is as smart as they come. I have never encountered a higher basketball IQ. As slow and hobbled as he was, Randy embarrassed even the quickest guards as he would just take his time and pick apart a defense, finding the open teammate. He would never yell at you for shooting it, only for not shooting it. He made it clear that failing to shoot the open shot was just as malignant as shooting a bad one. Randy could put a ball anywhere he wanted it. He would lead you with a pass to where you needed to go, as he could see the defense behind you when you couldn't. For the two years I spent in the D-League with Randy Livingston, he led the league in assists both years. He wasn't anything flashy. Straight to point with his passes and intentions. He made the game so simple. Randy would do all your homework for you. You just had to worry about putting the ball in the hoop.

My first game was against the Colorado 14ers. I scored fifteen points in twenty-one minutes. But we lost that game and then promptly lost the next five, sprinting out of the gate to an 0–6 record. Every day it was a constant battle in practice to see which of the two bruisers—Jeff or Pete—was going to make life miserable for us. They usually would just talk heat to each other, flexing their muscles, threatening to break the other's legs, but sometimes they ventured off to try to intimidate someone else on the team. Coach Gates would get in shouting matches with at least one of those two nearly every day, sending the whole team on sprints because of their petty grandstanding.

After starting off at 0–6, Coach knew his job was already on the line. He needed to change something. He cut a few players, and we eventually were able to turn the ship around, slowly but surely beginning to tick off a ten-game winning streak, climbing back into the standings. But even during the time we were winning, everyone was miserable. You never knew what you were going to get that day in practice.

I had roommate problems as well. My two roommates, who shall remain nameless, liked to smoke dope. And they liked to have women over, preferably mother-daughter combinations, through all hours of the night, laughing and screaming, slamming and banging doors until four in the morning. One day I'd finally had enough and told them that I didn't care that they smoked dope or enjoyed prostitutes at night but that they had to take it elsewhere.

They never stopped. They did, however, just stay in their rooms and smoke pot by the window, but that smell, that pungent smell that I hate so much, which flares up my sinuses, would always leak through the vent. Always. I'm all for the legalization of drugs. I really didn't care that they were smoking pot. I just hated the fact that they made me smell it and get sinus infections because of it.

At home or on the road, it was hard for me to be roommates with guys of such different backgrounds and preferences. Most of the guys loved to turn up the thermostat, preferring their room as hot as a sauna. They loved just falling asleep in a sweat on top of their covers. To me this was just about as unpleasant as trying to pop cysts in my armpit with a quilting needle. It was evident that I often didn't fit in and made people uncomfortable without even trying.

. . .

Then the economic aspect of the D-League kicked in. Seattle sent down Mohammed Sene, their first-round draft pick that year, who wasn't getting any play time up in the NBA. They wanted him to develop and get more playing time in the D-League. With one bimonthly paycheck, Mohammed made more than all of us combined for the entire season. The disparity was comical.

What player wants to leave the convenience of the NBA—where you fly on your own jet with all the food you want and stay in the nicest hotels in your own rooms—and go down to the D-League, where you fly on little commuter jets to second-class cities, traveling via vans and buses to your destination, stopping at Subways across the great American landscape? No one. The fact that an assigned player who is sent down to a D-League team can very well buy out that franchise makes it difficult for any such player to take playing there seriously.

People want in the D-League, but they also want out. No one wants to stay in the D-League. Everyone goes to the D-League in hopes of a better job: players, coaches, dancers, administrators, PR reps. Everyone. When an assignment (i.e., a player) was sent down, the NBA team he played for sent checks down to cover his expenses as well as his development. As they assign a player they're investing millions in, they expect to see him play. And he gets to play. That's the way it goes. An assignment gets x number of minutes regardless of his attitude or effort in practice.

It's not economically sound to send a player down to the D-League and not have him play.

When Mohammed came down, it knocked me out of the rotation. No matter how hard I practiced or hustled, it didn't matter. Mo was still going to get his minutes, regardless of his effort or interest. Resistance was futile. All I could do was shoot my extra shots after practice and then sit at the end of the bench and cheer my teammates on.

Sometimes I sat on the bench for stretches that went for games at a time. My confidence plummeted. I was making $12,000, and not even playing. How was this helping me in the long term? How was I hoping to have a better job the next year with minutes and numbers like mine?

My confidence was so bad that whenever I did get in a game for short spurts, I'd miss layups. Wide-open layups. And Gates felt that it was best to take me out, fearing I might otherwise compound one mistake with another. He subbed me out, and all I could do was sit and analyze that one minute I got to play.

I found myself once again staying up late at night, stressing and obsessing about the mistakes I had made in a previous game, never being given a chance to redeem myself. I was also concerned that I wasn't getting any younger. I began to develop ulcers and vomit blood.

I was unhappy and depressed, and I saw no light at the end of the road. I kept trying to get hold of John, wanting him to do something, to trade me—anything. On the eve of the year 2007, we were in Austin. I had played for only a few minutes, and again was just perseverating over all the little things that had occurred in the time I had been in the game.

I texted John: "John, I'm unhappy. Why are you not listening to me? I don't want to be here anymore. Where is this going?"

John had been MIA for a while, as there wasn't a thing he could really do for me. Gates didn't want to let me go or be traded. John finally sent a text message back: "Then go work at the 7–11 if you're so miserable."

As I walked down a quiet street in Austin, Texas, I put the phone back in my pocket and began to cuss obscenities at John, twenty-five hundred miles away. I'm sure he heard me. It was the only time I came near to firing him.

In February, my twenty-sixth birthday approached and the family gathered in Boise to meet up and see a game of mine. I played for one minute, getting two rebounds. And then, having done nothing wrong, I was subbed out. I looked up and saw my family in the stands. There I was, turning twenty-six, in debt, with nothing to show for myself, sitting on the bench in the D-League, making $12,000 a year. I couldn't even look at them from across the arena. The rest of my siblings were carving their way through the world, doing their best to make themselves a life, while I was chasing a pipe dream. Before the game was even over, I snuck off to the locker room and began to violently vomit blood.

That night the family gathered at the hotel, where they all gave me gifts. I have never been a fan of birthdays. I think that on my birthday, if anyone should be giving a gift to say thank you, it should be me. I couldn't look my siblings in the eye as I opened their gifts. They knew I was in pain. They knew it was difficult for me to accept their generosity when I had nothing to give them. I still owed them money. Yet here they were, giving me more.

That night as I lay in bed, my stomach churning, eating at my insides, I came to the conclusion that I was living in a fantasy and it was time to grow up.

That next morning I packed my bags and told Coach Gates I at least needed to take a medical leave of absence to get my ulcers under control. But I also told him I might not be coming back, and that I was pretty sure I'd be quitting.

I felt I had traveled this road as far as I could, that it had come to its end and life needed me elsewhere. Driving home to Salt Lake, I cried in the car as I recalled all those morning with Coach Rupp when the game was innocent.

I had given so much to this game. It had given me a free education. But other than that, nothing but heartache. Why were people who didn't respect it, who didn't touch the line every time when running sprints— why were they being rewarded while I wasn't? I believed that the game of basketball was a living, breathing organism, that she had a soul, and that she watched me doing the little things when no one else was or could even appreciate them. Why had she let me fail? Was I simply another candle in the wind? Was my lesson in all of this to take it to the very end, with no regrets?

She had broken my heart.

28

Comeback Dream

Often, things are never quite what they seem,
No matter how often you plead or ask why.
Will I see you there in a comeback dream?

Your yearning hopes flow with a steady stream,
Down into a barren womb, long since dry.
Often, things are never quite what they seem.

You find yourself in a tyrant's regime.
No more will you be dancing with the sky.
Will I see you there in a comeback dream?

There's no bright future of gold and gleam,
No giant crystal balls from which you scry,
For even those are never quite what they seem.

In a place that you could've never foreseen
You wonder if you're chasing a lie,
A lie that will mangle your comeback dream.

You laugh at my grief, busting at the seams,
Fool, yet you never even dared to try.
For even though things are never quite what they seem,
At least I have myself a comeback dream.

I sat at home for a week recovering from the ulcers and putting on some weight. In truth, I was ready to call it a career. But, then…

Ten days later, John called me late: "Lance, it's time to go back. A window is opening for you. Coach Gates will be giving you a call."

Coach Gates called me, and after a long phone call, we were able to at least get some of the issues on the table. "Jeff is leaving for Turkey in two days," he told me. "We need some bodies, plus Lukie may be leaving." Jeff Graves had had an offer ironically from Galatasaray, my team in Turkey the year before and Luke Jackson was looking at an offer from Spain.

I told Gates that I needed him to let me play through my mistakes. If I was continually looking over my shoulder toward the bench, afraid of making a mistake, I couldn't be as effective as I needed. He agreed and told me he would make a more concerted effort to do that.

I drove back up to Boise and met the team for the flight to Arkansas. Jeff had finalized his deal with Galatasaray, and all I could do was smile and wish him good luck. I found it so humorous that the same team that had mistreated me in the beginning, setting me off on this roller coaster of a career thus far, was now doing me a favor by taking Jeff Graves away, removing him from my path. Karma comes full circle.

In my first game back, against the Arkansas Rim Rockers, Pete Ramos broke his leg. He was done for the season. A week later, Mohammed Sene was recalled to Seattle. Within a week, I had gone from being a fifth and seldom used big on the bench to being the starting center. Things can change in the blink of an eye, and they often do. As bad as I felt for Pete and his leg, I also knew that one man's misfortune was another man's opportunity. I failed the first time, when opportunity knocked at the University of Utah after Chris Burgess broke his foot. I wasn't going to repeat that mistake.

What I did this time was dig way, way back to my high school days and dust off many of the moves and skills that Coach Rupp had developed with me.

In many ways, some of the skills that Rupp taught me were too advanced, too farsighted, for even the collegiate game, let alone high school. Rupp could tell that I had decent, but not the greatest, athleticism, but he foresaw that my size and quickness would be enough to compensate for lack of raw natural athletic ability. He taught me to be a face-up post player, to shoot over the smaller opponents and drive past the bigger ones.

Like college coaches in general, mine didn't want me to play the face-up game, preferring to have me play my back to the basket and pound my way inside. Part of the face-up game entails having a jump shot, and most college coaches don't like their big men "settling" for jumpers.

Rupp taught me to shoot the jumper. The rationale college coaches use against big men shooting jumpers is this: college coaches can go find shooters anywhere, while big men are a rarity; the big men, rather than trying to do what the other kids can do, should do what no one else can do, which is use their size and plow their way in.

This is a nice philosophy for the college game. But once I began to play professionally, I struggled. I'm not broad-shouldered enough or long-armed enough or thick enough to force my man back and muscle him into the basket, as the competition is now much stiffer and just as big as me—if not bigger, faster, and stronger. It wasn't until I finally told myself to go back to what Rupp had taught me that I began to excel in the professional ranks. Rupp told me to play not to my weakness but to my strengths—my speed and shooting touch—to counter the slow, brute force of most big men.

In my first two games as a starter, trying to dust off my old skills and mind-set, I averaged a respectable twelve points in about twenty-four minutes. Then in my third game, I exploded for a thirty-point and ten-rebound game and a win in Bismarck, against the Dakota Wizards. As I scored every which way with left- and right-hand shots around their shot blockers, everyone—the reserves on the bench, the players on the court, and the fans in the crowd—was asking, "Who is this white guy?" All they could think to do was yell at me from the front row, "Ivan Drago!"*

People were quick to pass my thirty-point game off as a fluke—none more so than me, as I didn't know that I was capable of scoring thirty points in a game anymore. A week later, I scored thirty again, against Austin at home.

Then Coach Gates did something no other coach in my entire career has done: he admitted he was wrong, without any *buts*. He told my

---

*Apparently I look like Ivan Drago (a fictional character played by Dolph Lundgren in the film *Rocky IV*). Throughout my career, countless hecklers, from Los Angeles to Pocatello, Idaho, to Sioux Falls, South Dakota, have chanted this to me as though it would hurt my feelings. Now, personally, I don't see the connection, but thousands of unlinked hecklers can't be wrong, I guess. All things considered, it could be worse, as Dolph Lundgren is a not the ugliest guy around. So I allow the drunken fan who is spilling beer all over himself to slur insults at me without much resistance: "Ivan Drago! Go back to Russia."

The more intelligent and/or less inebriated ones will take it a step further and holler "I must break you!" believing themselves to be the first to make such a cleverly concocted insult/compliment. I smile a little inside and reply, without looking at them, but loud enough so they may here me, "If he dies . . . he dies!"

father one day in Boise, "I made a mistake with Lance. He told me he could play. I should've believed in him." Gates finally understood me and the player I was. He came to appreciate me and knew how to coach me. He became my friend and my ally.

That last month of the season, I averaged twenty-two points and thirteen rebounds a game. We clinched the best record well before the end of the season. Randy Livingston and I would just pick and pop the other teams to death. If I couldn't get a jumper, I'd roll all the way to key, creating space for Ronnell Taylor to cut through an open lane or for Ricky Sanchez to drift off for a three-pointer. We were deadly and efficient. We were patient, as patient as twenty-four seconds allowed us. We perfected the art of spacing. We created so much room for everyone to score that the defense had to either let us have a lane or else be called for a defensive three-second penalty. They had to choose their poison.

Randy loved playing with me, because I never got cute. I never put the ball on the ground. He would just pass and I'd just shoot it, whether it was for a jumper from the elbow after drifting from a pick or for a layup while rolling. Randy would lead me with a pass and I'd finish. He got me buckets and I got him assists. If I didn't have an immediate look, I wouldn't try to force it and dribble my opponent down; I simply kicked it back out to Randy or to Ronnell as he cut through a lane.

We cruised through the rest of the regular season, and Randy finally was called up to Seattle for the last week of the season. This was an integral call-up, as it marked the tenth season Randy played in the NBA, thus making him eligible for pension upon retirement. After Randy left for the last week, we continued on and won our last two games, clinching the best regular season record in D-League history. Randy was named MVP, and Gates was named Coach of the Year.

A first-round bye was awarded to us from the playoff seeding, but since Randy had not been on the roster at season's end, as he was in Seattle for the last week, he wasn't eligible to come back down and play with us for the postseason. He did come down to sit on the bench and support us, coaching us through the West Conference semifinal game.

John Greig was at the game, and so were Pax and Sam. It was televised internationally on NBA TV, and I did an interview in the pregame show, talking about my writing and the books I was working on, but mostly answering questions about how I had managed to come onto the scene after sitting on the bench for most of the season.

"How did you manage to stay in shape?" one interviewer asked.

"You always take that extra stride in practice, whether it be in drills or in scrimmages, and if you're not needed down on the other end, you still run down there. That extra stride will always carry you just that much further, especially when you're asthmatic like me."

I had twenty-four points and seventeen rebounds in that playoff game, but we fell in overtime to Colorado.

I had no regrets. I had returned and left it all out on the floor, knowing I had done the best I could, lighting the D-League on fire, averaging twenty-two and thirteen in the last month of the season. But by this time it was too late to really be considered for a call-up. Time had run out.

I'd have to wait through another off-season of hype and politics, just like the NASCAR drivers do on a maintenance lap, allowing the others to catch up. I knew I was never the type of guy who'd get a job based solely on hype. I was going to do it only through my actions on the court. My comeback dream wasn't yet complete.

29

I started out that summer by joining my teammate Ricky Sanchez down at his home in Puerto Rico, playing for a club there, in Humacao. As tradition would have it, I left Puerto Rico with only half of what I had been guaranteed, because people who know I'm deaf and struggle to understand a foreign language also like to think I'm stupid and thus won't notice that they're cheating me out of money. But the team did give me a small shirt that fits on me like underarmor on a football player. It was gracious of them to give me that shirt in lieu of the $7,000 they still owe me. I framed that $7,000 shirt.

I flew to Seattle so that I could train with John Greig and several of his other clients for summer camp. The Boston Celtics had been energetic in getting me to commit to them for the summer, well before the NBA draft. I was hesitant to at first, not knowing what rookie they'd take in the NBA draft later that month. I didn't want to commit early to Boston for the summer only to have them draft a rookie big man. At the end of the day, I appreciated their enthusiasm, and they said I'd get decent playing time. I liked what I was hearing, and so I went to Seattle with John, getting in the best shape I could for the Celtics' summer camp in Las Vegas.

I was feeling good about things until the NBA draft, when Boston took Glen "Big Baby" Davis in the second round. He just fell to them. The fact that he went that late in the draft had surprised many. I knew I was done for. I was upset that I had locked myself in with Boston for camp. If I was gunning for an NBA team, the only way I was ever going to be considered was by being a deep reserve who would probably never see the floor during games but would find his use on the practice floor. Glen Davis was in that same role as an undersized but energetic and bulky rookie. A résumé like mine wasn't nearly as presentable as one like Glen Davis had: MVP of the SEC (Southeastern Conference) and a final-four appearance. The writing was on the wall. No matter how well I played, "Baby" was going to get the bulk of the minutes, and he would get the nod over me if it was anywhere close to debatable, because Boston fans would know the name and immediately be excited about him. Whereas for me, who is Lance Allred?

My fears were confirmed when I walked into the gym upon arriving in Vegas to see Glen Davis and Leon Powe being taken through individual workouts before any of us had arrived. Boston had already made up their mind. It was a done deal. All I could do at this point was just go play and have as much fun as possible, regardless of what happened around me. I played well with what I had been given. John came down and watched the games, and was happy with the way I played. "Just keep doing what you're doing," he told me. "You're making the most of your opportunity, and people notice that."

I left Vegas with no regrets, with people whispering to me, "Danny Ainge really likes you," Ainge being the president of Basketball Operations for the Celtics.

"Yeah," I said. "But how much?" They signed Glen Davis shortly after.

After camp was over, I was invited to go play in China with the NBA Development League all-star squad in the International Stankovich Cup. I was hesitant to do it, but John asked me to, feeling we needed that recognition on my résumé. Furthermore, Randy had been invited to be on the team and said he would go if I went. But Randy flaked out at the last minute, the day before we flew from San Francisco to China.*

It was a strange setup. There were ten of us, and yet four of us were centers. I don't know who put the team together, but someone obviously just went with those with the best available stats who were willing to go. Four centers to share one spot, a spot that can be played by only one man at a time.

The notion that China is our enemy, a future threat to our stability, is preposterous. They f-ing love us! Or at least us American basketball players, who are almost NBA players. "Tracy McGrady!" they'd yell at us as we walked down the street. You would think that Yao Ming jerseys sold the most jerseys in his home country, but really it's Tracy McGrady.

By the second day I had come down with food poisoning, and for the rest of the trip I was in pain, dehydrated, and miserable.

---

*Thanks, Randy.

When people find out I was in Hong Kong, they will excitedly ask if I had a good time.

"Yes. The knockoff shops were such a lovely attraction. If you're ever there, I recommend you go to the one just off the train at Lon Square. It was so much fun walking through sweatshops, taking advantage of all of those poor people to assuage our vanity."

The Chinese love their cameras. And they love to use their cameras to take pictures of Americans. Especially tall Americans. As I walked down a busy sidewalk, the sound of each step I took was drowned out by the clicking of cameras. I often turned around to see a tiny lady smiling, giving me a thumbs-up as she captured my confused look with another quick snapshot.

I learned to combat this nuisance by pulling out my own camera to take pictures of the people taking pictures of me. It really did cheapen the moment for them, as they'd pull down their cameras to give me their own look of confusion, which I in turn would capture.

One girl spoke to me in broken English as I immortalized the disappointed look on her face: "No fun!"

Once I got home from China, I needed money, and Aunt Jeanette lined me up with a landscaping job. It was OK money, and I enjoyed learning how to build and design yards for when my own time comes. But I didn't like the late-night phone calls from my lonely employer, who left long, inebriated diatribes on my voice mail, talking about how she was still angry that she was never blessed with a child.

Helga was a demanding boss, and very impatient. I was hired to do the grunt work and ditch digging, but she also had a hired landscaper, Liz, working on her lawn, and the two of them bickered constantly. Like a child of a divorce, I was caught in the middle. It reached its worst point one day while I was working in the back of a truck bed, unloading a shipment of landscape rocks in the snow. I had not expected it to snow in October, and I was trying to get this project done before I headed back up to Boise to start the season. Snow or not, though, I was going to finish. Helga came out holding the phone and said, "I can't talk to her. She drives me crazy. You talk to her."

I took the phone and apathetically asked, "Yes?"

"Lance!" Liz barked on the other end of the line. "What are you doing shoveling while it's raining and snowing out? You need to grow a backbone!"

As much as I enjoy lonely women calling my manhood into question, I wasn't really in the mood for it on this day. I rolled my eyes, standing there on a pile of rocks, which may as well have been a pile of shit.

No man can serve two masters, let alone two lonely women. I learned through all of this that no matter how much money I make, it's never worth the cost or hassle of having someone else do your yard work for you. Why pay someone to do something you can do yourself?

Throughout that summer, John called me often to inform me of offers to go overseas. Some were for ridiculously low pay, and some were quite enticing. But something kept telling me no. I needed to give it one more year in the D-League, give it one more push. I knew myself well enough to know that if I went overseas now, I'd be asking myself *What if?* for the rest of my life. I stayed. I was going leave no stone unturned. I was going to give this one last push.

"OK," John agreed. "But you have to resign yourself to the fact that the day may come where you'll have to go back overseas."

"I know, John. I'm only giving it one more year in the D-League. One more year is all I will allow myself. And if I don't get that call-up, I will just accept the fact that it wasn't meant to be, and we will finish my career overseas."

I had this feeling in my stomach that my experience overseas had been so bad because I wasn't supposed to be there, that I was supposed to be in the States. And it was more than just about me: I also felt that to be playing in the NBA would inspire kids with other disabilities. If it had been only about the money, I would have just gone back overseas for the quick check.

The clock was ticking. It was a strategic move to stay, just as it was a strategic move not to go to any fall preseason camps. I knew the system well enough now to know that I was never going to outjump anyone in the gym or steal the limelight. I was never going to be invited to stay on a team through power of name or reputation. Going to a preseason camp would have ultimately been an exercise in futility, leading to more disappointment, and I was still stinging from the letdown with Boston.

I chose to stay home and prepare for the season in Boise, which would start back up again in November. Coach Gates was back; so was Randy. There were several reasons why Randy decided not to retire after that year, in spite of earning his pension, being named MVP, and having a son on the way. But I know that one of the big reasons was for me.

"I need you to help me get there, Randy. You're the only way I can," I admitted to him on the phone when I asked him to come back. And he did. Randy Livingston was my last crossing guard, to a place I had been chasing for so long.

Coach Gates called to tell me he had three new guys coming to the Idaho Stampede: Cory Violette, a former Gonzaga standout who grew up in Boise; Roberto Bergerson, a Boise State legend who had played for the Stampede back in the CBA days; and Ernest Scott, a kid from Georgia who had played for Gates in the USBL (United States Basketball League) at one time.

Coach wanted all three of those guys and me to go on a semi-pro preseason team that toured the country, playing at various colleges, allowing the coaches to gauge their team for the upcoming season.

It was a chance for them and me to get acquainted with each other and grow familiar with our traits and tendencies. It was a clever way to get the rust and kinks out before the season began, allowing us to ease back into the pace of an officiated game. They all agreed to go, and I agreed to join them. I had nothing else to do. It was a quick way to pass time, get in shape, meet my new teammates, and collect six hundred dollars!

I was thrilled upon meeting these three, as I could tell they were quality people. In any business, if you want to win and be successful, before talent and skill, you need good people around you.

Cory and I took an immediate liking to each other, and we became roommates in Boise. We thought similarly politically and economically and could talk and debate for hours. Cory startled me the first night he and I shared a room on the road when I awoke to find him eating a pizza in the dark. He was either staring at me while doing so, or he was sleep-eating.

I was very excited about the upcoming season. Training camp started, and Randy flew into town. Camp began without any incident or ripped feet this year. I was in good shape, and it felt good to be back.

My choice to stay in the D-League proved immediately to be a wise one, as I charged out of the gates with the same fervor with which I had ended the previous season, scoring thirty points in the first game.

. . .

D-League travel is the best.

You're never departing from a major city for another one. You're always traveling from a small, secondary city like Boise or Bismarck to either Los Angeles or Denver or to another small city—the cities with markets in which a D-League team can thrive. Small cities like Boise, where there are no major pro sports teams, are the smartest markets for building a minor-league team.

With the D-League comes the luxury of the travel. This is the time when you're reminded of just how good you have it. You wake up at 5 a.m. every road trip and head to the airport, where you once again meander through the tedious security checks, sardonically reminding yourself that freedom isn't free as you take your shoes off and do your best to tuck in your big toe, which protrudes through the hole in your ratty sock. You walk through the scanner, with all eyes magnetically drifting toward your big toe, which has popped up to tell everyone hello, while holding up your pants by a belt loop as you wait for your gear to come off the conveyor belt.

Then awkwardly, with one hand, as the other is still holding your pants, you grab your things as quickly as you can and wrestle with your laptop, which you have to take out of your bag every damn time because for some reason everything metal, when wrapped in nylon bags—except, of course, for computers—shows up on X-ray scanners. Still holding up your pants, you try to clear out of the way as fast as you can for the sake of those behind, at least if you're someone who is polite like me, and then walk over to the two chairs that have to accommodate the thousands that pass through every day. You then just drop all your things on the floor and begin to dress yourself in public.

Then comes the plane flight, which is hardly an end to justify the means. Because of the simple, economic truth that we're in a small city, there are no 757s waiting for us. Seven-footers like me have to suck it up by getting on tiny two-seater commuter jets, with cabins that remind you of an MRI tube. A tube in which you do your best to refrain from wigging out in a state of claustrophobic hysteria, pounding the walls, begging for someone, anyone, to let you out.

You hit your head on all the open cabinet doors, each encounter more agitating than the last because you cannot see ahead but you know it's coming. You walk blindly down the aisle, as you cannot stand up straight. You can only bend at the neck and stare down at your feet and the white emergency exit lights, which will never ever light up for you and let you live to tell of it. At least for me, these dormant Valkyries earn their keep by serving the semiredeeming, offhand purpose of guiding me in a straight line back toward the rear of the plane.

People then laugh and point at you and ask, as though no one else before or after them has done so, "Are you guys a basketball team? . . . How is the weather up there?" They will then turn their heads and watch you maneuver, twisting and turning as you tuck yourself like a folding chair, a skill mastered over time. It's not pleasant or fun. It's simply what needs to be done.

"Is that uncomfortable?" the annoying woman a few rows up from you asks; she, of course, got to the airport early to claim the emergency-exit row and is now too self-absorbed for it to occur to her that she should probably trade you seats.

"Yes," you answer as politely as you can in a strained voice as you adjust your knee to stop it from digging into your ribs. You give her a polite smile and take out your book, which is the only painkiller you have to help get you through the torturous flight ahead. The book also serves a second purpose: letting exit-row lady know that you're not in a chatty mood. She checks back periodically throughout the flight to see if you have put your book down, hoping for conversation.

If you make the mistake of putting your book down, she may force the issue and ask over the heads of the people between you, "How tall are you?"

"Five-one" is your default answer to that question, which you have been asked more times than a soap star comes back from the dead. It immediately lets you gauge a person's intelligence by seeing how long it takes them to figure out that you're lying to them. Exit-row lady lights up with duly noted and impressed eyes, nodding approvingly at you, and begins to turn away, her body language conveying her internal dialogue: *Five-one, that's really . . . Wait, I'm five-six. That can't be right. . . .* She turns back around with a look of amusement on her face, thinking you're being funny and playing with her when really you're hoping it will let her know, for the love of all that's holy, that you'd like her to please leave you alone.

When you land at the airport closest to wherever your final D-League destination may be, you're packed away in a caravan of minivans and driven for hours to where you'll be playing, because money is tight and the owner sees no point in getting a bus when vans are cheaper. As you stow yourself away along with your luggage, you listen to rap music on the radio, because it's cool and cliché, while you munch away at your Fig Newtons, which you share with Coach Gates, because they're a white-man treat. You never have to worry about your teammates taking your Fig Newtons; they're black-man proof. Not because Randy thinks they're gross, but because he has no idea what Fig Newtons are, scared to try new things, choosing to remain on his steady diet of Big Macs and potato chips. You can eat only so healthy on a thirty-dollar per diem.

The pinnacle of your D-League experience will occur when you take that christening bus ride through the night along I–94 from Sioux Falls to Bismarck, North Dakota. As though it's an intro to a bad horror movie, the bus breaks down at two in the morning, thirty miles outside of Fargo. The frosty December winds that howl across the Dakota plains pound against the bus, rocking it, asking you to all come out and play. You sit there in the back of the bus with Randy, Cory, Ernest, and Berto, covered in blankets, your clothes layered, your beanie tucked to the lowest point possible, as you play poker through the night, doing your best to take your mind off the cold.

Randy will keep buying back in and playing every hand he has.

Ernest will sit and watch, because his girlfriend gets mad when he plays.

Cory will sit there and complain with food in his mouth that we're such terrible players and thus are impossible to read.

Berto will chew his fingernails in solitary frenzy.

And you'll look out the window, across the field, to see the ghostly silhouette of a Chippewa warrior riding out on his horse across the frozen Dakota plains.

30

I, Lance Allred, am a child of God, and I know that He loves me.
I will be an example of Him at all times.
I, Lance Allred, will live life to the fullest and never settle for less
*   than my best.*
I will be the best basketball player that I can be.
I, Lance Allred, will play in the NBA.
I will hand over my life to the Lord for his doing.
I, Lance Allred, will achieve all that I desire, for the Lord has
*   promised me so.*

This is my mantra, my goal list that I repeat every night before I go to bed and every morning when I awake. I repeat it every game while standing on the court, at the free-throw line, during the national anthem. This has been my mantra since I was seventeen years old.

I wrote a letter to my heavenly father at the start of the week of the annual NBA Development League showcase, which is here in Boise this week. It's the week of January 14, 2008. The showcase is a gathering of all the D-League teams, who play two games each in a four-day span. It's a convenient setup that allows all the general managers of NBA teams and European clubs to gather in one place and achieve all of their scouting in just four days in one place, rather than through weeks of traveling to various cities that they haven't the time to visit.

To My Father in Heaven,
*   I hope you enjoy my first letter to you, which is a bit odd considering how long it has taken me to write you one. My ability to write is nothing short of your doing and it is the talent I am most grateful for that you have given me.*

My Father, I am about to turn 27 and I feel my time is run-
ning out and my age is now just another to add to a too long list
of limitations that have been set upon me. I know I ask you for a
lot, and I know I can never repay you in full for what you have
given me. And I know that continuing to ask for more can be
viewed that I do not appreciate what you have given me thus far.
And that is not true, for my family, friends and loved ones, and
my life are the greatest gifts you have given and always will be.

With all of these blessings, I need one more. My Father, when
you gave me my patriarchal blessing 12 years ago, I took it to
heart, every word in the literal sense. With it, I assumed and
embraced my challenge of pursuing a basketball career despite my
limitations, knowing you would be with me every step of the way,
and that I may be an instrument in your hands to glorify you and
your mercy and compassion that you have shown to me despite
my flaws, pride and fallacies.

My father, it is 12 years later now, and I am very tired. I am
worn and fatigued and stressed beyond speaking, and I avoid
human interaction because of it. I know I ask for a lot, again
I know, and I know I don't deserve to ask for anything more.
But I beg of you to let me have this one moment. Just this mo-
ment in time where I can look back and say, "We did it. It was
worth it."

Even if a 10-day contract is all I ever get, it will all be worth it.
Our time has come, my Lord, and it is time for the world to see
how you have blessed and guided me through this life.

I wouldn't be asking this if you had not promised it to me.

My father, I do not care about the money, or the fame. I just
want to be able to say that I set an "unreachable" goal and I
made it. Please, help me to do so, so that I may glorify thee. This
is my one wish for this new year of 2008.

Your   son,
Lance Allred
P.S. Thank you for Mac, and tell Szen I said "Hello" and I
miss him.

This is a big week for me. I am not oblivious to that fact. I tell myself and
every reporter who asks me that the showcase is just another game, and
if you're playing harder than you normally would just because someone

is watching you, then shame on you. You should play as hard as you can every night. While I tell the truth, I'm also lying.

This is more than just another game for me. It will be a manifestation. The wheels of momentum have finally begun to churn for me, as my name is now trickling through the phones of NBA front offices. "Lance Allred?" they ask skeptically. "The one from Portsmouth?"

Yes, Lance Allred. As of right now, Idaho is on a ten-game winning streak. We hold the best record in the league. I lead the team in scoring and rebounding. I lead the D-League in double-doubles and player efficiency per forty-eight minutes. I'm rated as the midseason MVP.

My nerves are so uptight that the night before our first game, my back flares into spasms. I spend the evening on the ground, staring up at the ceiling, holding my tigereye stone in my hand. The next morning we have a shoot-around at Boise State in their auxiliary gym. A front-office executive from one of our affiliate teams is there to tell Coach he should be playing their assigned player more, which incidentally means more time for him and less for me. Coach Gates pats me on the back reassuringly and says, "Everyone will know your name."

Before the game I get a request to do an interview with Sports Illustrated, and since it has nothing to do with Rick Majerus, I agree. Ian Thomsen sits down with me in the locker room, three hours before the game. What was supposed to be a twenty-minute interview turns into two hours as Ian scribbles his notes and worryingly checks his recorder to make sure the battery is still charged. He asks me questions that range from polygamy and religion to sociological and economical philosophies and inquiries about my travels. John Greig comes in on the interview, introduces himself to Ian, gives me a hug, and wishes me luck. "Just go out there and have fun," he says encouragingly.

Ian ends the interview and lets me know he wants to continue it later in the week before the showcase is over. He leaves the locker room, and I'm finally able to sit in silence for just a few moments before anyone else trickles in. I sit at my bench, curling my toes in the carpet as the voice on the PA vibrates through the walls.

This is my time.

My teammates begin to filter in, coaches coming back and forth, scribbling scouting adjustments on the board. Coach Lopes, one of my all-time favorite assistant coaches, stands in front of me and says, "No matter what happens, I'm proud of you. At this point, you cannot fail. You have already achieved so much."

The game before ours finally ends. I look across the court and see my old teammate Britton Johnson walking off the court. He has recently come back from a shoulder injury that kept him out all season till this point. I want to say hello, but I also don't. I don't want to talk to anyone. I try not to look up, but even as I'm turning my head to face the hoop as I shoot my warm-up routine, my visual memory catches faces in the crowd that I recognize. Faces that decide whether or not I'm good enough.

The five-minute warm-up mark passes, and I go to the center of the court for the team-captain pregame meeting with the night's officials.

We run our layup lines, warming up our legs, as the home crowd files into the seats, making indistinguishable those faces that I want to pretend are not there.

The horn blows, and we walk to our benches as the starting lineups are announced. While waiting for the visitors to be called, I lie down on the floor in front of our bench. "Rebound and run," I say as I lie on my back. "Rebound and run. Rebound and run," I order, reminding myself to keep things simple. I stand for the national anthem. The lights go dark, and I begin to whisper my mantra, which I whisper every game during the national anthem:

I, Lance Allred, am a child of God, and I know that
 He loves me.
I will be an example of Him at all times.
I, Lance Allred, will live life to the fullest and never settle
 for less than my best.
I will be the best basketball player that I can be.
I, Lance Allred, will play in the NBA.
I will hand over my life to the Lord for his doing.
I, Lance Allred, will achieve all that I desire, for the Lord has
 promised me so.

The horn blows, and I step onto the floor.

I make my first six shots in the first quarter, recording fourteen points and seven rebounds before the buzzer sounds. I have to sit out the second quarter and split time with two assignments down from Seattle and Portland. I'm prepared for it. "Control what you can control," I tell myself.

Scouts and GMs waste no time at all and began to trickle over to John Greig, who smiles back at them with an "I-told-you-so" look on his face.

"John, he is a completely different player. Night and day!"

"John, where has he been?"

"John, why didn't you tell me he was this good?"

When the final horn blows and the final stats are recorded, I have twenty-four points and twelve rebounds in twenty-four minutes.

I'm named to the all-showcase team.

It's cold out in Boise today. I can see this even through my window shades. A dim gray seeps into my room. It's 6 a.m. Mac is lying next to me, sound asleep, while I cannot sleep at all.

I stare up at my ceiling, a ceiling in an apartment that I don't own, a place that I cannot call home. I have no place to call my own, I remind myself as I mentally sift through all of my possessions, which are stacked away in either Jacob Beebe's house or Tara's house or other places that I have long since forgotten.

All of my immediate possessions and a few of my many beloved books are with me. I reach over to pet Mac, who starts at my touch and stretches sleepily, only to fall back asleep.

It has been a month since the showcase.

"You're going to be called up real soon," they told me after the showcase was over.

Soon. Soon. You're going to be called up real soon. You're this close. You're so close. How close is close? How soon is soon? I'm still here in the D-League, and my play has deteriorated. Not drastically. But I'm not as sharp as I was two months ago. I'm thinking too much. I'm analyzing every game. I trick myself into fearing that each game is make-or-break. That I have to uphold the buzz I created for myself, which I fear is as capricious as the business I work in. Tomorrow they could all just forget about me. Or have they already done so? Did my buzz go as fast as it came?

We're on an eighteen-game winning streak. Last week, on the night of my twenty-seventh birthday, we broke the D-League record for longest winning streak, at sixteen games. It was a great birthday. I was proud of my teammates; I was proud to call them my friends. I will remember that moment forever.

Though we're winning, and will continue to win, I'm tired. I'm burned out. I have gone as high as I can go here. I don't know of anything else or anything more I can do. I have climbed this ladder to this level, from the very bottom rung to the very top, and I'm ready to keep climbing, but I cannot, as there's a ceiling blocking me.

Jaded. Jaded is the only way I can describe how I feel on this cold, gray-sky morning here in Boise. I'm not depressed. I'm not angry. I'm not bitter. I'm jaded.

I'm disheartened. Tired. Exhausted. Weary. How much more do I have to fight? Is this as far as it goes? Was the comeback dream a train of steam that could go only so far? Was I just another tragedy? Was I just another sad, sad story of life, and how it's never what we want it to be?

Is my lesson in all this simply that I had to learn to validate myself? That only I can validate myself? Yes, I have learned that true validation comes only from within. It was a beautiful lesson that has carried me across the globe, to faraway places that most can only dream of. I'm thankful for it. But I want more. I need more. I didn't come this far, so close, down and back and around again, every which way, trying to find my own way in, just to walk away.

We have practice today. Some more defensive slides that Gates has us do every day. I don't want to go to practice. I want to sleep. But I can't sleep. I'm void of all emotion except for exhaustion. I'm so exhausted that I can't even rest my eyes without the fears of falling short startling me back to my senses.

I don't want to practice today. What if this leads to nowhere? What if I don't get the call-up? Why should I keep going?

Why do I keep fighting?

"Because I choose to."

I nearly fail to recognize that it's my own voice that has startled me from my inner dialogue.

I sit up out of bed and stare at the claw scars on my hands and wrists that have accrued over the years of basketball. I put on my shoes.

"Because I choose to," I say aloud one more time as I stand up to take Mac outside on his morning walk.

Just another cold, gray-sky morning in Boise.

All-Star Weekend 2008, February 15–17, came, and Cory, Randy, and I were chosen for the all-star team. Coach Gates and Coach Lopes were coaching. Randy was excited for us to come down and see his hometown of New Orleans and give him the chance to show us around. When we landed, the bus picked us up, and I watched the city as we drove by, noticing the water lines on the freeway walls that showed how high the flooding had reached in the city during Katrina. From the freeway I saw houses by the sea, boarded up, with giant Xs marked across them to show they were still abandoned. I saw lots that had been sheared clean of everything; they were empty and lonely.

But to my surprise, downtown New Orleans was incredibly clean and presentable. I'd later learn that while the downtown area and the French Quarter had been hit, the French Quarter had not been dealt as hard a blow as other parts of the city. And New Orleans had made a smart move in cleaning up the main downtown area. Between downtown and the French Quarter, the city was attracting tourists again, and it needed the tourist revenue to help fund the rebuilding efforts in other areas. I was so impressed with all the history and the architecture in the old districts. I was even more impressed with how much the people loved their city, how proud they were of their heritage, and how warm and welcoming they were and eager to share their stories with outsiders.

People often go to New Orleans for the same reason they go to Las Vegas. I hate Vegas. I hate the superficial flair that coats the hollow city. I hate the heat. New Orleans is all heart and soul. There are casinos there and other outlets of vice, just like in Vegas, but accompanying these are things that Vegas cannot offer: plantation tours, the French Quarter, Jackson Square, St. Charles Cathedral, voodoo shops, steamboat rides, crocodile farms and other aquariums, fishing tours, and so many other things. And then there's the food.

I'm not a big food guy. I eat basically just to survive, as I grow bored and impatient when I'm eating, eager to get on with the daily chores of life. But in this place, New Orleans, the food was indescribable. When Cory and I arrived at the downtown Hilton, right off the French Quarter, we found Randy walking back in, as he had arrived a few days earlier to organize many of his NBA community events for his hometown. He told us to walk a few blocks down to Mother's. It was a red-brick building, and from the inside it looked a former slaughterhouse or meat-packing plant. The restaurant had been created in the 1930s. Their sandwiches—or "po'boys," as they call them—were very good. When you go, get the "Debris" sandwich. And let's not even talk about the pecan pie. It was the most delicious pecan pie I've ever had. Cory and I went back the next morning for grits and ham and eggs. Just a great place.

That first night in New Orleans, after we did our NBA TV interviews, Randy took us to a five-star restaurant in the French Quarter that a high school friend of his had inherited, named Brennan's. The atmosphere was incredible. When you sat down and looked out the window from the deck to the garden and absorbed all the sounds and the music, you knew you were in the Big Easy. His friend, who owned the place, was Alayna, a pretty blonde with an easygoing but sophisticated dialect who was very welcoming and generous, as most New Orleanians are. Randy led us to his favorite spot, asking to be served by his favorite waiter, Ray, an older gentleman who had spunk. We ate turtle soup and gumbo for appetizers and then some salad. Growing up with a turtle, I was very conflicted about eating the turtle soup, but it was delicious. I had to eat it, because food is a part of one's culture, and when Randy offered me a bit of his heritage, it would've been rude and closed-minded on my part not to try it. The main dish was an incredible trout with fresh crabmeat on top. I cannot emphasize enough how amazing this meal was. For dessert, Ray cooked us some bananas Foster in a giant pan with a huge scoop of brown sugar and some rum, topping it off with ice cream. And when we were done, Alayna wouldn't let us pay for anything. It was the greatest meal I have ever had, free or not.

After dinner I walked down Bourbon Street. You see and hear things about Bourbon Street, and as this was my first time in New Orleans, I wanted to make sure I walked along Bourbon. Two things stuck out for me: how short the street is, and how many strip clubs there are in the tightly packed street, hidden in the old French- and Spanish-style buildings. For as much free sexuality as there was, or was said to be, via beads on Bourbon Street, I had never imagined that there would be strip clubs. It just seemed like trying to sell water to a fish.

Randy is the King of New Orleans. He is a legend there, and you would think the New Orleans Hornets would consider themselves lucky to have him on their team, even as a fifteenth man. Even if he isn't playing, he is a great coach and tutor for the younger point guards, and he is a part of the community. People know and love him. Just by having him there on the bench, the people of the city would be more inclined to go to the games, knowing they have a guy there who grew up in, understands, and thrives in their intricate city and culture. As of right now, the Hornets have no natives on their team.

That night was dream-factory night for the Development League. Randy participated in the hot-shot competition, and made one shot, I believe. There was a three-point contest, and then there was a dunk contest, and two of my high-flying teammates, Brent "Air Georgia"

Petway and Mike Taylor, were participants, both facing off in the final round. There was also the H-O-R-S-E contest, which I was slated to participate in. In a H-O-R-S-E contest, one player puts up a shot, and the opponent has to duplicate the shot exactly or he gets his first letter, an *H*. The first player to spell *H-O-R-S-E* loses. It was the first-ever H-O-R-S-E contest for the D-League, and would be the first in the NBA for over thirty years. "Pistol" Pete Maravich and "The Ice Man" George Gervin faced off once. I'm sad we never got to see Bird and Jordan face off in an official game of H-O-R-S-E.

My father hated basketball, but H-O-R-S-E was a game, the only game, he would play with me. Utahns take H-O-R-S-E very seriously. There's a basketball court in every church house. And to stretch the letter of the law, Mormon boys play H-O-R-S-E on Sunday, so they won't break a sweat and thus the Sabbath.

I found out only the weekend before all-star week that I'd be participating in the H-O-R-S-E event. I had injured my shooting hand the week before, bruising the bone in a palm when I tried to break my fall after being undercut following a layup. I had spent the entire week resting, icing and rehabbing my hand, and it was very painful to shoot the ball, so I couldn't get into the gym to practice any creative shots. I went into the contest cold turkey. Seeing that I wasn't able to practice on anything tricky, my strategy was to simply shoot my bank shots from long distances and funny angles. These are game shots for me, and I have been shooting them for years. It was a safe way to go for the H-O-R-S-E competition. Now, I know most people want to see flair and jaw-dropping visuals, but that isn't me, and I didn't get invited to all-star weekend by doing any of that. I was going to simply keep doing what got me there.

In the final round, I was matched up against Morris Almond, an assignee from the Utah Jazz, who was the scoring leader in the D-League at the time. He had played around in the first round with lots of balancing, and sitting and kneeling shots, and he was having a good time. I, however, used the same approach that I did in the first round—straight for the kill. I ultimately ended up beating him with a bank shot, boring him into submission.

It meant a lot to me to hold up my first-ever trophy, winning the first-ever D-League H-O-R-S-E competition and the first in the NBA enterprise in over thirty years. I finally had a trophy to put on my shelf when I retire, and it was from playing the game that my father played with me on Uncle Saul's outside basketball court on summer evenings as a boy.

The next day was the all-star game, and though we lost, I was happy with the way I played. What was more important, I had a great time. I wasn't letting myself believe I'd receive a contract based on how I played at the all-star, because . . . well, because it was an all-star game. Though the trip would end on a sour note—I'd spend the entire next day, sixteen hours, in my beloved Chicago O'Hare Airport, that lovely loose organization of an airport, due to weather—I loved the trip.

I was proud to be in New Orleans. I was proud of that city for what it has overcome. I was proud that I could call these people my fellow Americans. New Orleans to me is what America is all about, or should be: various and strong cultures and history melting into one, with so much diversity and so many options for everyone to pursue. From now on, whenever someone tells me they want to go to Vegas, I tell them to go to New Orleans instead. I was so grateful that the NBA allowed me the opportunity to be there, to eradicate the impressions of chaos that I allowed, through the news and the words of others, to filter into my mind. And I'm grateful that I was there with Randy, my brother from another world, who was proudly able to show it to me.

31

March 12, 2008

I'm driving in Orem, Utah, away from the practice facility of the Utah Flash, with Cory Violette in my passenger seat and Roberto Bergerson scrunched up in the back, on our way back to the hotel in Provo, when Coach Gates calls me.

"Where you at?"

"I'm just bringing Cory and Berto back from the gym. They wanted to stay after and play some Ping-Pong."

"Well, get your things packed up. You're flying out tonight."

"Huh?"

"You're going to Cleveland, baby!"

"Really?"

"Yeah!"

I nearly wreck my car as Cory and Berto, who are never silent when they're in the same room together, sit there in dead silence, both staring at me.

"I'm going to play for the Cleveland Cavaliers?"

"Yep," Coach Gates confirms one more time.

I begin to cry. "OK, I will be at the hotel in two minutes."

"K, see ya."

Cory pats my back: "That's what I'm talking about."

"'Bout time!" Berto hollers in the back seat.

John Greig calls me right after I hang up with Coach Gates: "Congratulations, man. Call your family, and call me when you're at the airport tonight after you have settled down."

I call Dad and tell him, but my phone is about to die, so we make it short.

I arrive at the hotel in Provo, an hour south of Salt Lake, and charge up my phone as I wait for my teammates to gather in the lobby so I can say good-bye to them and the coaches. I cry as I hug Randy good-bye.

I drive up to Mom and Dad's, where my family and friends are waiting for me, but not before I quickly buy a new suit at Dahle's. I want to make a good first impression. Dad and Mom are at the door waiting for me. Dad cannot speak as he hugs me. Mom strains in outright joy to say, "You did it, boy-o."

After Mom and I split from our long embrace, I lean down to pick up Mac, my friend and companion, who has been with me through thick and thin. He looks me in the eyes, and he can see tears. He thinks something is wrong until I smile at him. "We did it, buddy," I say softly.

I hug my dear friends Max, Josh, Jared, Jacob. Court, Tara, and John are there to hug and congratulate me. They have never doubted me. Not even John Greene in his infinite skepticism, which he inherited from an accountant father, ever doubted me.

I call Raphael, who tries to cheer me up over the phone but cannot as her tears get in the way. I am only able to leave a message for Nathan and Vanessa. I call Coach Rupp and Coach Cravens and thank them for everything. I call Pax and Sam to let them know I couldn't have done it without them and their unconditional love for me. I ask them to tell Yaya that I love her. So many more people that I wish to call, but I don't have the time.

As Mom, Dad, Court, and Mac ride with me to the airport, we sit for a moment, the four of us talking, reflecting on things that were and things that are and things yet to come. Dad will be beginning his doctoral studies in education in the summer.

I say good-bye to them and Mac as I walk into the airport.

I'm going to join the Cavs in Washington, D.C., where they have a game against the Wizards. I can't sleep a wink on the plane. I'm in first class, and it feels awkward. Big seats or not, I never sleep well on planes. But I'm able to sneak back into coach, lie across a row of seats, and sleep for a bit. I guess I feel more comfortable there.

A town car picks me up at the airport, where I'm taken to the Four Seasons in Georgetown. I walk down to the team breakfast and meet Amanda, who has my contract ready for me. Ben Wallace walks in. I introduce myself. I then introduce myself to Mr. James. I'm too tired to say anything stupid.

I grab a small bite and walk up to my room, where I sleep until Max, the team trainer, takes me to get my physical. I pass with flying colors, return to the hotel, and sleep some more. I wake at four and prepare to leave early with Chris, the player-development coach, who is taking me over to the arena early to put me through a workout.

I lace up my shoes, which I brought with me, and walk out to the court. I stare at the floor, almost scared to step onto it—but I do. I feel the lights of the big stage warming my skin. I throw up during my workout, but swallow it back down so no one can see me and think I'm out of shape. I'm not out of shape. I'm just tired and nervous.

When I'm done, I walk back into the locker room and put on my very first NBA jersey, which is waiting for me. Allred 41, it says on the back. My very own NBA jersey. I stare at it and want to cry, but there are photographers from NBA.com taking shots of their "D-League poster-boy."

I sit in silence as my new teammates exceed my expectations by walking over to individually introduce themselves if they haven't already. Coach Brown comes in. I like his demeanor: calm and confident.

We say the Lord's Prayer out in the tunnel and then run out to the floor, where the boos from the Washington fans cascade over us. The adrenaline, which I felt was depleted, kicks into reserve. The rush is surreal as I run up and down shooting hoops on an NBA stage—where the lights are brightest, where the lights shine on a court that so many said I'd never see.

"Ivan Drago!" a heckling fan calls at me, indirectly letting me feel right at home. It's just another gym.

The buzzer sounds. The players are asked to assume their places for the national anthem. It begins. I look down to my feet:

I, Lance Allred, am a child of God, and I know that He loves me.
I will be an example of Him at all times.
I, Lance Allred, will live life to the fullest and never settle for less
   than my best.
I will be the best basketball player that I can be.
I, Lance Allred, will play in the NBA—

I stop. I look up to the flag, lit in the dark. And it all finally truly sets in.

I, Lance Allred, am in the NBA. . . .

I begin to weep.

In a quick flash of frozen yet endless time, I see the faces of my loved ones before me. I see my parents. I see my sisters. I see my brother. I see Yaya, Pax, and Sam. I see them all. I hear the voices of my childhood, floating along the Bitterroot River, laughing happily back to me, as innocence is reclaimed, if for but a fleeting moment.

I see Szen sitting on the side of the court watching me, having walked with me every step of the way, whether I could see him or not.

I see the pain. I see the hurt. I see the anger. I see the love. And I see the joy. I see it all in this moment that's now immortal.

This moment is mine. No one can take it from me. No matter what comes after or what came before, this moment is mine.

It will forever be mine.

Epilogue

To my reader:

As a child with my hearing impairment and my inability to speak properly, my parents encouraged me to read and write to communicate. Thank you for listening.

Having battled my own mind, and done so through many cultures across the globe, I wish to tell you all that life is good. Self-doubt is my greatest flaw and will always be, but I choose to fight it and will not let it rule me. If you find yourself at a bottom, know that in the blink of an eye it can all change, first and foremost in your own mind. By accepting disappointment and furthermore accountability for your actions and responses to life's heartaches, you'll take control of your life and find the happiness that we all look for.

We only have one life, so we may as well live it. You should never be afraid to try, to dream. Whether you fail or succeed isn't nearly as important as whether you try.

Friends and loved ones have come and gone, traitors and tyrants passing as quickly as they came, and through it all, I'm grateful. My memories are what make me. They're what define me. They're all I can take with me.

May you all find peace on your paths and journeys through this world.

Lance Allred

Acknowledgments

When I sent my draft to publication, I had over eight hundred pages. Due to publishing and marketing, the book is obviously no longer that length. If you feel that your name should have been mentioned in the book and was not, I can say with honesty that it most likely was in the original draft, and your helping hand along my way through life will never be forgotten. Thank you all, named or otherwise, for helping me to create my memories.

A few names that had significant impact come to mind that I am indebted to: the Swinton family, namely Jon-Jon; Tim Colman, my first basketball coach; Brian Maxwell, my arch-rival turned dear friend; Katie Tate, my first girlfriend and true friend, whom I met at the University of Utah (there is only one Katie Tate); Cary Addison, and finally, my saint, Ted Adams.

About the Author

Lance Allred lives in Salt Lake City, Utah as a father to his son, Simon.

He travels the world as a keynote inspirational speaker, empowering corporations, nonprofits and schools on Leadership, Perserverance and Grit.

Watch his TEDx smash-hit, "What is Your Polygamy?" which has garnered over 3 Million Views in its first six months.

To learn more about Lance, visit his website, www.lanceallred41.com

 L Squared

L Squared Productions, 2017

Made in the USA
San Bernardino, CA
12 March 2018